TO RESCUE THE FUTURE

TO RESCUE THE FUTURE

The Pro-Life Movement in the 1980s

edited by Dave Andrusko

LIFE CYCLE BOOKS

TORONTO, ONTARIO • HARRISON, NEW YORK

TO RESCUE THE FUTURE: The Pro-Life Movement in the 1980s

Printed in U.S.A.

Published by:
Life Cycle Books
2205 Danforth Avenue
Toronto, Ontario
M4C 1K4
(416) 690-5860

ISBN 0-919225-18-7

CONTENTS

Dedication

To my parents, who never lost faith, and to MCCL, which made it all possible.

PREFACE: HEARING THE SIGNALS

The trick, of course, is to be alert to changes around you, to anticipate their impact on your institution, and then to respond: to reconceptualize what you are up to. Disastrous results tell us something is very wrong. But we ought to be able to hear the signals before they get quite so strong."

JOHN NAISBITT, *MEGATRENDS.*

Although I did not realize it at the time, the genesis of this book was the public debut of infanticide. The date was April 15, 1982 and the location was Bloomington, Indiana, "the sort of academic community where medical facilities are more apt to be excellent than moral judgments are," as George Will observed. It is no exaggeration to say that I was thoroughly radicalized by the unspeakably brutal death of Infant Doe. Up until the time that tiny newborn baby died of starvation, I took my pro-life commitment very seriously but impersonally. Infant Doe's unnecessary death forever changed that for me, and I'm sure for many others as well.

The last day of that poor Down's syndrome baby's life is

engraved on my memory. National Right to Life General Counsel James Bopp, Jr., working feverishly with Monroe County Prosecutor Barry Brown and Deputy Prosecutor Larry Brodeur, had for three days tried to persuade the Indiana legal apparatus of the seemingly commonsense proposition that failing to feed the child for six days meant that the child was being neglected. (Infant Doe was born with an esophageal malady which meant he could not take in food. The remedial surgery was relatively simple. The parents would not allow the surgery, nor would they allow the child to be fed intravenously.)

The pro-life lawyers had absolutely no success. In a classic example of Orwellian doublethink, the courts decreed that the decision not to treat was a valid medical alternative to the decision to treat. In other words, the decision to withhold treatment was now a form of medical treatment. With all state options exhausted, Brown and Brodeur were able to convince Supreme Court Justice John Paul Stevens to allow an emergency appeal at 9 a.m. Friday, April 16. Accompanied by Patrick Baude, a professor of constitutional law, Brodeur left for Washington, D.C. by way of Atlanta. Brodeur called from the Atlanta airport. Brown told him Infant Doe had died just seven minutes before Brodeur's flight left Indianapolis.

I did not hear of Infant Doe's plight until the day before he died. Aside from helping to keep our national directors apprised of the deteriorating situation, there was virtually nothing I could do. When I learned at about 11:30 p.m. Eastern time that Infant Doe had succumbed, I wept for the first time since I had taken up the cause of defenseless life.

I wept for that little baby who died because his parents and his doctors decided a life of mental retardation was worse than death. I wept out of personal frustration and anger that here in the freest, most democratic nation in the world, I could do nothing to stop the torture of a baby whose only crime was that he would learn more slowly and less than you and I. I wept for my country; what happened to this little child of God was not worthy of the greatest country on the face of this planet. Most of all, I wept for the 16 million unborn children whose young lives had been so pointlessly, so callously snuffed out because they, too, were "unwanted."

The major media, pro-abortion to the core, at first criticized the (non)treatment of Infant Doe. Some, like the *New York Times*, found themselves in the unenviable position of trying to differentiate between the illegitimate killing of Infant Doe and the perfectly legitimate killing of unborn babies. (It was a remarkable editorial in the *Times*, totally schizophrenic, one that historians no doubt will someday read baffled and amazed.)

While I claim no particular powers of prophecy, what I predicted in May 1982 has come true with a vengeance. I cautioned that then the media heavyweights would not long be with us.

"One can predict," I wrote, "that after the first wave of guilt over Infant Doe subsides, the anti-life forces will come out of the woodwork. They will emboss infanticide with all the usual fuzz words — personal autonomy, freedom, choice, strength to choose death, etc., etc. — and after a while the *Times* will meekly fall into line. Undoubtedly, there will be lapses, such as Infant Doe editorials, but in the long run, without a base in pro-life principles, the influential opinion makers will relapse. Resourceful as they are, they will find some way to justify killing handicapped newborns."

Sure enough, no sooner had the Reagan Administration tried to promulgate regulations requiring that handicapped newborns be given the same level of care as non-handicapped children than the medical and media establishments went wild. Requiring the posting of a sign indicating that under section 504 of the Rehabilitation Act of 1973 it is forbidden to discriminate against the handicapped was described in a column published in the *Washington Post* as introducing "Big Brother in the Nursery." Good medicine would be the victim of "Baby Doe squads" (with all the Nazi overtones that that phraseology connoted) brought to the hospital by the 24-hour hotline number.

Rolling out the heavy artillery, they told us that the sanctity of the doctor-family relationship would be imperiled. The most vicious broadsides against the regulations, sadly, came from the American Academy of Pediatrics. Ominously, the APP, in their legal brief against the regulations, argued for the possibility that parents may have a "right of privacy" which would give them complete discretion in the decision whether or not to treat injured newborns. If accepted, such reasoning would be, as Bopp warned, the *Roe v. Wade* of infanticide. (A few months after this brief was filed, the AAP ran a commentary in their house organ unfavorably comparing the capacities of severely handicapped newborns to those of dogs and pigs.)

Infanticide had reared its ugly head and the media and medical establishments clasped it to their bosoms. The two most influential opinion making forces on questions of medical ethics had made it official: it is now as acceptable to starve babies to death outside the womb as it is to dismember babies inside the womb. A decision of almost unparalleled significance has been made and few beyond the pro-life movement have even blinked.

It is clear to me that if America can assimilate the deliberate killing of born babies virtually without missing a beat, the hour is much later than pro-lifers suspect. The time has come to reassess everything, most particularly our timetable. If we are ever going to have a chance to roll back the anti-life forces, we have to quickly dig in and define a perimeter of defense against further encroachment on the sanctity of human life. If we are to re-establish unborn babies as members in full standing in the human family, it is obvious that we must preserve what remains of the shrinking circle of common human decency.

This book is a preliminary look at where the pro-life movement is at and where it is headed; at what we've done and, more to the point, what else must be done to save the babies. What is important is not the particular conclusions any of the authors reach; each and every one is open to critical scrutiny. What *is* important is that the pro-life movement must update, revamp, refine, and expand its understanding of what is at stake in the battle between what we will call for our purposes here the "quality of life" ethic and the "sanctity of life" ethic. (Although this is an oversimplification, most people understand precisely what we are talking about.) We must re-evaluate the role our movement must play in the cataclysmic struggle between two philosophies that can not co-exist indefinitely. We are not providing a blueprint for that new role, only a sketch.

Consider, for example, the question posed to me by one advocate for the handicapped community. What chance, he asked me, does the pro-life movement have of ending the wholesale slaughter of unborn babies if our society accepts the premise that born babies must forfeit their lives if they do not live up to somebody else's arbitrary standards for "meaningful life"? Or, as another individual who is frightened to death by the casual acceptance of genetic engineering asked me, where will we be if we embrace a philosophy that life is "information in motion," that implicitly denies there is something uniquely irreducible about human beings?

This book is, then, a jumping off point for those who understand that what is at stake is nothing less than the fate of the human race. Divided into six sections, *To*

Rescue the Future: The Pro-Life Movement in the 1980s is composed of 22 essays written by many of the finest minds in the movement. My intention is quite specific: to suggest to the reader that our world is changing so fast, our society's decline into barbarism for the best of reasons so rapid that unless we move expeditiously on a number of fronts, we will be outflanked and overrun. We will look closely at what tactics the pro-life movement has used in the past and offer new avenues for possible exploration. Since a key ingredient in winning is the ability to anticipate what the anti-life forces will do next, we also look at what they have been doing and where we can expect them to strike next.

These goals explain why this book contains such vastly different kinds of essays, from scholarly examinations of the constitutional basis for the people's right to regulate abortion to very practical, nuts and bolts descriptions of how to organize your local community. The lengths are equally as varied. I was determined to provide something of interest to everyone regardless of level of commitment, from the novice pro-lifer to the 15-year veteran, from the closet sympathizer to the most outspoken pro-life advocate.

My special thanks go to former National Right to Life Committee President J.C. Willke, M.D. and current President Jean Doyle for their permission to write this book while I was serving as editor of *NRL News*. Needless to say, nothing in this book should be taken to represent official NRLC policy, nor should it be assumed that NRLC would necessarily agree with any or all of its conclusions. The contents of this book reflect the assumptions, value-judgments, and best guesses of myself and the contributors. My desire is to stimulate careful consideration of what the movement has done, is doing, and should be doing in the future.

To my wife, Lisa, my daughter, Emily Susan, my love

and profound gratitude for putting up with all of my long evenings in the den. They understood because we are in this fight as a family.

Dave Andrusko
Woodbridge, Virginia

INTRODUCTION: THE TRANSFORMATION OF ABORTION POLITICS

With the defeat of the Hatch-Eagleton Amendment and the particularly savage Supreme Court abortion decisions handed down in 1983, the abortion debate has settled into an odd sort of lull. Some commentators argue the issue has essentially fizzled out, a great example of the wish being father to the deed. Others ask of the pro-life movement the rhetorical question, If you haven't succeeded in eleven years, aren't your efforts doomed to failure? But the more astute appreciate that this moment of quiet is just the off-year calm before the presidential election year storm.

Whether cheering the putative demise of the movement or awaiting the enormously important 1984 elections, there is a common assumption: the partisans on both sides are plodding along on a treadmill, that nothing particularly different is or will take place, and like two armies dug into trenches, little will be gained or lost by either side in the foreseeable future.

Nothing could be further from the truth. Tremendous currents of change are quietly moving beneath the surface of abortion and other related life issues. The real issues at stake in the abortion dispute are becoming increasingly evident to more and more thoughtful people. The results may well be a complete transformation of the issue within five years.

AN INSATIABLE THIRST FOR KILLING

Dave Andrusko*

"Only when it's dark enough can you see the stars."
MARTIN LUTHER KING, JR.

The legalized execution of 16 million unborn children bears powerful witness to the infinite capacity of the human heart for cruelty and self-deception. As a culture, we have broken our moorings and set sail on the bloody seas of mass extermination. Having loosened the bonds that restrain parents from brutalizing their little ones, America has assured itself a prominent place in the history of mankind's bloodiest century.

So accustomed have we become to the bloodletting that many forget it wasn't always so. It is a sobering thought to know that, soon, an entire generation will have come to maturity never knowing a time when children did not have to thank their parents for not killing them.

Abortion on demand, once the exclusive agenda of

*Dave Andrusko is the editor of *National Right to Life News* and editor of this book.

cultural revolutionaries waging unconditional war on "bourgeois," "patriarchal" America, has now settled into the very marrow of our culture. Not so many years ago, the very word abortion was so abhorrent it was not used in polite company. The knowledge of this stern disapproval seems to have fallen into some memory hole. Abortion is so entrenched today that proponents have to be roused to wave their coathangers. This is understandable. Twenty-five years ago they were outsiders carrying the banner for a fringe cause. Today they are custodians of the status quo. Much has changed.

What will the Toynbees, the Gibbons, the Spenglers of the future say about the American Holocaust? How could a nation which as recently as the late 1950s embraced what Langdon Jones has called the "Procreative Ethic" change in less than a generation into a giant human abattoir in which every third baby conceived is knived, poisoned, starved, choked or dismembered?

Like scholars explaining, say, the origins of the First World War, each will fasten on certain cultural components which they believe shaped the temper of the times. Some will cast an explanatory eye on the general disarray of a culture awash in random acts of meaningless violence and depersonalized sex. Others will cite the "population bomb" scare of the 1970s, while still others will seize upon the passionate media embrace of a Woman's Liberation Movement which established its secular church on the rock of unfettered abortion. For the popularists, the most likely explanation will probably be cultural narcissism — "meism" — an inward turning so complete it made any concern for posterity problematic.

Explaining a change of this magnitude is probably impossible. However, while scholars may search in vain for the causes of this incredible turnaround, the horrific results will virtually jump out at them: incalculable brutality and limitless violence.

Second Generation Abortion Doublespeak

As professor William Brennan has demonstrated, the sine qua non of any program of mass killing, is the depersonalization of the intended victims. Their lives must be defined as "useless." In the case of abortion, witness the indispensible role played by the "fetus as blob" rhetoric that polluted the discussion about the fate of the unborn child in the sixties. However, by the late seventies and early eighties, even those who most adamantly clung to the flat earth credo that the unborn child was merely a part of his or her mother's body were forced to reconsider their position.

Faced with medical technology's amazing ability to "rehumanize" the unborn child, abortion strategists in the early 1980s began to reconsider their tactics. Al Moran, executive director of Planned Parenthood's New York affiliate sounded the warning at a 1982 media workshop sponsored by the National Abortion Federation. Moran warned that abortion proponents might find themselves "isolated" if they could not negate the effect of emerging technology, which was to "personalize" the unborn child.

Realizing that the traditional question, When does life begin? was rapidly becoming moot, abortion apologists turned to two new tactics: accelerating the desensitization process and cutting the abortion question in a way more favorable to their position. Each was intended to replace or shore up old justifications which were growing increasingly untenable.

On the surface, it might seem redundant to try to further "desensitize" a nation that was killing three to four thousand babies a day. But pro-abortionists were well aware that it was not enough merely to make abortion and childbirth (in the memorable words of Federal District Judge Jon O. Newman) "simply two alternative medical methods of dealing with pregnancy..."

Abortion proponents would never be safe from the moral indictment of pro-lifers until and unless Americans would accept abortion under any circumstances, no matter how grisly.

Thus, it was not only to make sure no second trimester babies survived abortions that clinics switched from the use of prostaglandins to "D and E," dismemberment and evacuation. Pro-abortion strategists grasped that if the public would accept something as ghastly as the dismemberment of babies identical in size to preemies, then any subsequent fallback position to the use, for example, of "menstrual extraction," or "morning after pills" would seem positively benign by comparison.

The other half of this shrewdly conceived and executed abortion counterattack was a largely successful effort to completely redefine the question. If it could no longer plausibly be argued that life did not begin at conception, abortion proponents understood that the question must be asked in a different way. The new question posed was, What *is* human life?

With a flick of their pens, abortion proponents breezily announced that it was obvious "mere biological life" began at conception, their previous all-out denials notwithstanding. The issue now before the house was either: What makes "biological" life "human" life?; or (in a pinch) when does this product of the union of a male, and female *Homo sapiens* become a "person"? It was, of course, a given that if one did not measure up, one was not entitled to the protection of the law.

The specifics of what constitutes humanness or personhood varied from ideologue to ideologue: consciousness, ability to interact, rationality, ability to communicate, sociality, etc., etc. If one is willing to believe that these people are not consciously deliberately malevolent, then the charitable view is that they did not have the first idea what they were unleashing. Nonetheless, what is abundantly obvious is that any or all of these criteria are completely subjective and liable to the worse kind of abuse, if ever put into effect. Abortion supporters, however, were serenely indifferent to the expansionary logic of their second generation abortion-speak.

Abortion and Infanticide: Six of One, Half-Dozen of the Other

Keener observers, however, realized instantly what had happened. The arguments that now justified abortion were equally adept at defending the practice of infanticide. Indeed, the fit could not have been any better. After all, children with Down's syndrome are not likely to meet the pro-abortionists' elitist standards for "interaction," or "communication." If by chance they do, "sociality" (whatever that is) offers grounds vague and all-encompassing enough to justify the destruction of Down's syndrome children.

Then came Infant Doe, the first instance of infanticide to be widely publicized. Born with Down's syndrome, that tiny baby boy was starved to death by parents who preferred death for their child to a life of mental retardation. It is impossible to overestimate what the reaction of the pro-life and pro-abortion forces to his horrible death signified. For what happened was not just that another category of human beings had been decertified, horrible as that was. Nor was it just that the powerful media elite had trotted out the same arguments to defend infanticide it had used to justify abortion, terrifying as that was.

What had transpired in the wake of the death of Infant

Doe was that the pro-abortion worldview had broken out of the confines of the issue of abortion. Abortion apologists found themselves either defending or not opposing infanticide. Given the evolution (or devolution) of their fundamental premises, this was unavoidable.

Even more important, by publicly taking up the cause of Infant Doe and by standing foursquare behind the Reagan Administration's efforts to prevent infanticide, the pro-life movement demonstrated both to itself and to the outside world that it was genuinely, consistently pro-life.

Each side was dramatically, permanently changed by their positions on infanticide. Abortion's inherently anti-life biases were revealed in all their pervasive ugliness. The reverence for all human life, always at the core of the pro-life movement, received national attention. The importance of this breakthrough cannot be stressed enough, and we will come back to it momentarily.

For the moment, what should be noted is that, predictably, the national media haven't the foggiest notion of what has happened. They still report the battle as if the issue of infanticide were a sidebar to the abortion issue and of only passing interest. The confusion over the momentous, agenda-shifting legacy of Infant Doe's death is typical of the media's superficial understanding of the politics of abortion and of the tremendous philosophic and ethical questions at stake. It can be said in all fairness that the major media misread the lessons of virtually every important abortion-related story of 1982-1983. Thus, a brief look at what really happened is in order before we conclude our look at the pro-life movement's "state of the union" and prospects for saving the babies.

1982-83: The Turning Point?

To those who do not or will not understand the pro-life

movement, the events of 1982-83 might look like something between a draw and a disaster. Politically, the movement added "only" two pro-life votes in the U.S. Senate, we were told. The Hatch-Eagleton Amendment garnered the votes of "only" half the Senate. Meanwhile, the Supreme Court far from "moderating" its position on abortion, as some pro-abortionists kept pretending it might, actually expanded abortion rights. And, as we have seen, infanticide acquired its own troop of apologists, including the *New York Times* and the American Academy of Pediatrics, no less.

If the pro-life movement was indeed the babies' only chance, and if it had fared as poorly as the media kept saying it had, then supporters could be forgiven if they put down their morning papers completely downcast. However the truth, as so often is the case with abortion politics, was far different.

Those who interpret the daily ebb and flow of events for us — the media — do not understand social movements in general, and most especially the pro-life movement in particular. They treat the movement as if it were a corporation motivated by a desire for profit. Thus, for example, if pro-lifers do not profit enough politically one year, the media immediately announces that the movement is, in effect, nearing insolvency.

Moreover, journalists are fascinated with the idea of politics as sport. Primarily concerned with "who's ahead," they find it virtually impossible to see the currents that are quietly moving beneath the surface.

Instead, the media settles into its favorite sport; the "expectations" game that presidential candidates know so well. The media decides how well we are supposed to fare, say, in the Senate vote on the Hatch-Eagleton, and when we don't make it, we have "lost."

The truth is the pro-life movement came out of 1983 in decidedly better shape than at any time in its eleven-year history. To its core membership have been added important new groups that supplement and expand the breadth of the pro-life issues. Despite the formidable forces arrayed against it, the movement is extending its influence and outreach in ever-widening circles. Each "defeat," when looked at in perspective, reveals a far-different pattern of events than a casual once-over would suggest.

Take, for example, the 1982 elections. Coming away from a perusal of the *New York Times*, the casual reader might ask himself if he hadn't just read the movement's epitaph. It is all there in black and white. We did miserably. As Senator Robert Packwood announced, it was only a matter of a couple of years before, the "battle for choice" would be won. After producing a net pro-life gain of nine seats in the Senate in 1980, pro-lifers added "only" two new voices in 1982. Therefore, the issue was on the wane... or so we were told.

But as David O'Steen and Darla St. Martin point out in their excellent essay, in both cases pro-life strategists pulled out the most that could have been hoped for. In 1980, the political landscape was replete with vulnerable pro-abortion senators. They were replaced with pro-lifers. In 1982, virtually the exact opposite was true. There was a realistic possibility of losing between three and five pro-life incumbent senators. In fact, all pro-life senatorial incumbents were protected and two pro-abortion Democrats were replaced by two pro-life Republicans. The real lesson is that in both elections, the movement accomplished the maximum possible, given what was available.

Similarly, far from a defeat, the vote on the Hatch-Eagleton amendment served a number of critically important functions. Only someone whose memory goes back no further than yesterday could fail to see what a landmark the vote represented. In 1974, pro-lifers could scratch out only 27 votes against federal funding of abortion. In 1983, one-half the Senate (49) voted against abortion on demand. Equally important, a vote against the amendment will be used against those senators who are now on record as unambiguously in favor of abortion for any reason throughout the entire nine months of pregnancy.

And as barbaric as the Court's decisions were in the *Akron, Ashcroft*, and *Simopolous* cases, only a child could believe that a court whose majority has invested ten years in defending abortion would change its mind. The major story was obviously the emergence of the Court's first female member as an articulate, thoughtful critic of *Roe v. Wade.* Justice O'Connor's dazzling dissent unquestionably offers a principled justification to reverse the legal absurdity that is *Roe.* Her argument was so convincing it is arguable that only one more new anti-*Roe* member needs to be added to the Court to construct a majority to overturn the decision.

Finally, the tragic death of Infant Doe will someday be identified as the turning point in the struggle over the entire "quality of life" ethic. While most people seemed unmoved by this injustice (or are unaware), the Reagan Administration bit the bullet and went nose to nose with the powerful American Academy of Pediatrics. When the AAP and other medical heavyweights screamed "Big Brother," the Reagan Administration did not blink; it merely made its intentions even more clear. Whatever the final results, the brake has been applied to the drive for infanticide. Had the death of Infant Doe occurred during the administration of Jimmy Carter, there is little doubt that the government would have added its sanction to the right of hospitals to discriminate against handicapped babies.

The martyrdom of Infant Doe also facilitated the first tentative working alliance between the pro-life movement and the disability groups. Although the pro-life movement has always opposed infanticide, it had not gotten publicly involved in the fight until the time of the death of Infant Doe. At that juncture, pro-life activists struck out on this new front and the character of the movement has been changed forever.

It is worth pondering as well that our ally in this fight represents the first instance of a group working with pro-lifers which has not been instantly savaged by the press. Advocates for the handicapped community are not viewed by the press as kooks. This authenticity rubbed off on pro-lifers; the movement continues to receive much, much better coverage in its opposition to infanticide than it ever had in opposing abortion.

Beyond the intrinsic importance of the emerging pro-life/disability group alliance is what it bodes for the future. As we have seen, with the death of Infant Doe, the anti-life genie has escaped the narrow confines of the pro-abortion bottle. It is free to find new masters to serve. And there is no shortage: witness variations on the euthanasia theme, such as "death with dignity," "living wills," and "assisted suicide." But this list just begins to scratch the surface of the club of death. If the twentieth century teaches us nothing else, it is that there will always be legions eager to turn mankind into meat.

What has this to do with the right to life? Grover Rees, III, the eminent constitutional scholar, tells a story in which the friend of a woman who had been declared brain dead came to him for help. He told Rees that the woman had communicated with him by blinking her eyes and squeezing his hand. The doctors who had taken her off the respirator and ceased intravenous feeding, refused to believe the woman's friend. He had come to Rees to ask him to do what he could, including going to a judge to compel the hospital to feed the woman until her status could be determined. However, she died before Rees could be of help.

After it was all over, Rees was puzzled why the man had come to him in the first place. He had not written on the topic of brain death or definition of death. Rees had no track record which would suggest he would be helpful or even sympathetic in such a case.

And then it struck Rees why the man had turned to him. Even though the man was not himself anti-abortion, to whom else could he turn but a pro-lifer and automatically expect that the person would take up the cause for life, devote as much time as was necessary, and all for free?

As the momentum builds to "do something" about the increase in the number of older citizens; as the seemingly benign idea of screening out "bad" genes becomes compulsory for certain "undesirable" traits; when doctors are so eager for spare organs they cease to observe such subtleties as whether the donor is really dead, where else will frightened citizens be able to turn for help but to the pro-life movement?

New alliances will sprout up right and left. As was the case with the generally very-liberal disability group advocates, coalitions will be cemented with groups that previously had kept their distance from the pro-life movement.

But it was not just in politics and the courts that the pro-life movement made important gains. Nineteen eighty-three may someday be remembered as the year in which several major non-denominational "electronic preachers" courageously decided to assume a high profile on abortion. The enormous audiences for the likes of Jim Bakker, Pat Robertson, and Jimmy Swaggart, are intuitively pro-life, but "uneducated in the life issues," as pro-lifers like to put it.

To many conservative Protestants, abortion smacks of "politics," which has no place anywhere near a pulpit. Nonetheless, Bakker, especially, for months turned the entire thrust of his ministry in the direction of opposing abortion. The benefits to the cause of the unborn will prove to be beyond anyone's wildest imaginings. An entire nationwide audience, instinctively pro-life, has been made aware of the Abortion Holocaust.

Conclusion

This brief essay is an attempt to place in context a few of the enormous number of changes that have occurred in the politics of abortion. Much, much more could be said about the organizational maturity of the movement, and the socio-political context in which we fight for life. The contributors to this volume will elaborate on most of the issues I barely touched on as well as many others.

But the bottom line is you. We can only contribute what ideas, insights and energy we have. It is up to you, the readers of this book, and the millions of other pro-life Americans to re-establish the protection of law for all God's children.

The battle for life is not between pro-lifers and pro-abortionists, traditionalists and feminists, but rather between justice and injustice. Our opponents and their allies in the media know this deep down in their hearts, which is why they denounce us so bitterly. The battlelines are clear: Either life is for everyone or the right to life is doled out at the whim of the powerful. Abortion represents in miniature a struggle that ultimately must result in the total victory of one answer to this question or the other, for the principles at stake are absolutely irreconcilable.

If the partisans of "choice" win, what remains of our tattered sanctity of life ethic will be dismantled, piece by bloody piece. Because it is based on the right of the more powerful to oppress the less powerful, the pro-abortion position is at war with the core principles of our nation.

So blinded are they by their own rhetoric, they hold "choice" to their bosoms as if it represented a kind of philosopher's stone that magically converts cruelty into kindness, selfishness into altruism. But barbarism with a human face is still barbarism.

What they will never understand is that if the pro-life approach to problem pregnancies wins the day, then everyone wins; no lives are taken. Pro-lifers are just that: pro-life. We will do everything we can to help women facing troublesome pregnancies, or parents grappling with the birth of a child with handicaps. What we will not do is promise a one-stop, once-and-for-all solution to the human condition. That is the province of the pro-abortionists. As great simplifiers, they promise what we can never promise: twenty-minute solutions to complex human problems. All we can offer is love, compassion, and a life-sustaining choice.

As pro-lifers, we toil for a cause that is just and no amount of money, no full-page ads in the *New York Times*, no stream of hate-filled editorials will ever convert the slaughter of defenseless children into a just act. Richard Neuhaus told pro-lifers at the 1982 National Right to Life Convention that the pro-life movement is radical not because of how far out it is, but by "virtue of how deep and central is the question we raise: Who, then, is my neighbor?"

Neuhaus said the abortion issue is one of the great tests the American experiment has ever undergone. He said we should not be discouraged if our hope of victory is delayed for "we are recruited for the duration, we must be long-distance radicals — we must never give up." We will not give up... but, of course, you know that already.

What we must remember is that the local neighbourhood abortion clinic did not just appear out of nowhere. It had a long and dishonorable lineage. Its parentage is the same mentality that brought us the slave plantations, the concentration camps, and the Gulag Archipelago. It is a cruel mentality, one that worships power. It represents a view of life that limits the quality of humanness to those who are powerful enough to throw off the chains of their oppressors.

When you think about it, there is a fundamental irony at the heart of the battle to save the children. For it is the pro-life movement, scorned and ridiculed by the media as a "reactionary" force, that is the principal defender of the most revolutionary idea of the America experiment — the idea that all men and all women and all children, born and unborn, are created equal.

It is our duty and our privilege to keep that beacon of hope shining in a time of great darkness. When the inevitable discouragement sets in, just remember, as someone once wrote, that in the long sweep of history truly human victories are always upsets.

PART I

ENLARGING THE PRO-LIFE MOVEMENT: OUTREACH AND COALITION-BUILDING

One of the cold, hard facts of life for any social movement is that it can never merely maintain itself at current levels of activity: A social movement either creatively explores new avenues for growth or it withers and dies. The pro-life movement organizationally is standing at a pivotal crossroads in its history. Past quarrels and disagreements have been placed on the backburner. The consensus is that it is time to return to what pro-lifers do best: grassroots organizing. The alternative is to be buried by the colossal financial power and media support enjoyed by our opponents.

Part of the growth will involve overtures to and from constituencies that share our commitment to the sanctity of human life, not just for the young and the perfect. The now-classic example of this is the inchoate but, nevertheless, developing alliance between the right to life movement and the advocates for the handicapped over the issue of infanticide. In the three essays that follow, the reader will be treated to a cram course in how to develop and expand your local, state, or national pro-life organization.

ROE v. WADE: AN ELITIST DECISION

Carl Landwehr*

"An organized, motivated pro-life voting constituency — the product of an all-out, massive voter identification process — represents the only way to outmanoeuver the pro-abortion elitists."
CARL LANDWEHR

In 1973, the United States Supreme Court legalized abortion on demand throughout the entire nine months of pregnancy. Even the most avid pro-abortionists were taken aback by the Court's sweeping decision. In its *Roe v. Wade* and *Doe v. Bolton* decisions the Court took away from all fifty states the power to regulate abortion in any meaningful sense at the same time as it redefined the unborn child as a nonperson. The Court willfully forced upon Americans an anti-life ethic

*Carl Landwehr is the author of "Organizing for Community Pro-Life Action," a text now used throughout the United States and in six foreign countries. He is also the author of numerous articles and pro-life booklets on working with the media, effectively using community resources, and designing ways to educate the public about abortion.

that for a majority is in direct violation of long held beliefs about the value and sanctity of all human life.

These results are well known. What is not so well known is that both before and after *Roe* public opinion polls clearly show that up to 75 percent of the American people oppose the Court's revolutionary decisions. The Court's 1973 abortion decision as well as subsequent abortion opinions are a classic example of elite decision-making.

It is vital to raise the question, "Are grassroots people opposed to abortion?" The answer is a resounding, "Yes!" Indeed, the cause of unborn children is a classic grassroots movement. Webster's Dictionary defines grassroots as "society at a local level... distinguished from the centers of political leadership." When the Supreme Court legalized abortion in 1973 it was grassroot citizens, not elite decision-makers, who felt a moral commitment to change the law.

The belief that every human being has a God-given right to life regardless of age, health, or handicap is a basic value held by grassroots people. It blends well with their other values such as a strong family unit, religious commitment and a strong work ethic. Research done by the Connecticut Mutual Life Insurance Company further proved this point. The Connecticut Mutual's *Report on American Values in The '80's: The Impact of Belief* compares the values of people who are for abortion with those of people who are against abortion. It revealed that people with high religious commitment were opposed to abortion and people with low religious commitment were for abortion. Less important (but still having a significant value on people's values) was where they lived and their annual income. For example, people living in small cities or in rural areas and those with lower incomes were found to be strongly against abortion. In contrast, people living in larger cities and people with higher incomes were in favor of abortion.

The sides of the abortion issue are clearly drawn. On one side there are grassroots citizens with a deep moral conviction that every life is worth living. On the other side are elitist decision makers who advocate abortion as a solution to social problems such as overpopulation, rising welfare costs, teenage pregnancy, and birth defects. Each side in this battle has its own inherent resources which are important to evaluate.

What are our Resources?

Let's first analyze the resources of the pro-life camp. The sheer numbers of people who can be mobilized to take action at the voting booth is the greatest resource of the pro-life movement. But are grassroots people willing to work for legal protection of unborn children? Yes, grassroots people will work because of their deep moral commitment. Commitment alone, however, is not enough. Effective organizing is crucial if we are to take advantage of this pool of potential volunteers.

At the grassroots level, effective organizing is the only way to get all of these people involved. This is no easy task. Many people find the political system to be ovewhelming and complex. They are victimized by the "You can't fight City Hall" syndrome. They need local pro-life leaders in their churches and communities who will speak out publicly against abortion which will, in turn, give them the self-confidence they need to also speak out and get involved. Local leaders are the all-important key necessary for turning on the untapped resource of the pro-life grassroots. Local leaders must rally the concerned people in their community into an organized effort to save unborn children and change attitudes and public policy. The following suggestions will help a local leader organize his/her community:

1) Identify people who feel strongly about the issue.

2) Motivate them by showing them that we face a crisis situation in this country.
3) Give them a specific and reasonably attainable job to do.
4) Follow them up, reward them, and give them another job.
5) Encourage them to find others to give jobs to. Once that has happened, chances are good the leader is intrinsically motivated and will continue in the movement.

Frequently, local leaders do not have the necessary resources to develop the pro-life movement in their community. They must, in turn, have statewide leaders who will help them. Here's what state leaders must do to assist and mobilize local church and community grassroots leaders:

1) Identify an active local leader in every community in the state.
2) Train local leaders on the issue. They need to know how to educate about abortion and how to hold their elected representatives accountable.
3) Set a goal, such as state legislation, that all local groups can immediately tie into.
4) Establish a statewide communication network, such as a newsletter but, better yet, a telephone tree.
5) Divide responsibilities at the state level into standing committees on legislation, education, and fundraising. These committees can help local leaders.
6) Introduce pro-life legislation during each session of the state legislature.
7) Launch a major campaign of letter writing and visiting elected representatives.

8) Bring the legislation up for a vote so that all elected officials are on record.
9) Use the vote as a barometer of the state's ability to ratify a pro-life amendment.
10) After the vote, begin political action to defeat the legislator voting against the measure.
11) When legislation is not pending, state leaders should maintain contact with local leaders by working on educational and development projects.

These are some of the ways state and local pro-life leaders can instill a positive attitude in their people, conduct activities of substance and meaning, and develop a functioning organization. At the national level, there are different ways of approaching the issue as well as unique problems. But at the national level, there is also one particular weakness that must be overcome.

There are many "undeveloped" states. An undeveloped state is one that does not have United States senators and representatives who will vote for pro-life legislation, does not have legislatures that will ratify a human life amendment, and does not have a statewide organization to implement pro-life action. This patchwork situation is a result of many pro-life leaders leaving development and expansion of the movement up for grabs. They mistakenly believe that this vast army of pro-life support will take action without nurture, cultivation, and mobilization.

Leadership in the movement seems to be following the classic educational model. So many leaders believe that to save unborn children all they have to do is give educational programs and hand out literature. Too many people think that once a person learns about the tragedy of abortion such shocking information will immediately launch them into action. This is not the case. *People get involved in the movement because someone asks them to do something.* Education should be viewed not only as providing information but also as a tool to identify new workers for the movement. Once they are identified they should immediately be involved. In other words, give them a job to do. Involvement means making a commitment to *do* something.

While vitally important, the education model is insufficient, particularly at the national level. People must not only be made aware of the reality and the horror of abortion, they must be plugged into pro-life organizations and activated to do something concrete. Here are some suggestions for leaders at the national level:

1) Undeveloped states should be identified and offered assistance.
2) All national organizations should jointly plan strategy to help organize these undeveloped states.
3) Each national organization should set development objectives for their constituencies in the state and then work together at the local level.
4) Undeveloped states should be helped to establish a basic organizational structure (division of responsibility), encompassing all levels in the movement.
5) Techniques should be provided to these states in the form of helpful guidelines for action.
6) Developed states nearby should be asked to share financial resources and trained personnel.
7) These states should be helped to set goals and objectives to develop a one-or two-year plan.

What Are Their Resources?

Now let's look at the resources of the anti-life forces. After the abortion decision in 1973 they did not take the pro-life movement seriously. They felt that it would quickly dissipate. However, with the defeat of pro-abortion Sen. Dick Clark in 1978, followed by the overwhelming pro-life victories of 1980, they realized the movement would not go away on its own; they would have to work for its demise.

They have begun to reach outside the "centers of political leadership." They are now marketing their anti-life philosophy in grassroots America. Our base of support at the local level is now under attack. They are concentrating on those states where they can defeat an amendment once it is passed out of Congress. If they successfully establish solid inroads into the value structure of the grassroots, the pro-life movement is in serious trouble. The battle is being fought for public opinion. Will society accept or reject abortion on demand? This is the crucial question.

Our opponents have many other valuable resources. Young people have grown up with abortion on demand and many of them accept it matter-of-factly. In a few years they will be voting. Abortion proponents have the money to buy prime television time to bring pro-abortion values into everyone's home. They have political, governmental, judicial, and media connections which can have a major influence on what laws are passed, the content of political party philosophy, and how the federal and state tax money is spent.

How the Other Side Works

A classic example of our opponent's effectiveness occurred in Toledo, Ohio, in 1980 when pro-abortion groups defeated a pro-life city ordinance. They were able to convince pro-life people to actually vote against the ordinance. The loss is also significant because it occurred in a city comprised largely of blue-collar workers, 30 percent of whom are Catholic. Catholics voted against the ordinance by a 2-1 margin.

A poll was taken two months before election day and over half the voters supported the pro-life ordinance. What happened between the poll and election day warrants serious observation. A campaign consulting firm was hired, and the pro-abortionists developed a campaign strategy which did not even address the abortion issue. Campaign rhetoric and TV strategy was non-emotional and concentrated on a woman's health. They argued if the ordinance delayed a woman's abortion, her health would be endangered. And since abortion is legal anyway, why should voters be in favor of the ordinance?

Television commercials ran showing a pregnant woman (presumably pro-life), talking with another lady. Here is what she said about the ordinance: "It is bad law for both sides. It is bad for anti-abortionists because it doesn't stop abortions, it just makes them more dangerous." So, in effect, the pro-life voter actually was tricked into voting against the ordinance by an effective campaign using what appeared to be logical arguments.

Pro-Life Growth and Development: A Look Ahead

It is important to ask a timely question: Is the pro-life movement growing? Yes, it is growing, but not fast enough in order to keep up with our opponents. The pro-life movement is now a strong force in America's politics, but this will change if we do not get back to basic grassroots organizing. Efforts to expand the movement into undeveloped areas are haphazard and too often left to chance. There are pockets of strong pro-life activity among oceans of inactivity and ineffectiveness. Many developed states border undeveloped states and there is all too often little if any sharing of resources.

Here is an example of what has to be done if the pro-life movement is to gain rather than lose ground to the anti-life forces. These are minimum requirements.

1) State leaders with help from the national organizations must take out a map of their state and circle the towns and cities where there is no pro-life activity.
2) Divide these cities up among state leaders.
3) Give educational programs in these cities until a nucleus of concerned citizens is found.
4) Teach these new people how to educate others as a way to find new workers.
5) Immediately involve the new people in on-going community and statewide activities.

The potential for pro-life victory *is* there. There is enormous potential for overturning *Roe* if we remember that *Roe* legalized abortion on demand for the entire pregnancy and that up to 75 percent of the American public opposes unregulated abortion. The amendment process is an awesome undertaking; it requires education, political resources and savvy, and a resolution that will never take no for an answer. Consider the obstacles: an amendment must first receive a two-thirds vote in both houses of Congress and then be ratified by three-fourths of the state legislatures. Formidable as that prospect unquestionably is, there is potentially enough support out there among grassroots people.

However, those people are not going to just spontaneously fall into place. Unless the pro-life forces are thoroughly, thoughtfully, cleverly organized, they cannot take full advantage of their considerable potential to educate, pass legislation, and elect prolife candidates. An organized, motivated pro-life voting constituency — the product of an all-out, massive voter identification process — represents the only way to outmanoeuver the pro-abortion elitists.

MAINSTREAMING: A CASE STUDY

Denyse Handler*

"When our message becomes mixed up with sectarian, political, or cultural values, people who do not share those values do not disagree — they simply dismiss our message as having no relevance to themselves. The purpose of 'mainstreaming' and other techniques discussed here is to make the message relevant to those whom we have a chance of convincing. Only then can we talk about agreement or disagreement in principle."

Handler's maxim: A foot in the door is worth more than an army in the street.

DENYSE HANDLER

This is a story about "mainstreaming." It is the story of how one pro-life publication consciously decided to break out of the pro-life ghetto to reach a larger audience with its message. The story of how our

*Denyse Handler is the managing editor of The Human, a Canadian magazine of life issues. She lives in Toronto with her husband and two children. She has also published a number of articles and pamphlets on various life issues.

magazine, *the Human* changed might encourage others, whatever their field, to reach out and try to mainstream their efforts. Believe me, it can work!

Once upon a time, back in the early Seventies, there was a "really great little pro-life paper" run by a band of dedicated volunteers. It had lots of enthusiastic movement support. It weathered a formidable series of storms to bring the news of the life issues to pro-lifers. But after seven years the editors were not happy. By the standards of other 'cause' magazines, *the Uncertified Human*, as it was called, was terrible. We had no government money, for one thing. Much worse, we were very inbred. We were satisfied as long as we were appreciated by pro-lifers, but we did not realize what a valuable tool a magazine can be in affecting public opinion, especially in a country such as Canada, with about 27 million people (only about 17 million of whom speak enough English to have read *the Uncertified Human* anyway).

It was not worthwhile continuing if we were going to spend the next decade talking to our own faithful little band, changing few minds and making little impact on the way the life issues developed in Canada. Unless people who control media or social agencies can be interested in at least considering our view, no headway can be made in changing public opinion. Moral certitude and political muscle will not accomplish this. Imagination is essential for moral leadership in a bioethical age. Coincidentally, at the time (1981), our dedicated printer had formed a partnership with a public relations man who agreed to look at our efforts. Almost his first concrete suggestion was, "Change your name."

Our name, *the Uncertified Human*, was very precious to us. It was clever in an ingroupy way, referring to the decertification of people as human beings that precedes their destruction. But what did such a name communicate to people who knew nothing of this? Nothing. It was a formidable barrier to public acceptance of this magazine. Once we got past the trauma of contemplating a name change, we suddenly realized that, among ourselves, we had always called our magazine *the Human*.

In October 1981, under a new masthead and all new artwork, the first edition of *the Human* came out. Since then our input into public discussion of the life issues in Canada has broadened considerably. Subscriptions among institutions, professionals, and libraries soared. Media interest increased sharply.

But there was more to come. We recognized that in order to be accepted as a magazine with a legitimate viewpoint, worthy of inclusion in library collections, we had to be accepted by other magazines. (Not *loved*, just accepted.) We applied for membership in the Canadian Periodical Publishers' Association (CPPA) while still in the old *Uncertified Human* format. We were rejected. There may have been prejudice in that.

But this rejection caused us some soul-searching. We had always prided ourselves on being an all-volunteer, home-grown, kitchen table operation. It really showed, too. Our self-image, of which we were proud, was totally inconsistent with our desire to reach and influence opinion-makers and trend-setters. They were the very people most likely to be turned off by this sort of thing.

We faced the fact realistically that, while the CPPA may have its flaws, it is responsible for maintaining minimum standards of publication in member magazines. The old *Uncertified Human* was a borderline case at best and therefore highly vulnerable to prejudice. The new *Human* sailed in without a fuss (though, it must be confessed, a few discreet visits to granting agencies were made, just to make sure there was no unnecessary difficulty). Now we are available on selected newsstands — we compete on equal terms with magazines with an opposite editorial policy — instead of merely hollering about them from the sidelines, as in the past.

What about content? We wanted to be mainstream in our appeal, yet retain our editorial values — concern for human life in all forms and stages. We soon learned how we were going wrong in that department. A young medical student who attended church with our executive editor, Jessica Pegis, told her that we ran terrific articles, full of facts, but that their overall effect was frequently ruined by some preachy or pompous closing paragraph, reminding the audience that pro-life people understand the evils of the world and that they are either going to fix things or tell people how much worse it's going to get. She thought this approach alienated people who did not officially consider themselves "pro-life" — and who, after all, were we trying to reach? She told Jessica that she could not show *the Human* to her professors or fellow students.

Jessica checked out some of her own stories and discovered the woman was right. Stories by other staff writers, including myself, fell into the same trap. Suddenly, a lot of questions about our public appeal came into sharper focus. Jessica realized that whenever we said that something "upset pro-life people," we were limiting our audience by assuming that membership in the ideological camp of pro-life was a prerequisite to having any worthwhile opinions about abortion or infanticide or aging.

She realized that "posing the issues" as opposed to "stating the answers" is the key to success. We have never, then or since, attempted to conceal our anti-abortion bias. But we allow the reader to perceive himself as a vital participant in an exchange of information. This is the basis of effective persuasion.

We all but eliminated the word "pro-life" from our copy, except where it occurred as part of the name of a group. Instead we talk about ourselves or others being "concerned about human life issues," "concerned about abortion," "anxious to get legal protection for unborn children." This forces people to think about the issues in new ways.

Our editorial slant is obvious anyway. Our writers' guidelines advise the would-be freelancer that we don't accept material "that argues against the right to life of any group of human beings, including the unborn." We will be listed in the 1984 *Writer's Market*, so that soon hundreds of American and Canadian writers, by sending $1.00, will receive a copy of *the Human* and the guidelines. By purchasing manuscripts in this area, we are helping to increase the flow of material supportive of our cause.

We now bill ourselves as a Magazine of Life Issues. This implies, as Jessica Pegis points out, that everyone is interested in life. The reader can learn the latest on the issues that draw together the disciplines of science and ethics. This is quite different from stating one's bias at the outset, since a reader is far more likely to be lured by a promise of information than by a threat of a lecture. We also do features on contemporary trends and problems that anyone who rejects solutions like abortion, infanticide, or mercy killing must face — for instance, how to provide social services for single parents, retarded and physically handicapped people during a recession. We also provide regular film and book reviews.

We do not supply the answers before we ask the questions. We ask some questions ourselves. The result is that people now accept us more readily on *our* terms. Instead of dismissing us as an "anti-abortion propaganda broadsheet," they're apt to say something like, "Oh yes, you people do a lot of things on the handicapped — and you're anti-abortion too, aren't you? Very interesting. You raise a lot of difficult issues."

Our biggest reward to date came on June 22, 1983, when an award-winning Canadian columnist called us "Canada's most relevant social issues magazine" in his regular column on page 2 of the *Toronto Star*, the fourth largest daily in North America. Much other notice has followed since then. We feel that we are succeeding in mainstreaming the issues, so that our point of view ceases be viewed as the preserve of conservative Catholics, small-c conservatives, fundamentalist sects, and assorted cranks.

The techniques we used can be adapted for use by anyone. Here is a convenient list that you could use to do the same thing:

1) Get rid of quirky, in-group features that guarantee limited public interest and exposure. Be ruthless. It is not the Old Guard you need to convince, but the public.
2) Go professional as soon as you can. Properly conceived, well-planned, well-executed efforts attract more attention and pay for themselves.
3) Get in Everywhere. A foot in the door is worth more than an army in the streets.
4) Don't have all the answers. Talk as if all sensible people agree that these concerns are important and present your views for discussion. Avoid the use of "limiting" words like "the pro-life view is" when what you really mean is "the view that would give due protection to *all* parties involved is..." People want to develop ideas that will help them confront these issues without putting on a mental uniform.

There is much more that could be said on these topics. There is, for instance, the useful art of "counter-stereotyping," deliberately reversing a stereotype of your group. If, for instance, your group is believed to be the preserve of middle-aged doctors' wives, make sure that *every* speaker at your rally is a woman under thirty in blue jeans, until the stereotype changes. There is also the question of how to make use of government largesse, etc. For now, let's just say, it can be done and if you have a mind to, you can certainly do it.

COALITION-BUILDING AND THE PRO-LIFE MOVEMENT

Paul M. Weyrich*

"As pro-life leaders, our job is to activate the constituencies represented by these spokesmen. We can win if we think creatively, implement our strategies aggressively and honestly, and work unceasingly to broaden our coalition."

PAUL WEYRICH

All too often, many of the fine people seeking to build a new political majority in America fall victim to hopelessness. They weigh the enormity of the task before us and they say, "This problem is too big,

*Paul M. Weyrich is Executive Director of the Committee for the Survival of a Free Congress (CSFC) and a prominent conservative theorist and leader. Weyrich also serves as President of the Free Congress Research and Education Foundation, a public policy research organization, and as President of Coalition for America, a non-partisan organization. A veteran pro-lifer, Weyrich is married. He and his wife, Joyce have five children.

it's just too much. There's nothing I can do about this because I am only one. The media is pro-abortion (or anti-family). I can't succeed so I won't try."

As I travel around this great country, I hear variations of this lament time and time again. Sometimes it will fall more along these lines: "Well, it is true that you and your colleagues in Washington have managed to accomplish some positive things. But here in our town, the other side is entrenched and we will never be able to succeed." My reply to the good people who say such things is simple and direct.

The modern pro-life, pro-family movement was not built in a day; nor for that matter, was the sophisticated, liberal coalition that reigned largely unchallenged from the days of FDR until the 1980 elections. None of the varied elements of the coalition which brought us a substantially more pro-life Congress in 1980 was formed easily or quickly. Even more to the point, not all of the important activity going on in our movement has taken place in Washington, D.C. In fact, the basis for our activities is a lot of people doing things at the local level. Prominence and effectiveness are achieved slowly, through simple hard work. The thrust of this paper will be to examine the theory and some of the practicalities of putting together a winning coalition. Although I'll be referring to the experience of "Library Court*," it is my opinion that the lessons are directly applicable to the pro-life movement and its need to build a broadbased coalition.

*I wish to note that the examination in this article of the Library Court concept as a coalition-building tool is based on conversations with my colleague Connie Marshner, who directs the Library Court group. In addition, portions of the discussion of leadership are adapted from an article which first appeared in the July 1983 issue of *Conservative Digest*.

A Theory of Coalition-Building: Winning Through Increments

Increments. That is the key word. Majority coalitions and political progress are achieved one step at a time, in small incremental pieces. To start building your local coalition (and thus help build the national pro-life coalition) first look at the total picture in your community. Do not let that total picture, which will seem overwhelming, intimidate you. Break the solutions to your problems down into achievable steps. Further, do not let yourself be intimidated by the resources and expertise our opponents bring to the political fray. Remember, they did not succeed in winning all they have all at once either. Their objectives and goals evolved over a long period of time. We must appreciate the virtue of winning a little bit at a time.

For example, on abortion, many of our people have taken the position that either we get the ultimate bill or amendment that stops all abortions or we do not do anything at all on the issue. I happen to believe that that is an ineffective, perhaps immoral, position because if one can take any steps toward stopping some abortions that is a correct step *provided* that one keeps the ultimate objective in mind and continues to strive toward it.

How National Coalitions Work in Practice

The way any national legislative coalition works — and the thinking process behind it — was brought home to me early in my tenure in Washington. As a young aide to Senator Gordon Allott of Colorado, I was assigned to attend a strategy group meeting supporting expansion of existing open housing legislation. Present at the meeting were: Hill staffers like myself, decision-makers for the various civil rights organizations, a potpourri of left-of-center groups (even those not directly concerned with civil rights questions), liberal newspaper columnists, and assorted other folks.

My eyes were opened by what I saw. I was amazed at what transpired. First, the legislation was explained in down-to-earth terms and its importance to the entire liberal movement was emphasized. Then, the chairman of the meeting took one aspect of the bill at a time and noted "action items" — areas in which support for the legislation was weak. I saw Hill staffers volunteering to produce either statements for the *Congressional Record* or means of forcing floor votes. I saw outside research groups volunteering to produce background papers by a specified date. Various groups promised to be sure to insert guidance targeted to their memberships in the next issues of their newsletters. A prominent newspaper columnist promised to produce a column supporting the thrust of the legislation.

What I saw was coalition politics practiced at its best. All the promised actions indeed took place and the proposal was ultimately enacted. Nothing was particularly mysterious or incomprehensible about the process. When people speak today of "inevitable decline," I object. The prevailing anti-life, anti-family bias was not inevitable; rather, it was revolution from the top down, the result of hard work and planning by our opponents who understood thoroughly how the system works. I have argued and continue to argue that we need to learn some political lessons from our political opponents. Which leads me to my next point:

There are no such things as inevitable victories or inevitable losses. Those who built — and for so many years sustained — the FDR coalition always understood that Washington was not built in a day. Elements of the liberal coalition have always held out for the ultimate while gladly accepting the gradual along the way. A lot of people try to make our political opponents seem ten feet tall. They are not nearly as formidable as they seem. How they operate is no mystery, nor are the tactics they employ the exclusive property of liberals. With the right combination of humility and aggressiveness, we will ultimately win the right of safe passage for all unborn babies. But we must remember the battle will be won one step at a time.

One other preliminary point. It is absolutely imperative to understand that in coalescing with other groups, we are talking about politics, not theology. By that I mean when we witness to a friend we are attempting to convert him totally. But with public policy questions, we are not necessarily going to get 100 percent conversion, nor should we necessarily try for it.

An illustration may make this point more clearly. When we look to someone who agrees with us on infanticide, but not on abortion *per se,* if we refuse to work with him or her to curb infanticide in the local hospital, we are making a major, perhaps fatal, tactical error. In a broader political context, this is like saying to a potential ally in any number of causes: "If you will publicly repent of every wrong position you have ever taken, I might condescend to let you work with me." How many allies do you think you will secure with that attitude?

You have to take people where they are. If you do that and do not surrender your own views, if you are good and you work hard, you will gain the opportunity to witness to new allies. I know of literally hundreds of people who reluctantly entered a pro-family coalition who subsequently became enthusiastic co-workers in the cause. The more they found out about the organizations in the pro-family movement, the more they became convinced we were what they were looking for in politics.

Let me give a practical example. Suppose you are, like me, a pro-lifer who is also a political conservative. You find yourself in a community where you have excellent prospects for reducing the number of abortions or abortion referrals at the local hospital. Further, you find that your strongest potential ally is the left-of-center clergyman who, unfortunately in your view, strongly favors the nuclear weapons freeze.

If you insist that such persons have sound conservative views on the nuclear freeze before you will work with them to stop local abortions, you will in all likelihood not have them with you. If, however, you take the opportunity to get to know them, you might be able to persuade them of the wisdom of your point of view on the freeze. Even if you do not change their views on the freeze, you might be able to save the lives of some innocent human beings who would otherwise be killed in the local hospital. The lesson for coalition builders is if you never get to know your potential ally in the first place, neither of you will ever have the chance to save those innocent lives.

What I am arguing against here is a mindset as much as anything else. Some people take the old view that goes like this: "There are only two reliable pro-lifers left in the country and that's me and you, and I'm not too sure about you." You *cannot* make political progress with that attitude. Without ever compromising our most essential principles, the key to building a pro-life governing coalition is an attitude that is as *inclusive* — not exclusive — as possible.

This view has lead to something unusual for me. For the first time in 25 years of political life, I am being accused of being in the middle! I have never considered myself a moderate, but rather a staunch (albeit realistic) conservative. Yet, I maintain that it is an indefensible position to say: "We are here and we want to get over there, but unless we can get there all at once, we're not going to move."

Leadership and Coalition-Building

A key element in building a successful, enduring

governing coalition is, of course, leadership. We need champions — presidential, congressional, state and local — for our cause. Despite a more sympathetic Executive Branch and a much improved situation in the Congress, we have had it rough the last few years. We have more followers and activists than ever, but things have been rough because we have too few leaders. But leaders are not selected, they choose to lead. It is true that events often thrust leadership upon otherwise unassuming individuals, but those individuals become leaders because they pick up the banner offered to them.

What are the qualities a coalition or organization leader must possess? First, a leader must be able to convey a sense of hope to the troops. From Winston Churchill to Phyllis Schlafly, all leaders of "hopeless causes" who won against the odds projected inevitable victory, even at the darkest hour.

Many fine people wait for others to select them as leaders. But genuine leaders simply act when it is necessary to move forward for the good of the many. Even in a democractic system, people make themselves leaders; they step forward when necessity requires it.

Second, a leader must be decisive. He must have the capacity to act and to step forward in a manner that combines boldness and humility, even when the old pros say an idea is doomed to failure. Third, a leader must have the ability to accept input, to make the troops feel a part of the process, and to allow worthwhile alternative strategies to surface while avoiding the aimlessness of constantly searching for consensus. Fourth, a leader must be willing to shift his strategy and tactics to suit changing situations, while never negotiating on basic principles. Finally, a leader must be able to communicate to the troops and to occupy the moral high ground for the sake of his ultimate objectives.

Building a Permanent Coalition: The Library Court Concept

There are permanent coalitions and there are temporary coalitions. Each is useful for different purposes. Temporary coalitions on occasion evolve into permanent coalitions. What we will talk about in the next few pages is the construction of a permanent, on-going coalition at the national level. However, this model can also be imitated for the construction of similar forums at the state and local levels.

A clearly thought-out, long-range goal for our movement must be the creation of a governing coalition which will provide not only electoral victories but also a range of meaningful public policy alternatives for the country once we secure legislative majorities. The question is: How do we build a permanent coalition which will form the basis for both electoral and policy victories? Put another way, the problem is how to get like-minded groups to cooperate and work with each other.

Political commentators like to focus on the "New Right" implying that its focus on "single issues" is somehow detrimental to the political process in America. Nothing could be farther from the truth; the New Right is nothing more than a functioning coalition of issue focus groups who work together for common goals. The New Right, in turn, seeks to be part of a still greater governing coalition that combines those who share a commitment to traditional moral values (including the right to life) and traditional conservatives. Thus, while the groups composing the New Right are uniformly pro-life, at the same time they represent other issues as well. While the pro-life movement is, and should be, single-issue, there is no reason why it should not work with New Right and traditionalist groups when their interests overlap. For example, they have a shared interest in putting an end to abortion and infanticide.

Such groups, focusing their energies on special concerns in the political arena, are not new. They are absolutely essential in an era, such as ours, when political party leaders (members of what David Lebedoff has called "The New Elite") become unresponsive to the popular will. Far from being a threat to coalition-building and consensus, as so many liberal commentators seem to imply, the New Right has been effective *because* of classic coalition-building. It is New Right leaders who have been most vocal in calling for a permanent alliance between those committed to the social justice issues and those supportive of a strong role for America in the world and, in general, those who are friends of liberty everywhere.

Beyond this, it is the New Right which has moved to build coalitions with all Americans who value traditional beliefs and the sanctity of innocent human life. Many pro-abortion commentators, such as former *Washington Star* religion columnist Jim Castelli, argue that the New Right is not a legitimate pro-life force because its emphasis is so distinct from the emphasis of, for example, the Catholic bishops.

In a briefing prepared for Catholics for a Free Choice — a pro-abortion group — Castelli claimed that, in contrast to the bishops, "The New Right is completely judgmental on abortion, treating the woman who has an abortion as evil and undeserving of sympathy." Further, he claimed that "the Catholic church respects the American political system" while the New Right, presumably, does not.

Well, you don't have to be a socialist to be compassionate and caring. Virtually every social justice activist I know has been involved, in the past or present, in programs designed to aid unwed mothers or others involved in an unplanned pregnancy, so that they will have an alternative to the horrors of abortion. Further, it is the New Right which has worked to forge majority support for innovative programs designed to address social needs in education and other social service programs without undue reliance on federal or other governmental mechanisms which rarely work. Finally, how does one show respect for the American political system more clearly than through active, principled involvement in that system — involvement designed to improve and build up the viablility and vibrancy of that system?

Those who believe in the sanctity of human life and the centrality of the family are working to build a permanent governing coalition in American politics. One mechanism for achieving that goal emerged in the 1970s. We call it the "Library Court" concept. It has proved to be a useful tool for coordination and consultation among the leadership of the burgeoning pro-family movement. In many ways much of the following description of that mechanism will seem like a psychology treatise on interpersonal and group relations. In truth, it is common sense applied in a careful way to practical political problems. And, again, while these lessons come from the experience of those groups that make up what is called the New Right, it is my opinion that the theory and practice behind it is completely applicable to the pro-life movement.

In any coalition, communication has to be regular, and it has to be steady. When you talk about trying to win long-term battles, you are talking about planning and executing a strategy which will enjoy broad support over time. Thus, you are talking about building a *permanent* coalition. In order to build a permanent coalition which will plan effective strategies, you need before anything else a regular forum in which you get together all your "chiefs" in a "war council." Understand that regular planning sessions of this sort are difficult to bring about and maintain — but they are absolutely critical to success. If you are in this for the long haul, however, and actually hope to change the country, you must think in these terms.

Since July 5, 1979, the Library Court group — consisting of a broad range of pro-family, pro-life, pro-traditional values organizations — has met every other Thursday to plan strategy and share information informally on behalf of the entire pro-family movement.

The Library Court group (named after the location of the early meetings) is an absolutely indispensable ingredient of our success in Washington. The meetings work because they constitute a forum, not another organization. There are no by-laws, no elections, and no letterhead. Thus, every participating organization maintains its independence. The sole reason for existence of the Library Court Group is to cause action to happen.

Action in this context means specific individual or group activities designed to promote specific political objectives. These specific objectives are always, of course, related to the larger goal of building a pro-life, pro-family America. Because these meetings are action-oriented, speechmaking and grandstanding must be discouraged.

One person must be on-going chairman and focus of the group. As my colleague Connie Marshner, who directs the Library Court meetings, has said, the meetings must be "as regular as sunset." They must be held often (at least every two weeks) in the same place, the same time and on the same day. Always.

At these meetings, we only talk about things we can take action upon and can move to implement. A key to success of this coalition concept, as intimated above, is strong, principled leadership. A core of leaders must direct this group with the important caveat that group input must be encouraged and utilized.

Who should be involved in such meetings? This is where the role of strong leadership becomes essential. Take your own community as an example. Look around. You want the decision-makers from the key organizations, those who can actually commit themselves on the spot to do something, whether that "something" be generating letters to the editors from the organization membership, getting a certain number of people to a political rally or whatever. You certainly want to include your known allies and groups with proven productivity, but you should look beyond known quantities to potential allies who could broaden the coalition's impact.

To start with, however, begin with a small group consisting of those you know and can trust. It is usually a good idea to work on more than just one issue. Although your various coalition members might not be articulate or active on some issues, they should be made welcome as long as they are in general agreement on overall principles.

Look at potential coalition members in a very pragmatic manner. You owe this to your beliefs and principles. Remember, the purpose is not fellowship, although fellowship will often develop. Neither is it friendship, although life-long friendships will certainly be forged. Rather, the purpose of such coalition meetings is *action* for the pro-life, pro-family movement. The most basic question of all about potential coalition allies is: Can they deliver? Everyone's good friends are not enough. You must have people who can produce. You want activists *and* decision-makers.

Similar decisions will be required in other areas. Can this person you are considering for the coalition get along in a general way with other people? Be generous on this point. I am not talking about excluding hard-workers who may have personality quirks. Only exclude chronic malcontents or "disagreers" or those who simply will not let others take the lead or those whose organizations simply have no credibility.

This will not be easy for you or for other leaders in the coalition. You will get some people angry at you. That is the way it has to be. Efficiency is absolutely required of a coalition meeting such as this in order to change things for the better. Changing things for the better is what is important, not whether or not everyone likes you.

You will be surprised, however, at how successful such an operation can be. If people come to know that the coalition you have built is effective and principled, they will want to join in. If they are willing to play by the basic ground rules (see below) and they fit the sort of criteria outlined above, invite them in.

The basic ground rule for a coalition is common sense. Civil conduct is a requirement. Filibustering is not allowed. In other words, speakers make their point, suggest action, and sit down.

Because the purpose of the meeting is action, brief minutes must be kept for internal use. These minutes will note what was discussed and who promised to do what. One of the chairman's jobs is to follow up on commitments for action, to remind, cajole, and encourage fulfillment of such commitments. At the next meeting, action items must be reviewed and summarized by the chairman in order to encourage responsible behaviour among the membership.

Confidentiality is critical. Folks have to know they can speak openly at these meetings and that what they say will not be in the paper tomorrow morning. It is important to be sensitive to the concerns of the various organizations which make up your coalition. Similarly, government officials must be certain they can attend your meetings to speak openly and honestly about their needs and how you might be able to help them.

In a similar vein, it is not proper to ask for any coalition group's membership list. If you want material sent to their membership, provide them with the materials and let them mail to their members. The coalition chairman establishes the agenda based on the suggestion of *all* coalition members, who are called before every meeting and asked if they have agenda items.

When there is disagreement among two members of the coalition (as has occurred in pro-life ranks on more than one occasion), the proper way to handle it is to encourage a thorough discussion of the issue(s) *once,* letting all sides have their say. After that, do not beat a dead horse. Let any member offer information to the rest of the coalition, but do not allow a new round of fruitless debate to occur. Remember, the purpose of the coalition is to encourage external action, not to quibble on internal battles. This is not a group, it is not an organization, it is a forum, a coalition.

If you follow these broad ground rules for regular meetings under the leadership of a strong personality who is just, fair, and action-oriented, you will be amazed how soon a feeling of achievement begins to pervade the group. You will make a difference in your local community and in your state.

The functioning coalition will become a mechanism for forming the long-range goals of the movement and providing strategy for current situations. The coalition meetings will also become a source of invaluable, regular dissemination of information throughout your local government. The simple act of sharing success stories with one another will become a means of building a collective (movement-wide) memory of which tactics are effective and which ones are not.

You will soon discover that if you approach your duties in the practical manner outlined above, fellowship and friendship will follow on the heels of meaningful political impact. There is nothing that says we cannot have fun. Yes, this is serious business. We are talking about human life. On the other hand, we do not have to be grim and dour as we go about our work. When people in your coalition find that these battles — win or lose — can be fun and interesting and meaningful to them as individuals, you will be a lot more likely to attract and retain contributing members to a (potentially) governing coalition.

Building Temporary Coalitions Around Issues and/or Elections

Coalitions are essential to the efficient workings of our democratic system. I have already discussed one means by which the pro-family movement constructed a permanent, on-going national coalition, and I have noted that the model can be applied at the state or local level.

Besides permanent coalitions, of course, there are circumstances which can bring together unusual political allies whose desire to serve the public interest — or the occasional confluence of mutual self-interest — dictates cooperation for the purpose of promoting or opposing legislation or electing candidates to political office. Occasionally, such temporary coalitions can develop into more permanent, ongoing cooperation.

Some highly visible recent examples of temporary coalitions for varied purposes include: 1) the involvement of both liberal and conservative religious leaders in activities designed to focus public attention on the serious ethical concerns raised by genetic experimentation; 2) the unusual pro-education alliance formed, however tentatively, between conservative critics of the education establishment, reform-minded elements of the education establishment, the American Federation of Teachers (AFT), and President Ronald Reagan, 3) the cooperation of liberals such as Stewart Mott and Eugene McCarthy with conservatives such as Terry Dolan on the issue of public financing of federal elections; and 4) the cooperation of liberal and conservative members of the Congress (working with a similar range of "outside groups") in opposition to increased U.S. funding for the International Monetary Fund (IMF).

In each of these cases, unusual circumstances dictated that individuals normally opposed to one another on a variety of issues came together to support or oppose particular public policy alternatives. Part of the art and science of politics is fusing such disparate interests together for the common good. It is worth noting that such unusual coalitions are absolutely essential to the construction of a genuine consensus for progress and orderly change in a democratic society.

Temporary coalition building can be most effective in both legislative and electoral politics. Space allows me to cite only two examples without elaboration: the highly unusual coalition that formed around the Criminal Code Reform Act of 1982; and the 1980 victories of conservative Republicans such as Don Nickles of Oklahoma and Jeremiah Denton of Alabama. Senators Nickles and Denton scored upset victories in traditionally Democratic states, due in large part to their success in fusing traditional Republican constituencies with pro-life, pro-family Democrats.

My own belief is that the pro-life movement is an essential segment of what I anticipate will one day be a conservative governing coalition. But it is worth noting a 1980 "war story" which illustrates the potential of temporary coalitions for Democratic candidates who may be liberals.

Michigan's old Tenth Congressional District was located in the heart of the state in traditionally Republican territory. From 1952-1978, conservative Republican Eldord Cederberg served this district in Washington. In 1978, he was defeated (in a year in which there was a Republican trend) by liberal Democrat Don Albosta.

Albosta, a committed pro-lifer, is a moderate liberal by most standards. As this was written in mid-1983, Albosta was gaining some notoriety as chairman of the House committee investigating the "Debategate" affair. Back in

1980, Albosta faced a stiff challenge from Republican state Senator Richard Allen. Although Allen was conservative on many issues in what proved to be a good year for conservative Republicans, he was staunchly pro-abortion.

In the general election campaign, Allen spent $410,995 to Albosta's $355,147. Nevertheless, Albosta received 53 percent of the vote to Allen's 46 percent. This, in a district which gave Ronald Reagan 55 percent to Jimmy Carter's anemic 35 percent and John Anderson's 8 percent. Simply put, Albosta, the liberal Democrat, ran 18 percent stronger than Jimmy Carter despite being outspent in a year which had a heavy Republican trend.

What could account for this rather remarkable outcome? *Other things being relatively equal*, it was the fervent support of pro-life activists in the district. As evidence, it is worth noting the following breakdown of funding for the two candidates:

Albosta	**Allen**
United Steelworkers	American Medical PAC
Postal Workers	Michigan Doctors PAC
Carpenters PAC	American Dental PAC
AFL-CIO COPE	Homebuilders
AFSME	Farm Bureau
UAW	Michigan Petroleum PAC
NEA	Dallas Energy PAC
Railway Clerks	American Vets
Machinists	American Bankers
National Pro-Life PAC	Free Enterprise PAC
National Right to Life PAC	United Tech PAC
Michigan Right to Life PAC	NARAL
	Friends of Family Planning

Coalition-Building and the Pro-Life Movement

The pro-life movement is a community of shared values. Our strengths come from two main sources. First, there is the traditional constituency of the pro-life movement. These good people are often blue collar ethnics from the northeastern United States. They are frequently Catholic and Democratic by tradition.

The second main source of the pro-life movement's existing strength is the New Right and the Christian Right (although closely affiliated, the two are not always synonymous). These folks are often southern and western fundamentalists and evangelicals, with traditionally Democrat or non-political leanings. Recently, they have become much more Republican in their basic sympathies. On a range of traditional political issues, this element of the movement is quite conservative, although this conservatism is by no means monolithic.

These are the foundational pillars for the movement. To have ultimate success, what is needed is a greater sense of genuine coalition building — getting non-traditional constituencies into our coalition. In the early 1970s, the organized pro-life movement consisted almost exclusively of the traditional right-to-lifers described above. By the end of the 1970s, the movement had begun to broaden through the infusion of the "Moral Majority" or fundamentalist element. The practical advantages of further expansion are apparent from a review of the 1980 results.

Different groups can deliver certain percentages in an election and, subsequently, in legislative battles. The use of grossly misleading "landslide" terminology — particularly when applied to the 1980 elections — assumes that most voters still vote straight party tickets. Some voters do, and in a given state there is always a "bedrock vote," which means the number of votes a Republican or Democrat candidate will get just for being on the ballot. But most voters exercise a surprising degree of independence.

One example is Iowa, one of several states where conservative GOP senatorial candidates provided "coat tails" to Ronald Reagan in 1980. Reagan won the state with 51 percent of the vote, just over 676,500 votes. But

Charles Grassley garnered some 684,700 votes, or 54 percent of the total. Clearly Grassley aided Reagan.

Different groups deliver certain "increments" in an election. Although abortion is not a critical issue to all Americans, it is the deciding issue to enough voters to make the difference in certain races. Exit polling in Iowa showed that 10 percent of those who voted for Chuck Grassley did so because of his pro-life stand. Since he won by 8½ percent of the vote total, the pro-life segment of the electorate obviously played a key role. Despite the fact that the Moral Majority and similar groups have been criticized in some sectors, they added percentage points in key races which turned out to be the winning margin for pro-life candidates.

If the pro-life movement circa 1983 consists of these two main branches — the traditional right-to-lifers and the new religious conservative element — the question is whether or not there are other elements in American society which can be activated in the years ahead?

Certainly, there are remaining elements of the religious community in need of activation for the pro-life cause. My own summary of the fundamentalist component might betray some regional bias: Clearly, these folks are not restricted to the South and West. Any examination of recent trends demonstrates that such voters play a crucial role in elections in Illinois, Iowa, and Missouri, to name only three. These voters need access to more pro-life information on a regular basis. Providing such information would be wise both politically and educationally.

Two other groups deserve special attention from pro-life political organizers. Members of the Church of Jesus Christ of Latter Day Saints (Mormon) have been reliable pro-life voters *when the issues are made clear to them.* A more consistent political outreach to these voters could raise their pro-life consciousness and firm up their commitment to pro-life political action. On the other hand, it is a troublesome reality that pro-life organizational progress in the black community has been nearly non-existent. It is true that most black establishment leaders are pro-abortion; more important, however, is that all polls indicate significant pro-life sentiment among average blacks. Some major black spokesmen such as Dick Gregory and Rev. E.V. Hill are avowedly pro-life. Since a vastly disproportionate percentage of babies aborted are black, black Americans should be at the forefront of the pro-life movement.

It is one of the great tragedies of our time that so much of the business community has quietly aquiesced or actively promoted the denigration of human life. In a similar vein, it is difficult to accept the apparent enthusiasm of most feminists for abortion on demand. [Editor's note: See essay by Rosemary Bottcher in this volume.] I could continue naming other organizations and segments of American society which should be on our side, but my point can be made simply.

The key to the future is the same as in the past: reaching out to bring in new allies. They do not have to agree with us on everything as long as they agree on the sanctity of human life. Depending on the circumstances in your particular community, you might want to approach such individuals to work in either a temporary or a permanent coalition. While it is true that there is not a business community leader known nationwide for his pro-life stance, there *are* such pro-life businessmen and businesswomen who could serve as pro-life spokesmen in your community.

Dr. Mildred Jefferson, a Massachusetts physician and conservative, and Erma Craven, a Minnesota social worker and liberal, are black women known throughout the pro-life movement for their articulate defense of human life. Do similar individuals exist in your community? John Jimenez is the hardworking Hispanic fundamentalist who organized the Washington for Jesus rally a few years ago. Is there someone like him in your town?

Such diverse spokesmen are the lifeblood of a vibrant political movement at the local, state or national level. But spokesmen alone are not enough. As pro-life leaders, our job is to activate the constituencies represented by these spokesmen. We can win if we think creatively, implement our strategies aggressively and honestly, and work unceasingly to broaden our coalition. Right now, pro-lifers are not sufficient in number to form a governing coalition. But, working in concert with those who share our views on many issues of human life, we can build a movement which will govern as we move into the Twenty-First Century.

PART II

POLITICS AND LEGISLATION: DOING THE POSSIBLE... AND THE IMPOSSIBLE

*What **really** happened and why in the highly successful 1980 elections? Why did the pro-life movement gain "only" two pro-life U.S. senators in the 1982 off-year elections? In the face of unyielding Supreme Court hostility, what can pro-lifers do at city hall and in the state legislatures to keep the issue boiling hot? What legal sleights-of-hand would pro-abortion litigants employ if **Roe** ceased to have the force of law?*

These are just a few of the intriguing questions explored in this section. For those long accustomed to hearing how poorly the movement has fared, the essays by Sandra Faucher, David O'Steen and Darla St. Martin, Professor Lynn Wardle, and Tom Marzen will be welcome news. The pro-life movement is alive and doing quite well, thank you.

THE BEST KEPT SECRET

Sandra Faucher*

"Will the fact that it's politically beneficial to be pro-life continue to be the best kept secret in town? Probably, but that's all right. When the Human Life Amendment is finally ratified, newspapers will probably bury the news on page 16."

SANDRA FAUCHER

Although the pro-life movement has been winning regularly since first entering national politics in 1974, ten years later the best kept secret in town remains that it is very beneficial politically to be pro-life. One would imagine after making a critical contribution to unseating twelve pro-abortion senators and electing an outspoken pro-life president, the movement would, in 1980, finally have been accorded the respect it so richly

*Sandra Faucher is the Director of the National Right to Life Political Action Committee and has been since its beginning in 1980. She has been actively involved in numerous phases of the pro-life movement, including lobbying, organization development, fundraising, and alternatives to abortion.

deserved. But only a few political analysts were shrewd enough to grasp what had transpired; a peaceful political coup.

Not since 1974 when the tide of revulsion to Watergate carried a wave of Democrats into the Congress has a single issue so transformed the political landscape as did abortion in 1980. Long consigned to irrelevancy, the pro-life movement proved to any genuinely open mind that an upfront pro-life position could be *the* deciding factor in elevating a competent man or woman to national office.

But by and large, the successes of the movement, like that of Ronald Reagan, were explained away. Each candidate had won, we were told, not on the strength of what he or she stood for, but on the weaknesses of their opposition. For example, it was not that the American people were growing increasingly uneasy with abortion on demand; it was not that the movement organized brilliantly; it was not that pro-life candidates had for the most part solid backgrounds in politics and business. No, the reasons so many pro-abortionists went down to defeat in 1980 was because of (take your pick) the comic incompetence of Jimmy Carter, the Iranian hostage situation, the drift toward conservatism, the candidates' ages, etc., etc. Why was the media's received wisdom so contrary to facts? Quite possibly because the media elite, who exert such an incredible power in shaping the political conversation of this country, would not accept that the values *they* found appalling might well be the values the American people found congenial, a point we will come back to later.

But bias aside, it would seem difficult to deny the oft-times deciding influence of the pro-life movement, particularly in close elections. As far back as the 1974 election of Senator Robert Dole of Kansas, his opponent, Congressman Roy, was telling the *Kansas City Times,*

"That's what beat us, we lost on one issue (abortion)." But it was not until 1978 when Iowa's pro-abortion (and media favorite) Senator Dick Clark went down to defeat to pro-lifer Roger Jepsen that the national media began to pay attention to the rising influence of the movement. For example, the *Wall Street Journal* wrote that year "... it indisputably shows abortion was a major factor in Dick Clark's defeat. One out of four votes switching from the pro-abortion Senator Clark to the anti-abortion Mr. Jepsen said they did so on the abortion issue..." A new political force had begun to flex its muscle.

Given 1980's enormous successes, 1982 was bound to be something of a letdown. But it is vital to understand precisely what did happen and what could — maybe should — have happened. Because the media's attention span is so short, and its sense of historical development so limited, the wrong questions were asked about the off-year elections of 1982. Although they would deny it with their dying breath, 1982 presented abortion supporters with a historic opportunity to defuse the abortion issue, perhaps permanently.

Every possible advantage belonged to the pro-abortion forces. The nation's attention was riveted on the ailing economy and the unhealthy spectre of double digit unemployment figures. Moreover, there were far fewer instances of electable pro-life candidates challenging pro-abortion incumbents than there were in 1980, and there were numerous highly vulnerable pro-life senators up for re-election. To further tip the scales, historically the party not controlling the presidency makes substantial gains in non-presidential election years. This served to give the upper hand to several pro-abortion Democrats who were already mounting strong challenges to incumbent pro-life Republican senators. To make matters still worse for pro-lifers, on the congressional side creative state legislative gerrymandering had redistricted many pro-lifers out of their house districts.

Taken together, the electoral prospects were ominous. Competent, unbiased reporting would have observed that the real measure of victory and defeat was not whether the pro-life movement would duplicate its successes of 1980, but whether it could overcome the considerable odds against it and hold on to what it had, particularly in the Senate. The real question of the 1982 elections was whether the pro-abortion forces would capitalize on a golden opportunity to quash the pro-life movement.

If ever it could be honestly said that the movement had its collective back up against the wall, this was it. The response was magnificent. In race after race, the pro-life increment proved the margin of victory. To take just a few examples, following incumbent Minnesota Senator David Durenberger's defeat of Mark Dayton, headlines in Minnesota pronounced, "Dayton's downfall: youth, wealth, abortion stand." In a heavily Democratic state wracked with sizable unemployment in Democratic strongholds, Democrat Mark Dayton was unable to overcome the adverse effect of his pro-abortion position, despite pouring millions of his own dollars into his candidacy. Charles Backstrom, a political scientist at the University of Minnesota, told the *Minneapolis Star and Tribune* that abortion played a "significant role" in Dayton's loss. "There is no question that Dayton's pro-choice standpoint hurt him...," Backstrom said.

An even more obvious example of the role of the pro-life vote was in Missouri where pro-life incumbent John Danforth had become the number one target of the National Abortion Rights Action League (NARAL) and all of the other pro-abortion feminist groups. Overnight, their candidate, Harriet Woods, became the darling of the media, sharing the limelight with only one other female senatorial candidate. Missouri was also a heavily

Democratic state with high unemployment. Polls as close as a week before the election showed Woods either even with or slightly ahead of Danforth. Danforth won by a razor-thin margin of one percent. Two days later, an analysis in the *St. Louis Post-Dispatch* headlined its conclusion: "Anti-abortion Forces Put Their Weight Behind Danforth."

Electorally, the movement had dodged a bullet. Not only did it help re-elect all pro-life senatorial incumbents, it added two more senators. The lesson was there for all to see: In close elections, it is extremely valuable to be pro-life. Why, then, does this fact remain a secret? To answer this, one must look at the attitude of the national news media on the abortion issue. Every pro-life group believes it has been victimized by media bias. However, our subjective assessments were given scholarly support by a 1979-80 survey conducted by Robert Lichter of George Washington University and Stanley Rothman of Smith College. Lichter and Rothman surveyed 240 members of the "media elite," journalists, anchormen, producers, editors, and so forth who work on what are generally accepted to be the most influential media outlets: the *New York Times*, the *Washington Post*, *The Wall Street Journal*, the three weekly news magazines, the three television networks, and the Public Broadcasting System.

Among the many fascinating results of their surveys were two particularly relevant points: Ninety percent of the "media elite" agreed that a woman has the right to decide for herself whether to have an abortion; and of the major leadership groups in the country, the one that most members of the media elite believe ought to have the most influence is... the media! These two factors — the media elite's overwhelming pro-abortion stance and its growing sense of its own destiny as a shaper of American society — reveal why, no matter how successful the pro-life movement is politically, that success will either be explained away or ignored completely by all those "anchormen" whom the American people have come to believe are paragons of objectivity.

The lengths to which this pro-abortion establishment/media symbiosis can go was nicely illustrated by coverage of the 1982 elections. The headlines could not have been any more flattering if the pro-abortion spokesmen had written them. For example, when the pro-abortionists held their post-election press conferences they talked of the high percentage of races in which they participated and their candidate won. The media, in turn, dutifully parroted the line, "Defenders of Legalized Abortion Recover After '78, '80 Setbacks" is a typical headline. No one bothered to examine the reality behind the rhetoric. For instance, when one takes a closer look at NARAL expenditures, one sees that of the $233,300 spent on Congressional races, $122,250 (52 percent) was expended in "no contest" districts. "No contest" means either that the incumbent was a sure winner or there were only pro-abortion candidates in the race.

Ditto for the $68,000 spent by NARAL in Senate races. Forty percent ($27,125) was thrown away on "no contest" races. It is not hard to have a great winning percentage if one assists only sure-winners. (NARAL even went so far as to introduce Harriet Woods as a winning candidate because she was a winner "in all our hearts." With creative language like this, uncritically reprinted by the media, small wonder the world was told of the demise of the pro-life movement.)

Unfortunately, there were those within the pro-life community who inadvertently fueled the premature reports of the movement's demise. The two national pro-life political action committees (PACs) who contributed most to candidates in 1982 and were active in the most elections are the National Right to Life PAC and the Committee for a Pro-life Congress. Neither publishes "hit lists" of senators they wish to defeat. But other pro-life PACs do, which has hurt the movement.

Publicly announcing that one is going to "get" Senator Jones as much as two years in advance of his election has practically no positives and a truckload of negatives: The incumbent and his pro-abortion allies are put on guard that you're after him; you've given him the opportunity to start raising money early to fight the "outside agitators"; many voters are turned off by hit list tactics; Senator Jones may not have a pro-life opponent or, if so, his pro-life opponent presents, in fact, only token opposition; a relatively obscure senator can be catapulted into national prominence; and, worst of all, pro-abortionists are provided with the opportunity to shout victory because you did not defeat Senator Jones as predicted.

For example, NARAL was able correctly to announce following the 1982 elections that "Not a single U.S. senator targeted for defeat by Right to Life groups... was defeated..." Lost in this statement is the fact that the incumbents were all but impossible to beat. (It also happened that the very groups who "hit listed" many of these "targets" spent no funds to defeat them.)

In approaching future elections, the pro-life movement is confident because we know from our voter identification surveys how voters really feel about abortion on demand. We also see that the pro-life increment continues to provide the margin of victory. As recently as June 1983, in an analysis of the hotly contested primary race for the Virginia House of Delegates between pro-lifer Gwendalyn Cody, targeted by feminists groups, and Lynne Purvis, a newspaper article observed that, "Her victory reaffirmed the get-out-the-votes power... of Right-to-Life groups, who are a strong part of Cody's base."

Will the fact that it's politically beneficial to be pro-life continue to be the best kept secret in town? Probably, but that's all right. When the Human Life Amendment is finally ratified, newspapers will probably bury the news on page 16.

SINGLE ISSUE POLITICS AND THE DOUBLE STANDARD: THE CASE OF THE PRO-LIFE MOVEMENT

David O'Steen and Darla St. Martin*

"Successful single-issue politics demands both actual success and a perception by otherwise reluctant politicans that it is in their best interest to support that group's issue. The freeze movement has had extraordinary success in creating a perception of political power while demonstrating miniscule success at the polls. The exact opposite has held true for the pro-life movement."

DAVID O'STEEN and DARLA ST. MARTIN

*David N. O'Steen, Ph.D., and Darla St. Martin are Executive Director and Associate Director respectively of Minnesota Citizens Concerned for Life and co-directors of the Committee for a Pro-life Congress, a national pro-life political action committee. Together they consulted in 19 U.S. Senate races in 1980 and 1982.

Imagine in the 1982 elections that ten incumbent senators on record as opposing the nuclear freeze were defeated in their primaries or in the general election and that each was replaced by a proponent of the freeze. What would have been the political result? A panicky Congress would quite probably have raced to halt American production of nuclear weaponry.

What the nuclear freeze movement *failed* to produce politically in the 1982 elections was precisely what the pro-life movement did produce politically in 1980. No less than ten incumbent pro-abortion U.S. senators were replaced with new pro-life members; overall, pro-lifers made a net gain of nine seats in the Senate. Yet paradoxically, after the nuclear freeze movement failed in 1982 — it did not appear to substantially affect the outcome of even a single congressional election — Congress still is clearly worried about the nuclear/peace issue while there has been, since 1980, no discernable stampede on the part of uncommitted or "pro-choice" senators to appease the pro-life movement, which had demonstrated real political muscle.

This is all the more curious when one considers the way people were talking going into the 1980 elections. In a letter written just prior to those elections, Gloria Steinem predicted that if the pro-life movement succeeded in defeating a single pro-abortion politician, Congressional thinking would be "let's just send this constitutional amendment along to the states for approval or rejection... and get the monkey off our back..."

While this may have been exaggerated to rally her troops, there is no doubt that Ms. Steinem would have been panic-stricken had she been able to see what was coming. Ms. Steinem, like most political observers, irrespective of their view on abortion, expected the political effects of the abortion issue to conform to patterns observed in the issue politics of the 1950s, '60s, and '70s.

But it did not, and much of the explanation why the political structure did not respond to pro-life successes the same way it responded to the other single issue groups can be found in the grossly unfair way the media framed the issue and in the stranglehold pro-abortionists have on the leadership of the Democratic Party.

Successful issue-oriented political action has two principal effects. The primary one is, of course, to elect friends and defeat enemies. Following this, one expects a secondary psychological effect upon elected officials, many of whom don't really care about the issue in the first place. As indicated earlier, some issues have enjoyed the psychological benefits without proving themselves politically. When abortion is the issue, it would seem that in the political world, at least some of the usual rules and conventional wisdoms must be discarded. Pro-life political power is real but greatly misunderstood, both within and without the movement. To understand why a little history is in order.

Most state abortion laws stricken by the *Roe v. Wade* decision date from the latter half of the nineteenth century. Their implementation was the result of what has been called the Physicians' Crusade, the determination of the leadership of the American Medical Association to protect the life of the unborn from abortion except in those instances where an abortion was needed to preserve the life of the mother. There is no evidence that great controversy surrounded the passage of these laws. At the time there was a general consensus against the taking of innocent life, and the laws were sought by a portion of the country's professional elite.

However, in the 20th century the configuration changed completely as new social forces, national and international, converged to form a new elite consensus favoring abortion. The rise of the radical left with its utilitarian view of humankind and strong anti-clericalism was the first of these major trends. Abortion was legalized in the Soviet Union soon after the 1917 revolution, and in the Eastern European communist satellites after World War II.

Another force was the eugenics movement with its aim of improving the stock by eliminating "undesirables." Abortion was legalized in Nazi Germany for Jewish women and women carrying potentially "defective" offspring.

To these forces were added in the 1950s and '60s the sexual revolution with its reaction against anything that might hint of restraint; the population control movement, later augmented by the ecology movement; and the feminist movement. Note that none of these were inherently pro-abortion; i.e., family planning did not have to mean destroying members of the family after conception and women's rights might have included equal rights for unborn women. However, elements of these movements were usually taken over from the top down by pro-abortion activists.

Planned Parenthood shifted from an anti-abortion position in 1963 to become not only an abortion provider, but a leading front for pro-abortion politics by the 1980s. The feminist movement was also completely taken over by pro-abortionists and pro-life women excluded from any leadership positions. In the 1980s, their representative organizations had come to oppose even an Equal Rights Amendment if amended to be neutral on abortion.

The patterns of thought and opinion generated by these trends were enthusiastically supported by the American media which by the 1960s had emerged as a force with sufficient power not only to define for the public the problems for consideration, but the range of permitted solutions as well. With this addition of the most powerful public propaganda network in the history of the world, there was again an elite consensus on abortion, but this time in favor of its legalization.

By 1960, abortion was once again a legislative, but not as yet a political, issue. Armed with progressive professors, countless study committee reports, and American Law Institute recommendations, the new pro-abortion elite descended upon unsuspecting, and often very uninformed, legislators. They claimed that current abortion laws had created a horde of problems which could be solved only through "liberalization" or repeal of abortion laws. (Liberalism, of course, in the sense that it was understood in 19th century western Europe and America would have meant care and protection of the weakest rather than destruction of the unwanted or "useless." But while the 20th century radical left infiltrated the camp of western liberalism with its ideas and attitudes, it misappropriated the name as well.)

In the first wave of "abortion reform" in the 1960s, the pro-abortion movement met little opposition. They were clever enough not to push for abortion on demand laws in the beginning. For example, the first fourteen abortion statute reforms that expanded abortion rights beyond the single commonly accepted exception (the life of the mother) had all been to accommodate the so-called "hard cases," such as rape and incest. Moreover, these changes received additional support because they were modeled after the recommendations of the prestigious and highly influential American Law Institute.

Eighteen states had relaxed their abortion laws by 1970; sixteen of those states did so between 1967 and 1970. The only abortion on demand laws were enacted in 1970 and even those did not extend the right to abortion past the twenty-fourth week of pregnancy. The oldest affiliates of the National Right to Life Committee — the Minnesota Citizens Concerned for Life and the Virginia Society for Human Life — were formed in 1967. By 1970, there existed a number of state organizations, all depending on grassroots organization and mobilization, in direct contrast to the style of their opponents.

By 1971, the steam had definitely gone out of abortion "reform." In the 1972 referenda in North Dakota and Michigan, abortion proponents lost heavily. They were losing in the legislatures as the pro-life groups conducted effective grassroots lobbying efforts.

Then the U.S. Supreme Court, the most elite of all American institutions, changed all the rules. In seeking to impose its view, the Court in *Roe v. Wade* unwittingly set the stage for abortion to enter national politics.

Getting Ready: 1973-80.

Ironically, the Court's decision was so outrageous that both sides in the abortion struggle completely misread its meaning for abortion politics. The pro-abortion coalition at first thought that *Roe* was such a knockout blow that the pro-life movement would dissolve. On the other hand, the pro-life movement greatly underestimated the difficulty of undoing the damage wrought by the court.

Even the more cautious and analytical within the movement underestimated the ability of the media to enhance the top-down power of the abortion establishment. It was understood that the damage could be undone only by the Court reversing itself or by pro-lifers passing a constitutional amendment. But the confidence of victory was such that many predicted a victory within five years. The chief subject of debate within the pro-life movement was whether or not an amendment with an explicit life-of-the-mother exception would be "accepted."

The Court went on in the next few years to widen rather than to constrict the abortion liberty. New as well as old legislative restrictions on abortion were wiped out. Thus, while state legislative victories were important to restrict public funding for abortions and for later ratification of a constitutional amendment, it made sense to turn the political skills developed in those races increasingly towards Congressional races.

As early as 1974, the pro-life movement had an impact in national races: the Kansas Senate race of Republican Senator Robert Dole and the Democratic primary in Minnesota's eighth congressional district where the pro-life challenger upset the party-picked candidate and went on to win the congressional seat. In 1976, pro-lifers skillfully organized for the Iowa Democratic caucuses and gave Jimmy Carter, then in his pro-life mode, an important initial boost toward the presidency.

Hard lessons were learned in those years, particularly the importance of not wasting valuable financial and human resources on unwinnable races. By 1978, some overly-optimistic dreams had died out but there were real accomplishments to be proud of. Hope burned bright as five pro-abortion U.S. senators that year were replaced with pro-lifers; one each in Colorado, New Hampshire, and Iowa, and two in Minnesota. It was at this juncture that the pattern of media response to pro-life victories was first established. It has not changed to this day.

First, prior to the elections, there are determined efforts to ferret out pro-life plans and to expose them, thereby aiding the pro-abortion campaign. A secondary goal is to discredit pro-lifers with the public at large during the critical election months by putting the worst possible face on whatever it was pro-lifers are doing. Whatever pro-life victories follow are greeted with media outrage. More important, the victories are explained away as a chance happening, often based on the use of "dirty tricks" that right-thinking people should be on the alert not to let occur again. At no time since 1973 has the media, especially the "media elite," ever slipped out of character: the life issue is never accepted as a legitimate issue to be addressed in the political arena, nor are pro-life citizens given the courtesy of being accepted as legitimate participants in the democratic process.

1980-82: Victory and the Politics of Perception

1980 presented a golden opportunity for the pro-life movement to use the newly-polished and honed political skills it had acquired. A number of pro-abortion senators up for re-election were vulnerable. The increment of voters that the pro-life movement delivered played a decisive role in creating a far more pro-life U.S. Senate.

When the votes were counted in November 1980, the pro-life movement had been victorious on all fronts. In the U.S. Senate, the prime target, eleven seats had switched from the pro-abortion to the pro-life column. In every one of those cases, pro-life citizens and political action committees were deeply involved in the successful efforts. In six of the races, the evidence strongly indicates that the net increment provided by pro-life political efforts was more than the margin of victory.

Those six were the election victories of Mac Mattingly in Georgia, John East in North Carolina, Al D'Amato in New York, Bob Kasten in Wisconsin, Steve Symms in Idaho, and Jeremiah Denton in Alabama. Each of those six election margins was less than three percent and in each case, the pro-life vote in the state was sufficient to secure the usual three-to-seven percent net pro-life increment that is attainable.

By pro-life increment we mean that percentage of voters who vote for a candidate primarily because of his pro-life position minus that percentage of voters who vote for the pro-abortion opponent because of his pro-abortion position. For example, a poll taken following Chuck Grassley's 1980 victory in Iowa showed that ten percent of the voters in Des Moines voted for him specifically because he favored a human life amendment and five percent voted for incumbent John Culver specifically because he opposed such an amendment.

Thus the pro-life increment in Des Moines was five percent. Since Chuck Grassley won by 8.6 percent the pro-life victory in Iowa may not have equalled his margin of victory, but certainly the movement played an important role in it.

In New York, however, Al D'Amato received more votes on the Right to Life Party line alone than his margin of victory. The evidence also indicates that the surprise victories of Bob Kasten in Wisconsin and Mac Mattingly in Georgia were won because of strong pro-life support. In Idaho pro-life efforts to educate citizens on the relative positions of the candidates just days before the election probably provided Steve Symms with more than his one percent margin of victory. In North Carolina, the closest race, John East won by only one-third of one percent and a county by county analysis showed the decisive impact of the pro-life vote.

Moreover, in Alabama a major pro-life effort probably provided the increment equal to or slightly exceeding pro-life champion Jeremiah Denton's overall 2.8 percent victory. And in the victories of Jim Abdnor in South Dakota, Frank Murkowski in Alaska, and Dan Quayle in Indiana over pro-abortion rivals, the pro-life movement provided a significant part of their margins of victory. In addition, two new pro-life senators, Paula Hawkins of Florida and Mark Andrews of North Dakota were elected with pro-life support which meant that two already pro-life seats were retained.

Only two pro-life seats were lost. One was the seat of retiring Pennsylvania Sen. Richard Schweiker. The only pro-life incumbent senator defeat was New Hampshire's John Durkin, whose pro-life voting record was generally unknown in the state. That was unfortunate since his 17,000 vote loss might well have been averted if he had made the effort to gain the pro-life vote. He was probably under heavy pressure from "expert" political consultants who didn't want their candidate "tarnished" by being linked to the pro-life movement in spite of his clear Senate voting record against abortion. Apparently they listened to the media better than they counted votes. In addition, twenty seats were added in the U.S. House and Ronald Reagan proved that, yes, you could admit to being pro-life on national television and still be elected President of the United States.

The effect of the pro-life effort on American government was more than almost anyone was allowed to know. Although the movement was nonpartisan and helped re-elect liberal Democrat Tom Eagleton in Missouri as well as aiding many Democratic candidates for Congress, the pro-abortion senatorial incumbents defeated were all Democrats. Since the pro-life increment equalled or exceeded the margins of victories in at least six cases, and since the Republican Senate majority was only 53-47 seats, it seems that without the pro-life effort, the majority would have remained in Democratic hands.

At the 1980 Democratic National Convention, a pro-life member of the Democratic National Committee had stood before the convention and pleaded with that body not to adopt a strong pro-abortion platform plank. "I'll warn you that many, many pro-life Democrats will turn away from pro-abortion politicians," she said, adding "...in many states there are Democratic senators in deep trouble this year because of their pro-abortion record. How much must this party lose before it will listen to the voters?"

Her speech was largely ignored by the media and totally ignored by the convention which went on to adopt stands favoring unrestricted abortion and public funding of abortion. But the pro-life committee member's question remains unanswered.

By all that is rational in politics, the Democrats should

have led the charge to take the issue out of Congress by passing a Human Life Amendment and return to "politics as usual." That they didn't shows the deep entrenchment of the pro-abortion elite in the Democratic party structure itself and the power of the nation's media to interpret those most personal of events — elections — for the public officials the people entrust to chart the course of the nation.

The media's treatment of the 1980 elections was not surprising, but its success at minimizing the pro-life success really was. The usual attempts to discredit and "expose" the pro-life citizen involvement in the political process had all been done in vain. Pro-life candidates had won. But after a brief bit of righteous indignation and finger pointing to the effect that dirty tricks by zealots had fooled the public and stolen victories from deserving progressive candidates, the dramatic switch in the Senate was then explained away as being the result of anything but abortion.

The overall perception created was not that a smashing pro-life upset had occurred, but rather that abortion probably had no real impact on the election, and in any place it did, it was because of the kinds of people and tactics that no real statesman could afford to be involved with. Besides, didn't all of the polls show that the public supported a woman's right to choose?

There were nervous jitters in the pro-abortion camp after the election and some politicians seemed almost ready to jump to the pro-life camp. But even the pro-abortion lobby underestimated how much Congress would allow the elite to interpret the evidence for them. Slowly, but surely, 1980 was explained away and the pro-life movement had no platform from which to tell what had really happened. Obviously, it didn't help that the movement itself had not developed to the point that it could take full advantage of such victories in the months that followed the election. Disagreement and discussion over strategies can be fine and healthy when they are kept in the family, so to speak. But a real disservice was done to the cause of life when the fight by some against the Hatch Amendment was taken out of the movement's board rooms and into the press. This allowed journalists and the pro-abortion lobby to gleefully portray the movement as weak and divided. In the politics of perception it provided just one more excuse to rationalize away 1980.

In 1980 the political environment was such that a number of key races were close enough that the pro-life issue could make the difference between victory and defeat. However, in 1982 a reaction against the Republican adminstration, fueled by the economic slowdown, made most pro-abortion Democratic candidates almost invulnerable and forced several pro-life Republicans to run for their political lives. Further, four of the natural targets for the pro-life movement in 1982, Quentin Burdick of North Dakota, Robert Byrd of West Virginia, George Mitchell of Maine, and James Sasser of Tennessee had all cleverly presented mixed records on abortion funding. Moreover, each had given some indications that they would vote against abortion on demand.

Evidently, each however had privately decided that a pro-abortion position was politically advantageous within the Democratic Party. Each campaign still maintained an image of some opposition to abortion even while receiving money from pro-abortion political action committees. It was not until 1983 with their votes against the Hatch-Eagleton Amendment that all four clearly demonstrated their support for abortion on demand.

Four pro-life incumbents fought off serious challenges in 1982: Republicans Orrin Hatch in Utah, David Durenberger in Minnesota, John Danforth in Missouri, and Democrat John Melcher in Montana. Their wins were in no small measure due to sustained pro-life political efforts, especially for Danforth and Durenberger.

While these vulnerable friends in the Senate were being protected, the pro-life movement proved the political edge in two other races. Pro-life efforts for James Santini in his primary against pro-abortion incumbent Howard Cannon in Nevada played a role in weakening Cannon's base of support, setting the stage for Republican pro-life challenger Chic Hecht's less than one percent victory in November. In Virginia, pro-life and pro-abortion political action committees went head to head in what was probably the clearest contest of the 1982 elections. Neither candidate had the advantage (or in some cases, disadvantage) of incumbency and both candidates, Democratic pro-abortion Lt. Governor Dick Davis and Republican pro-life Congressman Paul Trible were known political figures in the state.

Trible ran into the same problems most Republicans did in 1982 and his early lead evaporated giving Davis an apparent slight edge in the last week of the campaign. Without doubt, the specialized program in Virginia to bring out the pro-life vote for Trible more than provided his less than one percent margin of victory.

All in all, only four U.S. Senate seats had changed hands. Two previous pro-abortion seats were retained by pro-abortion challengers, both going from Republican to Democrat. The other two changes were Nevada and Virginia where two pro-abortion seats were filled by pro-lifers, both going from Democrat to Republican. Thus in terms of new senators elected in 1982, the pro-life movement posted a net gain of two in spite of a strong political tide running against many of its incumbents and against the party of the two new senators it had helped to elect.

Such was the political landscape that there were very few opportunities to make pro-life gains in 1982. The principal goal had to be to hold on to what we had. This was accomplished magnificently. Just as it had in 1980, the pro-life movement in 1982 made the very best of what it had available. Yet the perception within the Senate was not that the pro-life political forces had held on and posted a modest gain in an awful political environment, but rather that the movement had "lost." In this sense, the efforts of the media and the pro-abortion elite to perpetually downgrade pro-life successes had paid off.

The constant portrayal of the pro-life movement as some illegitimate force on the political scene unfairly trying to oust qualified incumbents has created among many members of Congress a mindset which leads them to judge pro-life political effectiveness by a standard unusual for issue politics. Thus, when the movement wins big, its considerable successes are explained away, trivialized, or ignored as much as possible. Meanwhile, the failure to unseat pro-abortion senators who are virtually invulnerable is offered as proof that the movement lacks political clout. The double standard is obvious when one considers the efforts of the pro-abortion forces. They failed to unseat a single targeted senator in 1982, and, as in 1980, lost those contests which were close enough for the issue to affect the outcome. But we heard nothing of the waning of the pro-abortion coalition.

While the House victories in 1980 paralleled those in the Senate, such was not the case in 1982. Re-districting by largely Democratically-controlled statehouses eliminated a number of Republican seats. In most cases the Democratic Party fielded pro-abortion candidates in these new districts which had been drawn to eliminate Republican incumbents who were often pro-life. This, combined with the Democratic tide which swept away a considerable number of Republicans who had won for the first time in 1980 eliminated the gains the pro-life movement had made in the House in 1980, returning the

House to a division on abortion very similar to what existed in 1978. This, too, contributed to the general feeling of safety felt by pro-abortion politicians in 1983.

What We've Learned: The Pro-Life Edge

The pro-life movement is a potent political force in a large part of this country. Thanks to the media, however, this fact remains pretty much of a secret. By examining the strengths of the pro-life movement and the pro-abortion forces, we will have the tools to understand why the movement has succeeded and what it has to do in the future to continue to be a strong political force.

The abortion battle has been likened to a class struggle between a socially powerful materialistic elite and a larger lower-middle class for whom individual life and rights are still held sacred. This oversimplification does contain elements of truth and helps explain the differing strategies that seem most successful for the two sides.

Of course, the vast majority of voters and candidates are really part of neither movement. A 1981 Gallup poll showed that only nine percent of the population would like to join either an anti-abortion group or a pro-abortion group. Significantly, six of the nine percent wished to join an anti-abortion group. While only a small percentage of these actually belong either to a pro-life or a pro-abortion organization and could be considered movement activists, they probably constitute a significant percentage of those who will base their vote solely on the position of a candidate on the abortion issue.

But experience shows that a somewhat larger percentage of the electorate above and beyond the potential activists identified by the Gallup poll will actually base their vote on the abortion issue. Close examination reveals that the net pro-life advantage is usually between three and five percent. Curiously, only the most perceptive politicians seem to recognize this significant fact of political life. In close races, where a candidate is hovering between 46 and 49 percent of the vote, the pro-life increment is critical.

In plotting strategy, another lesson pro-life tacticians must bear in mind is that the media will almost always attempt to foil pro-life political efforts. This would suggest that it is wiser to announce which politicians we are trying to defeat after the election, not before. Moreover, since the goal for pro-life efforts should be to make a difference rather than a statement, scarce resources most often should be expended only on those races in which we have a chance to win. This means that some races are best ignored while others that may at first appear less glamorous may prove very fruitful. The results of the Gallup poll cited above also help explain the clear pro-life organizational advantage over pro-abortion forces at the chapter level. In most parts of the country, the pro-life movement is capable of producing volunteers down to the precinct level and this is a second big advantage it holds.

These volunteers, if properly integrated into a campaign, can assist with various phases of campaign work designed to bring out votes for their candidates for reasons not related to the abortion issue. Once again this means long, hard hours and often little excitement. But it is just as significant as the increment that should be added through a "get out the pro-life vote" drive properly designed and executed to fill the unique needs of a particular campaign.

Another advantage for pro-life political activists has been an ability to reach demographic blocs that are more likely to oppose abortion. For example, polls have consistently shown that church attendees in general are more pro-life than non-churched persons, and it is always easier to reach people who belong to something than those who belong to nothing. The larger pro-life volunteer base has also given the movement an edge in the difficult, but invaluable, task of identifying supporters.

One more pro-life advantage is the attitude that the public still holds on abortion. This is an advantage, however, only if properly understood and honestly recognized.

The Politics of Public Opinion

What the American people actually believe about abortion and what most people probably assume the public believes are two very different things. Even many leaders of the pro-life movement have very little idea of the basic facts about public opinion on abortion. Pro-lifers have justly criticized the wording of many major public opinion polls taken on the abortion question. Almost always, they see that the questions themselves and the way the data from them are explained are skewed to perpetuate the fallacy that a majority of Americans favor the Supreme Court decisions: abortion on demand.

Unfortunately, in criticizing the pro-abortion manipulation of polling data, much of the pro-life movement has tended to discount them altogether. However, there is a wide range of opinion polls that, if properly analyzed, presents a fairly consistent picture of public opinion. It may not be the picture pro-lifers would most like to see, but it should be even more distressing for those fighting to maintain abortion on demand. Without a clearsighted reading of public opinion, pro-lifers can be led to make damaging strategic political and legislative decisions.

The average newspaper reader or television viewer either digest a summmary of the results of polls in a matter of seconds or hears about the results second-hand. Thus, the way the question is framed and the way the results of the poll are reported have an enormous influence on an audience, 99.9 percent of which will never read the poll itself. Pollsters know that how a question is worded can have a very significant impact on the outcome of the survey. To take one example, a *New York Times/CBS* 1980 poll found that while only 29 percent of those surveyed favored "an amendment to the Constitution prohibiting abortions," 50 percent of the same group favored "an amendment to the Constitution protecting the life of the unborn child." To the latter question there were 39 percent opposed and 11 percent undecided.

It's therefore easy to understand why abortion advocates in media and political circles try to cut the question in terms of forbidding, prohibiting, or banning all abortions. This ability to frame the question under consideration actually allows the pollsters to shape, rather than reflect, public opinion.

Another effect of this ability to frame the issue is more subtle and probably more damaging. Since the major national polls are represented by the media conglomerates as "news," over time their choice of questions tend to be accepted as truly representing what the issue is all about and the facts surrounding it. Thus, for example, not only the polling samples, but the entire news-conscious public, has been taught for years that the 1973 Supreme Court decision allows abortion in the first three months of pregnancy and that the sole alternative to the nation's current abortion policy is banning all abortions. Of course, the pollsters know better than anyone the fact that public support for abortions performed after the first trimester greatly diminishes and that there is substantial majority support for earlier abortions only in cases where the mother's life is threatened or if the child was conceived by rape or incest.

It is not surprising that after years of distorted

presentations of popular opinion on abortion that many, if not most, feel that there is majority support for an unrestricted right to abortion. What is surprising is that in spite of the best efforts of the pro-abortion media monopoly, actual public opinion has shifted much less on abortion that would be expected even given the natural human proclivity to accept the familiar with time.

Probably the single most useful poll in analyzing the public's real feelings is one that has been conducted by Gallup almost yearly since *Roe v. Wade*. The poll first asked if abortion should be legal under all circumstances, no circumstances, or certain circumstances. In 1975, 21 percent supported legal abortion under all circumstances, 22 percent thought it should be illegal under all circumstances, and 54 percent thought abortion should be legal only under certain circumstances. By 1980, 25 percent supported legal abortion under all circumstances, 18 percent under no circumstances, and 53 percent only under certain circumstances. By 1983, 23 percent supported legal abortion under all circumstances, 16 percent under no circumstances, and 58 percent only under certain circumstances.

To give some idea of the power of choice in headlines, the 1983 results could be characterized either as "81 percent support legal abortion," or "74 percent support abortion restrictions." Indeed, as an indicator for support of the real effects of the *Roe v. Wade* decision, the second heading is much closer to the mark. This becomes more obvious when the feelings of those who support abortions only "under certain circumstances" are analyzed.

When Gallup has broken down the responses of those who support abortion "under certain circumstances," the results often surprise both supporters and opponents of abortion. During the first trimester, Gallup has found substantial majority support in cases of rape and incest, and majority support if the woman's physical health is at risk. There is also just under 50 percent support during the first trimester for those cases where the fetus may be handicapped, or if the woman's mental health is threatened. (Other polls show slightly over 50 percent support in these latter two cases; either way, it is obvious the public is closely divided.)

Contrary to stereotypes, the only circumstance under which there is consistent majority support for abortions *after* the first trimester is where the mother's life is endangered. What is also important here is that most abortions are performed for social reasons. There is no majority support for abortions for social reasons in any trimester, even the first trimester, according to these Gallup polls, except in the case of rape or incest.

Since between 90 and 95 percent of the abortions are performed for social reasons (economics, lifestyle, number of children, etc.), or as a means of birth control, what these figures make clear is that there has been a consistent majority of public opinion in opposition to over 90 percent of the abortions allowed by *Roe v. Wade!*

Both because polling questions can be loaded and because most Americans do not understand the unlimited right to abortion that currently exists, the same majority that opposes the *results* of *Roe v. Wade* may not realize it should oppose the *Roe v. Wade* decision. For example, in the same poll that Gallup asks his sample whether they support the Supreme Court decision, the results of that decision are described as allowing a woman to "go to a doctor to end a pregnancy any time during the first three months of pregnancy." In a few words, this question manages adroitly to neutralize the considerable objections to second trimester abortion, subtly imply some medical need, and virtually disguise the fact that the subject is abortion. In a 1983 poll, Gallup found that 50 percent of the sample support the Court decision described in this manner. In 1983 43 percent said they opposed the ruling and 7 percent were undecided. In 1974 the favorable response was 47 percent, and in 1981 45 percent.

Pro-abortion strategists are well aware of their vulnerability regarding unrestricted abortion. In a 1981 speech to the National Planned Parenthood convention, Jeanne Rosoff, president of the Alan Guttmacher Institute, the research arm of Planned Parenthood, stated that most abortions "are performed for social and economic reasons, things such as age and things such as lifestyle, and when you try to get to these to measure public opinion, the support dwindles very, very rapidly."

The original Hatch Amendment and later the Hatch-Eagleton Amendment were proposed, in part, in order to re-frame the question in terms of whether or not it should be possible to restrict abortion at all, rather than in terms of banning all abortions. Either version of the amendment would overturn *Roe v. Wade* and permit abortion to be restricted or prohibited legislatively. Pro-abortion leaders were quick to recognize the Hatch Amendment as an attempt to isolate those who favored keeping abortion legal under all circumstances and build a popular majority for overturning *Roe v. Wade* from among those who would make abortion illegal in at least most circumstances. The director of the National Abortion Rights Action League at the time that Sen. Hatch first announced the amendment called it "the greatest threat to abortion rights since the 1973 Supreme Court decision."

It's unfortunate that this type of amendment was first voted on in the summer of 1983 rather than in 1981 when the sting of the 1980 elections was still fresh. By 1983 the perception of the safety of a pro-abortion position had been restored. Further, it was not expected that some elements in the anti-abortion movement would in the end oppose the amendment, which was not their ideal, as hard as those in the pro-abortion movement did. This left some senators whose positions were "soft," for example

Delaware Senators Joseph Biden and William Roth, in the position of being able to vote against the amendment and feel politically safe since they were pleasing both the pro-abortion movement and part of the anti-abortion movement in their own state.

However, the vote on the Hatch-Eagleton Amendment did accomplish two very important objectives. For the first time ever, senators had to vote up or down on whether they supported abortion on demand throughout the entire nine months of pregnancy. The record of the vote should be extremely useful to pro-life political activists in future elections. Those voting against the amendment can rightly be characterized as opposing any restrictions on abortion; up to that date, many of them had maintained ambiguous positions. In effect, the vote on Hatch-Eagleton forced many closet pro-abortion senators to show their true colors.

The second salutary effect of the Hatch-Eagleton effort was that the mainstream pro-life movement for the first time was able to fight the issue on terms which the majority of Americans could support. It was not an easy thing for the pro-life movement to do, but hopefully it represented only the beginning effort to cut the question as disadvantageously as possible for abortion supporters. However while the pro-life effort grows more sophisticated each year and better able to reach a higher percentage of its own hard core support, the pool from which the staunchest pro-lifers are drawn may be diminishing. The evidence would seem to suggest there is an increasing acceptance of abortions in the "hard cases" by people who would seem to be logical recruits to support the maximum pro-life position. At the same time, albeit at a slower rate, there may be a growing acceptance of unlimited abortion among others who formerly took a middle position.

Clearly, opponents of abortion retain a decided

advantage on the question of support/opposition to the issue of abortion on demand. They also have a significant advantage in terms of the net difference between the number of voters who will vote for a candidate because he is pro-life versus the number of voters who will vote for a candidate because he is pro-abortion. However, because abortion proponents control essentially all national information outlets, if they were ever able to narrow this gap, then the pro-life course would indeed become difficult.

This would seem to indicate that pro-life political strategists must multiply their efforts to convince the so-called "mushy middle" to identify with the pro-life cause. These are people who support abortions in some cases but whose basic opposition to indiscriminate abortion puts them much closer to the pro-life position than to the pro-abortion position. Even as this group is brought into the pro-life camp (where it properly belongs), the pro-life movement must simultaneously embrace and promote the ultimate goals of reverence and protection for all life.

In the same vein pro-life political strategists have an obligation to help their candidates articulate their position in such a way as to make the middle majority realize they are really closer to the pro-life candidate than to "pro-choice" politicians. While this probably won't produce "single issue" anti-abortion votes, it may help neutralize the creation of more "single issue" pro-abortion votes. Simultaneously it should also improve techniques designed to increase the percentage of the most solid abortion opponents who actually do vote based largely on the issue.

Despite the realities behind often misrepresented polling data, abortion advocates seem to have more successfully used public opinion polls with politicians, both before and after elections, than have pro-life advocates. This isn't surprising since the majority of the polls couch the language in terms most likely to elicit responses favorable to support for abortion. This is an area of weakness that should receive considerable attention from pro-life political strategists. For example, there is clear evidence that interpretation of polling data aided the pro-abortion movement to solidify such senators as Robert Byrd and Quenton Burdick against any amendment to overturn the *Roe v. Wade* decision.

To counter this, two actions can be taken. First, unbiased polls can be commissioned from reputable firms to be used to show politicians where the public really is. Second, there has to be a willingness to take existing national polls and any which are commissioned and very accurately analyze them for candidates, legislators and members of Congress in order to show the fallacy of pro-abortion claims.

In some ways this is painful because the results are not all that we would want, but they do show that when a politician must choose, it is not only safe but decidedly advantageous to be pro-life. Self-deception on the part of abortion opponents regarding public opinion is simply that, self-deception. If abortion opponents do not set the record straight in this area, then the pro-abortion perception will prevail. When all factors are considered, public opinion on the abortion issue, if accurately used and understood by the pro-life movement, can be a real advantage. If ignored, it can lead to disaster.

There is also a real need to bring the issue back into the legislative process, thereby forcing abortion supporters to argue their true case which is clearly a minority position. The ability to pass significant abortion restrictions will bring the teaching force of the law back on the side of life, besides beginning to save countless innocent lives. This momentum could propel those favoring life towards the kind of ultimate victory that after eleven years still eluded the best efforts of the pro-abortionists. So a primary goal will clearly remain overturning *Roe v. Wade*, either by a legislative authorization or through a reversal of *Roe* by the Court itself.

The Opposition — Parasitism, Perception and Intimidation

The pro-life approach to politics has been conceptually simple; i.e. identify your supporters, let them know where the candidates stand, and then get your people out to the polls, caucuses, etc. The pro-abortion coalition, by contrast, employs political techniques better suited to a top-down, elite movement that must protect a legal situation for which there has never been full majority support. Grouping some of these techniques together into three general categories, one might say that abortion advocates practice parasitic politics based on perception and intimidation.

Perception has always seemed more important than substance in pro-abortion rhetoric. Pro-life advocates who have debated the issue know first hand that their opponents would rather talk about anything (contraception, nuclear war, Catholics, population growth, the New Right, freedom of choice, etc.) than abortion. This is an old debater's trick and is useful when trying to defend an ignoble position.

This technique also carried over into politics in several ways. Efforts are often made to have the opposition to a pro-life candidate be perceived as stemming from something different than the candidate's position on abortion. The candidate may find himself or herself attacked in the media as a "New Right extremist" or against women's issues regardless of what positions he or she really takes on issues other than abortion. This technique is also carried over to attempts to discredit, or at least neutralize, support and sympathy for the pro-life movement. The media is employed to characterize the pro-life movement as being for or against other issues or as part of some larger political or religious conspiracy.

Pro-abortionist's politics of perception has also been used to create a general image of the pro-life movement and especially its political wing as somehow unseemly, while enhancing the image of their "pro-choice" position as the only one a civilized politician can possibly hold. One naturally expects that politicians to whom public opinion and elections mean everything would be far more immune to the politics of perception and manipulation of public opinion polls than the public at large. This doesn't seem to be the case, however, and one might wonder if the pro-life movement will be seen as losing until the last pro-abortion politician is defeated.

None of the elements of the politics of perception would work very well without the ability to determine the national media's portrayal of the controversy. Unfortunately, much of the media has been an integral part of the overall pro-abortion movement since the '60s, and political activists do not hesitate to use this ally.

While the right to life movement is confident that its goals will be attained through open and equal participation in the democratic process, this has not been the case with the pro-abortion movement. While purporting (falsely) to represent a majority view, the defenders of unrestricted abortion have repeatedly used attack and intimidation to try to drive pro-life citizens and organizations from the public arena.

Pro-abortion politics of intimidation takes several forms. Like much of their strategy, it depends on their media network. The consistent use of the media to stigmatize and denigrate the pro-life movement deters appointed or elected officials who are most concerned about image. In states where caucuses play a large role in the process, there is often strong discouragement of pro-life participation. Where pro-lifers have been successful in gaining measureable influence in caucuses and conventions, abortion opponents are accused of the crime of weakening the parties, especially the Democratic party. Such concern does not seem evident about the participation of other issue-oriented people such as environmentalists, nuke-freeze types, or labor delegates.

The politics of intimidation is played at the highest levels. Any individual associated with the pro-life movement who moves into an important bureaucratic post will usually be subject to considerable harassment. Dr. C. Everett Koop and Marjory Mecklenburg, Surgeon General and Deputy Assistant Secretary for Population Affairs, respectively, in the Reagan administration, were both quickly made centers of controversy when their appointments were announced. Their competence is beyond question; the real issue was their identification as movement pro-lifers.

Still another familiar type of harassment is the continual filing of complaints against pro-life political activities with government regulatory bodies, such as the Federal Elections Commission. Most of these complaints eventually come to naught in spite of the plethora of regulations which are often ambiguous and sometimes honestly misunderstood. However, the experience of a bureaucratic investigation is, at the least troublesome, and can be most frightening to those new to the world of politics. The pro-life movement could play this same game, but its style has really been to encourage, not discourage, participation in the process. Pro-life time is better spent improving methods to increase the increment we can deliver at the polls.

No discussion of pro-abortion intimidation should fail to mention religious harassment. The more general appeals to religious bigotry may have lost some of their effect because of the way abortion advocates have kept changing the message.

In the beginning all pro-lifers were characterized as Catholics and the movement was described as a conspiracy to impress Catholic dogma on the nation. This was later shifted to imply that pro-lifers were part of the Protestant Moral Majority, since broadened to include most of the range of fundamentalists and evangelicals. Somewhere along the way "New Right" was thrown in as an overall characterization, and we may be close to the point where the public is not sure just who they are supposed to believe make up the pro-life movement.

More troublesome have been pro-abortion attempts to keep political information away from pro-life members of various churches. Likewise, while pro-abortion political strategists use their media allies at every opportunity, they attempt to intimidate religious publications that oppose abortion in an effort to keep their readers ignorant, both on the issue and on the positions or voting records of candidates. Similarly, members of the electronic ministry come under attack. The pro-abortion movement seems to believe that not even the smallest fraction of the media should be allowed to represent any other views but its own.

In combatting the politics of intimidation, pro-life activists must remember that it has been precisely those techniques the opposition fears most and feels will be effective that will come under the strongest attack. The pro-life movement does have an advantage in being able to identify and reach out to certain religious constituencies opposing abortion and has the right and obligation to do so.

Much of the pro-abortion constituency is harder to readily identify and not as committed or likely to vote on the issue. It's no wonder they would like to change the rules and take pro-lifers out of the game. Such bullying cannot be tolerated and pro-lifers have the courage and determination that will usually face down a bully in the end, anyway.

In addition to the strategies we have discussed, the pro-abortionists have in recent years shown evidence of working harder to build grassroots political and organizational structures to compete with the broader-based movement against abortion. The best answer to this is simply accelerated pro-life organizational development, since the pro-life base is still only a fraction of its statistical potential.

While abortion proponents have not matched pro-life organizational efforts, they have been successful in attaching themselves to other movements, thus making the host's organizational basis their own. To detail this important strategy would take a chapter alone; we have space here only to list some of the many groups pro-abortionists have either successfully attached themselves to, or are trying to. Planned Parenthood is a perfect example. Not so many years ago, they, too, understood the unborn child within a woman was a baby; not anymore. The woman's movement is another tragic example. Today all of the major "women's rights" groups are not only pro-abortion, its advocacy seems to have become their primary, if not almost exclusive issue.

More recently, the pro-abortion movement seems to be attempting to encroach on groups representing the interests of minority groups such as Blacks. The labor movement is still another target. Finally, the Democratic party itself stands in danger of much greater pro-abortion control exercised at the highest levels. While it is definitely not to the interests of the pro-life movement that any of these groups be taken over, it is even worse news to the organizations themselves.

There are steps the pro-life movement can take to slow, and in some cases to halt, the spread of this activity. At the same time, pro-life political strategists should explore the formation of coalitions and specifically determine under what circumstances such coalitions further the goals of the pro-life movement.

The Future

Almost never must a political cause earn every political supporter at the ballot box. Ordinarily a show of electoral strength that holds the promise that the issue may endanger political careers, or sometimes even just continue to be an irritant, is usually sufficient to motivate politicians to seek some way to accommodate, or at least somewhat appease and neutralize, the forces that threaten to disturb their equilibrium.

For the pro-life movement it has not been politics as usual. Perhaps no cause in this century has been forced to win so often on the campaign battlefield with so little acknowledgement of its successes. Often abortion advocates have had the extraordinary ability to have only their interpretation of events heard. The media, which interprets for most of us, have been largely part of the pro-abortion coalition, and much of society's elite, which interprets for many would-be movers and shakers, has always been a crucial part of the pro-abortion movement's base. It seems politicans listen to both.

Yet the pro-life victories and accomplishments have been real. In 1974 on one of the U.S. Senate's first votes on pro-life legislation, only 27 senators supported curtailing federal funding of abortion. In 1983, when the Hatch-Eagleton Amendment came to the floor, there were 49 senators willing to vote to overturn *Roe v. Wade* and end abortion on demand. A significant indicator of what has been happening was the votes of first-term Senators. Of the 41 senators elected to their first terms in 1974-1980, 26 voted in favor of the amendment and only 15 voted against it.

Pro-life political action committees, together with the skillful lobbying efforts of such groups as the National

Right to Life Committee and the National Committee for a Human Life Amendment have been largely responsible for retaining restrictions on federal abortion funding During fiscal year 1979, only 4,430 federally funded abortions were performed in contrast to 294,600 in fiscal year 1977. If only 20 percent of those who were denied publicly-funded abortions gave birth to their children as is claimed by Planned Parenthood's research arm, the Alan Guttmacher Institute, then 58,000 lives a year are being saved. While only a small fraction of the goal, that is in itself worth all the efforts that have been made.

Attainment of the larger goals remain for the future; there will be many intermediate steps on the way. More than any other wing of the movement, pro-life political strategists are charged with keeping the issue front and center in the public forum and making the kinds of real gains that will enable the movement to take advantage of the yet unseen opportunities that tomorrow may bring. In our secular republic, the law is essential for restoring respect and protection for life, and the most skillful application of political action will remain necessary to affect all three branches of government that determine the law.

The experience gained in both success and failure teaches many valuable lessons for tomorrow. Techniques and strategies that work should be refined and expanded and creative new techniques should be developed by the political action committees. Pro-life political activists should not let themselves be intimidated and driven away from what must be done to win.

Yet, strategic flexibility and creativity will be necessary to retain the campaign advantages pro-lifers have enjoyed. The basic differences between the two movements and the advantages and disadvantages each has will probably continue to shape the nature of the battle. Pro-life activists must do what they do best — out-organize, out-motivate and ultimately out-vote the abortion advocates in the races that make a difference. The pro-life movement is becoming increasingly aware of its real strengths and weaknesses relative to the range of opinion on the issue of abortion held by the population at large. If realistically understood, there are many demographic factors that ultimately can be quite advantageous to abortion opponents. More than ever the movement's political strategists at least must press real advantages and pursue courses of action based upon a realistic view of the nation as it is, rather than as we would like it to be.

The pro-abortion movement has the mechanism to make statements, whether they are true or false. Pro-life statements may not be heard, and when they are, they may well be turned back against the movement. So the task of pro-life political efforts is always to make a difference rather than a statement. Because of the media there is no spillover effect to pro-life victories; if, therefore, we have to elect sixty-seven solid pro-life senators, then that two-thirds majority must be built, step by step. Concentrating on making a difference rather than a statement should also help pro-life political activists avoid the kind of intramovement battles that have been so damaging to the cause in the past. Those battles have largely involved which philosophical statement elements of the movement thought should be made, and which they felt they could not accept.

Hopefully, most have learned by now that while there is ample room for debate and discussion within the movement, differences should be kept out of the public arena. Tacit acceptance, if not support, should be given whenever we clash with the real opponents in issue over a pro-life initiative. However, no comparable movement in American history has ever enjoyed internal unanimity, and so politically active abortion opponents must realize that their crucial task demands that they cannot wait for unanimous support before they embark upon an essential course of action.

For the near future, pro-life and pro-abortion activists realize the immediate stakes. Justice O'Connor's brilliant dissent in *Akron v. Akron Center for Reproductive Health* signaled that the Supreme Court may be only two votes away from substantially reversing or vacating *Roe v. Wade.* Four of the pro-abortion Justices at the time of that decision were age 74 or older. Thus the retention of a pro-life administration that would name appointees to the High Court who would vote to overturn *Roe v. Wade* has become a top priority for pro-life strategists. Securing a pro-abortion administration is a top priority for the opposition.

Likewise, it has become essential to say that the Senate make-up is such that a pro-life Supreme Court Justice would be confirmed. In addition, the pro-life House majority has to be increased to equal, and then exceed, its 1981 level. The ability to have recorded test votes on the issue in the Senate must be protected as the number of pro-life members is numerically increased. Clearly, the most important challenges for pro-life political forces are yet to be faced.

As preparations are being made for perhaps the most intense battles yet over abortion, the spectre of infanticide and euthanasia has already risen. The parallels with the early days of the abortion struggle are all too obvious: judicial complicity, media misrepresentation of the issues, and "softening" of public opinion. We hear respected voices crying singly and in committee that only a new ethic, making the heretofore unthinkable accepted practice, can solve the new dilemmas.

Preventing this logical extension of abortion on demand must also fall into the realm of pro-life politics. It won't be easy, but the movement's ability and skills are far greater than they were in the 1960s and early 1970s. This time, the tide of anti-life sentiment must be turned much sooner.

Pro-life political ideals embody the best of both the nation's liberal and conservative traditions: the liberal concern for human equality and for the need to protect the weak and defenseless; the conservative desire to preserve the most fundamental ideals and values of the nation's heritage. America herself may be viewed as an experiment to determine whether free men and women can build and preserve a society that protects the equality, common worth, and dignity of every human being.

If so, then the pro-life cause is really one whose successes will determine whether America honors its own founding principles. With all the disadvantages that may exist, this political arena is one where there is still freedom to act. If the battle for these most basic human rights, the right to life and the right to protect life, is lost here, then there is little left for America to give the world.

RESTRICTING ABORTION THROUGH LEGISLATION

Lynn D. Wardle*

"Although it is not widely understood, there is much, much more that legislatures can do to extend to the unborn and to victimized pregnant women the legal protections permissible under the current rule of Roe and its progeny."

LYNN WARDLE

Introduction: Looking Beyond the Present to the Possible.

The summer of 1983 brought double disappointment to the American pro-life movement. On June 15, the Supreme Court announced its decisions in the *Akron*, *Ashcroft* and *Simopolous* cases,

*Lynn D. Wardle is a professor at the J. Reuben Clark Law School, Brigham Young University. He has written extensively about abortion in scholarly journals and in the popular press and has authored two books about the legal regulation of abortion in America. He and his wife, Marian, are the parents of two children and live in Orem, Utah. Professor Wardle is a member of the Board of Directors of Americans United for Life.

emphatically reaffirming *Roe v. Wade* and the doctrine of abortion on demand. The Court rejected with a vengeance the argument that state and local legislative bodies constitutionally have some discretion in merely regulating (not restricting, much less prohibiting) the performance of abortions. And on June 28, less than two weeks later, the U.S. Senate rejected the proposed Hatch-Eagleton Amendment to the Constitution. Fifty Senators (18 more than necessary to defeat a proposed Constitutional Amendment) voted against the simple proposition that: "A right to abortion is not secured by [the] Constitution."

The double defeat of June 1983 sharply illustrates the abortion-favoring disposition of the present Court and the *status-quo*-accommodating disposition of the present Congress. In the wake of those discouraging, public defeats, the task of restricting abortion through legislation might seem to be hopeless.

But it is not. Certainly the current Court's myopic dogmatism and the current Congress' unprincipled expediency are exceptionally disappointing. But these unpleasant realities ought not to blind us to past practices which suggest future possibilities that are very promising for the pro-life movement.

Specifically, as a matter of historical practice and constitutional principle the creation of public policy in our democracy is primarily accomplished through legislative enactment, not judicial decree. Thus, the right of the people to enact legislation to protect the unborn (and to protect the neglected victim of abortion — the pregnant woman) will ultimately prevail.

Legislative Predominance in Establishing Public Policy Through Law.

The establishment of public policy through law in America is primarily accomplished through the enactment of legislation. In this sense, most "law" is legislated.

The drafters of the Constitution were committed to the concept of self-government; they had instigated an unprecedented revolution to obtain the right of self-government, and they deliberately included a system of checks and balances in the charter of their government to preserve the right.[1] The record left by the framers leaves no doubt that they intended that the legislature would have primary responsibility for the establishment of public policy through the enactment of legislation.[2]

They did not contemplate a judicial branch active in the establishment of public policy. Rather, the judiciary was intended by the drafters to be "the least dangerous" branch of government.[3] In his well-known essay on the judiciary, Alexander Hamilton argued that the judiciary would be "least in a capacity to annoy or injure" the political rights secured by the Constitution.[4]

He distinguished the judicial function from that of the executive (which he said "holds the sword of the community") and the legislative (which he said "prescribes the rules by which the duties and rights of every citizen are to be regulated"). Hamilton concluded that the judiciary "may truly be said to have neither *force* nor *will* but merely judgment...."[5] Indeed, Hamilton's principal concern seems to have been to ensure that the judicial and legislative powers would not be merged.[6] Thus, as a matter of constitutional structure and design, the establishment of public policy in our nation should be achieved primarily through legislative enactment.

Moreover, as a matter of American history, the establishment of public policy through law actually has been a legislative, not a judicial, responsibility. Beginning in the century after the adoption of the United States Constitution, a great codification movement swept through the United States. The tendency of the times was (and, in large part, still is) to embody in positive, statutory form all significant points of law dealing with a particular subject, including a great deal of law which had been created and developed in the courts. The effect of this legislative activity was to reduce the relative significance of the judicial branch in creating public policy through law.

But the role of the federal judiciary underwent a profound metamorphosis in the twentieth century. If a turning point were to be specified, the year 1938 might well be chosen as the beginning of the modern era of judicial activism. Until then the U.S. Supreme Court had consistently maintained that the term "laws" — as used in a federal statute that requires federal courts to follow the "laws of the several states" — did *not* include most state court decisions (judge-made law.)[7]

That position was rejected in the landmark 1938 case, *Erie Railroad Co. v. Tompkins*.[8] In that case, the Court emphasized that "whether the law of the state shall be declared by its Legislature in a statute or by its highest court in a decision is not a matter of ... concern."[9] Perhaps in abandoning the fiction that judge-made law is not really law, the Court also lost its grip on the principle that it is not the proper function of courts — at least not the federal judiciary — to create public policy on substantive matters.

It was also in 1938 that the Federal Rules of Civil Procedure were adopted. These rules, which are a landmark in progressive judicial administration and procedure, allowed the federal courts to hear and resolve bigger, more complex controversies, and to render more far-reaching judgments than previously had been possible.

The consequences of those two significant changes upon the law-making activities of the federal courts were not immediately apparent, for those changes took place at a time when the federal judiciary was under attack from the political branches of government for invalidating a lot of New Deal legislation and other economic regulation. President Roosevelt succeeded in changing the posture of the Court through his power of appointment of federal judges and through political threats and public intimidation.

But the seeds of judicial activism sown in the 1930s eventually ripened and bore fruit. Beginning with the Warren Court in the 1950s, the federal courts have assumed a much more active role in creating public policy by exercising their judicial decision-making power.[10]

It has been suggested that one reason judges in the last half of the twentieth century have become more active in creating public policy is because that was necessary if the courts were to keep the balance between the legislative and judicial branches of government.[11] I would suggest, however, to the extent that the great surge in legislative activity after the adoption of the U.S. Constitution represents a clear deviation from the pre-1789 practices — i.e., the relatively modest role that legislatures had taken in determining public policy previously — that change was the intent of its drafters. Indeed, the framers of the Constitution believed that an abundance of legislation would be "one of the inconveniences necessarily connected with the advantages of a free government."[12]

However, in the past decade the Supreme Court has captured the subject of abortion and improperly preempted the establishment of public policy through law dealing with that subject. Virtually all of the law regarding abortion's legality is now judicially-created law. State legislatures have been reduced to codifying much of what the Court has decreed, but the boundaries of the legality of abortion have been set almost exclusively by decisions of the Supreme Court and lower courts. There has been virtually no new development in the law regarding the subject of abortion which has not originated in, been modified by, or been sanctioned by judicial decree since 1973, the year of the Supreme Court's *Roe* decision.

Roe v. Wade and its progeny are the clearest example in American legal history of judicial legislation, i.e., the creation of public policy by judges.

Legislation is Subject to Judicial Review

The previous analysis does not dispute the constitutionally sanctioned right of the judiciary to review legislation to determine its constitutionality. The Constitution is the supreme law of the land. Thus it prevails over any other source of law that conflicts with it. By the same principle that every act of a delegated authority which exceeds the delegated power is void, every legislative enactment which conflicts with the Constitution is invalid. Thus, legislative law must not violate constitutional law.

The responsibility to review legislation to see if it is constitutional is a judicial function. But the power of judicial review was not meant as an exception to the principle that judges would have no "will." Rather, it is intended to underscore the fact that judges, like legislators, are subject to the Constitution. Moreover, the Constitution, because it represents the supreme will of the people, is superior to the legislative will of the people's elected representatives.

As a practical matter, however, the power of judicial review has turned out to be the trump card. The anticipated risk of judicial review, i.e., "that the courts, on the pretense of a repugnancy, may substitute their own pleasure to the constitutional intentions of the legislature"[14] has become a reality.

The Need for Legislative Action

Thus one important challenge facing the pro-life community is to restore the Constitutional allocation of power. The word "restore" deserves emphasis. The task is not to enhance the power of the legislature or abolish judicial review, but to restore the constitutional balance.

The Constitution delegates the power to establish public policy on matters such as abortion to the legislature. The Supreme Court violated this principle when it decided *Roe* as it did; constitutionally, the Court had no business trying to establish a national policy on abortion through judicial decision. But it would not be a solution to the tragedy of *Roe* to go to the other extreme and take from the courts their proper judicial power to interpret the law and decide specific cases. The solution, rather, is to restore to the legislatures the power to determine public policy regarding abortion.

The overriding question raised by *Roe v. Wade* and its legal progeny is not simply whether abortion will or will not be prohibited but whether the people of this nation do or do not have the power to protect human life through the enactment of laws by their elected representatives. That question must be addressed and answered *before* the question of the rightness or wrongness of abortion is reached. For if the elected representatives of the people do not have the power to protect, then even if abortion is immoral, we have no remedy; we are stuck with a corrupt rule of law imposed by a corrupt judiciary.

The ultimate challenge facing the pro-life community is to restore respect for life as a fundamental value and protection for the defenseless as a basic commitment of our society. In *Roe* the Court dismissed, with a flick of its pen, the argument that these profound, historic values justify *any* restriction on abortion during approximately the first six months of pregnancy and any meaningful restriction on abortion after viability. Thus the challenge in a moral and ethical sense is to restore in law the value of humanity and respect for life.

But the specific and immediate challenge is to stop the killing — to restore protection in law for the unborn child and for the distressed, victimized pregnant woman. The reality facing us is that more than 14 million abortions have been performed in the past eleven years, over 1.5 million abortions per year for the last five years. The longer abortion on demand remains the rule of law the more difficult it will be to change.[15]

Legislative action is a necessary but insufficient, condition for the reversal of *Roe v. Wade.* A legislature does not have the authority under our constitutional system to reverse a judicial interpretation of the Constitution. Nor does any legislature have the sole authority to amend the constitution by merely enacting legislation. Nevertheless, legislatures have key roles to play in both the process of judicial reversal of prior precedents and the alternative process of amending the Constitution.

One role is to extend the maximum permissible protection for the unborn and to focus public attention on the inadequacy and extremism of the current rule of abortion on demand. The other significant role for legislatures is to enact bills or resolutions designed to advance the process of judicial reversal of *Roe v. Wade* or of amending the Constitution. This legislative action must occur at two distinct levels, preferably simultaneously. The first level of legislative action is federal, i.e., action by the U.S. Senate and House of Representatives, and by federal agencies. The second level is state and local, including action by state, county, municipal, and special district elected officials.

Extending Maximum Protection by Enacting Effective Constitutional Abortion Regulations and by Focusing Public Attention on the Extremism of Abortion-on-Demand.

The task of extending maximum constitutional protection to the unborn and enacting provocative legislation falls primarily upon the state and local governments. This is so because the regulation of abortion has historically been a matter of domestic relations and criminal law primarily dealt with by the states rather than the federal government. For instance, prior to *Roe*, every state had enacted laws restricting and regulating the performance of abortions. By contrast, at the Congressional level, during the entire decade preceding *Roe v. Wade* only ten bills were introduced relating directly to abortion.[16]

The regulation of abortion is not one of the functions specifically vested in Congress, but it appears to come within the powers reserved by the Tenth Amendment to the states. Thus, state and local legislative bodies must take the initiative in extending the maximum permissible protection under law for the unborn and for pregnant women.

From the pro-life perspective, this presents a decided advantage, for it is in the state legislatures where the pro-life movement has its greatest strength. The state legislatures are closer to their constituency than their federal counterparts, and considerably more responsive to the will of the people than politically-insulated judges who sit on the federal bench. In the decade since *Roe*, states have persistently attempted to regulate and restrict abortion. Between 1973 and 1982, a total of 228 separate abortion laws were enacted in the various states.[17] This is a good start, but it is far from adequate.

Although it is not widely understood, there is much, much more that legislatures can do to extend to the unborn and to victimized pregnant women the legal protections permissible under the current rule of *Roe* and its progeny. For example states can do a great deal to protect the post-viable unborn child. In the recent *Ashcroft* case, the Court upheld a Missouri law requiring that a second doctor, responsible for the welfare of the viable unborn child, be in attendance at all post-viability abortions. Even prohibitions of post-viability abortions not performed for life or health reasons are constitutionally permissible. Yet some states do not have *any* restrictions on the performance of post-viability abortions.[18]

Ashcroft also demonstrated that there is much that states can do to encourage parental (and spousal) participation in the abortion decision without violating the Supreme Court's dogma of privacy. The Court upheld a Missouri law requiring either parental or judicial consent to abortion (or judicial determination of the question whether the minor girl is "emancipated"). Again, unfortunately many states have absolutely no restriction against the exploitation of distressed pregnant minors who are vulnerable to unethical abortion-promotors.

Furthermore, state restrictions on abortion funding can be enacted or toughened. States and local governmental units can require *much closer* regulation of abortion practices and practitioners than is presently the case. Some abortionists are getting away with murder in the careless, high volume practice of abortion-for-profit. State legislatures can and should enact (or require state agencies to enact) professional standards applicable to training, professional conduct, precise reporting, frequent administrative review, and adequate follow-up.

The other purpose of state and local governmental legislation is to focus public attention upon the abuses and the inconsistencies in the rule of abortion on demand. For instance, state agencies and legislative committees can undertake fact-finding missions or fund research regarding the risks of abortion, the abuses of abortion clinics, the need for informed consent, abuses of parental rights by abortion counselors and clinics, fetal pain, the incidence of abortion, the increase in abortion repeaters, etc.

The facts of fetal development can and should be highlighted and disclosure of those facts in public sex education/family preparation courses can be required. Every suit against a clinic or doctor for malpractice or lack of consent to abortion should be the subject of legislative special committee investigations and responsive legislation. Every year at least one new anti-abortion bill or resolution should be enacted by every state legislature with as much attendant publicity as possible.

On the federal level, the principal area of activity should be abortion funding. The Constitution gives the Congress control over the federal purse strings. The power of Congress to supervise federal agencies and specify what will be done with federal funds (i.e., specifying specific research to be undertaken, etc.) is a field which the pro-life community has neglected too long. For instance, must we wait until pro-life parties are driven out of federal court before Congress amends the attorneys' fees statute to prevent the punitive imposition of fees against pro-life litigants? Moreover, Congress can address selected issues dealing with the civil rights aspects of abortion. Congress is a wonderful forum for calling national attention to the abuses of abortion through hearings and legislative debate of carefully selected issues. Moreover, Congress conceivably has the authority to provide extensive regulations indirectly (if not directly under the Fourteenth Amendment) concerning abortion. But it is important that the issues be carefully selected and that the bills and legislation be carefully drafted. National publicity is too important to be wasted on irresponsible, extreme, or poorly-drafted proposals.

Legislative Action Designed to Overturn Roe v. Wade.

It is, of course, the responsibility of the courts to say what the Constitution means. There is nothing in the legislative arsenal sufficient to overcome a judicial interpretation of the Constitution. Nevertheless, legislatures have two avenues through which to instigate the rejection of an interpretation of the Constitution. One way legislative action can contribute to overturning *Roe v. Wade* is to prompt the Supreme Court to reconsider its decision. Legislatures can do this modestly by enacting legislation which directly challenges or subtly invites reconsideration of specific premises of *Roe.* There is no question that *Roe* rests upon as shabby a legal fiction as has ever supported any judicial doctrine.

Legislatures can challenge that shallow legal fiction. The courts can *only* decide — and usually *must* decide — questions that are raised in genuine cases or controversies that are brought before them. Since every abortion case that has been decided by a federal court has involved an attack on an abortion law or regulation, legislatures can determine what future abortion issues will be decided by the federal courts by enacting laws designed to raise those issues.

As a practical matter, Congress is in a better position to challenge the Supreme Court than is any state or municipality. The Court is much more aware of and concerned about the power of Congress than it is of the power of the separate states. Thus, it would be wise for

Congress rather than the state legislature to directly confront the fundamental premises of *Roe.* But state legislatures can very effectively chip around the edges of the doctrines of abortion on demand, and subtly challenge the basic premises of *Roe*.

The other way in which legislatures may play a direct role in reversing *Roe* is through the process of amending the Constitution to explicitly reverse *Roe v. Wade.* Article Five of the Constitution outlines the amendatory process. Amendments can be proposed in two ways: (1) by passage on two-thirds vote in both houses of Congress, and (2) upon petition of two-thirds of the states that a constitutional convention be convened. To date, only the first method has been used to amend the Constitution. This emphasizes the predominant role which Congress plays in overturning *Roe v. Wade*.

The second step in the amendment process involves ratification by three-fourths of the states either by vote of the state legislature or by convention. Only one amendment, the Twenty-first Amendment repealing prohibition, was ratified through the convention method.

The problem with a constitutional amendment is Congress. The recent experience with the Hatch-Eagleton Amendment highlights the problem. Although half of the members of the Senate voted to repudiate abortion-on-demand, revealing the strength of the pro-life position, the Hatch-Eagleton proposal fell far short of the two-thirds vote (67) necessary to propose an amendment. The votes against the Hatch-Eagleton amendment by many nominally "moderate" senators underscores the difficulty of adopting a constitutional amendment. As Professor John Hart Ely noted when the Supreme Court outlawed abortion restrictions: "The sighs of relief as this particular albatross was cut from the legislative and executive necks seemed to me audible."[19] Thus, the American Congress, which has seldom been distinguished for its institutional courage or integrity, is not likely to willingly assume a leadership role in the difficult and controversial process of amending the Constitution to reverse *Roe v. Wade.*

However, it is imperative that the amendatory process be aggressively pursued. The Hatch-Eagleton proposal or some other proposed Human Life Amendment should be brought up for a vote on the floor of the Senate or House of Representatives at least once every Congress (i.e., every two years). By so doing the pro-life movement can capitalize on and actually benefit from 1983's unfortunate defeat of the Hatch-Eagleton proposal. If even just a few additional votes can be swung to the pro-life column every time the Hatch-Eagleton or HLA comes up for a vote, the comparison will convey the powerful message that the pro-life movement is *growing* and that public dissatisfaction with *Roe's* doctrine of abortion on demand is *increasing* over time. Moreover, if the vote for a Human Life Amendment grows at just the modest rate of two votes every two years, by the turn of the century our amendment would be passed (unless the Court or Congress grew weary or embarrassed before then, which is not unlikely if we commit ourselves to a program of deliberate, steady progress).

Conclusion

It is not unlikely that the ultimate reversal of the outrageous doctrine of abortion on demand and recognition of the right of the people to protect human life will be accomplished through judicial reconsideration of *Roe v. Wade*. But the Supreme Court will only take that unpleasant and self-embarrassing step if it is forced by sustained and widespread public opinion and political pressure. That is why legislative activity of the type previously described is a necessary predicate of any plan to reverse *Roe v Wade.*

Despite the disappointments of June 1983, the future of the respect-for-humanity movement is very bright. The eloquent dissenting opinion of Justice O'Connor in the *Akron* case is the most important statement on abortion to come out of the Supreme Court in over a decade. And the public vote by *half* of the U.S. Senate to repudiate *Roe v. Wade* is a significant achievement.

I believe that the events of June 1983 mark the beginning of the end for abortion on demand. If we persevere, we shall write the conclusion to this ugly chapter in the history of human rights before the end of this century.

1 The Federalist No. 47 (J. Madison);The Federalist No. 48 (J. Madison).
2. "A voluminous code of law is one of the inconveniences necessarily connected with the advantages of a free government. To avoid an arbitrary discretion in the courts, it is indispensable that they should be bound down by strong rules and precedents which serve to define and point out their duty ..." The Federalist No. 78 (A. Hamilton). See further the Federalist No. 48 (J. Madison) (the legislature is "superior" to and its constitutional power "more extensive" than that of the executive or judicial branches).
3. The Federalist No. 78 (A. Hamilton).
4. Id.
5. Id.

6. Id. Hamilton apparently was particularly concerned that the legislature would assume the judicial function In the last two decades of the twentieth century, however, it appears that the greater threat is that the judiciary may assume a significant part of the legislative function.
7. At least since Swift v. Tyson, 41 U.S. (16 Pet.) 1 (1842), this had been the rule.
8. 304 U.S. 64 (1938).
9. 304 U.S. at 78.
10. During the administration of Chief Justice Warren the Supreme Court was characterized by selective, principled activism. During the administration of Chief Justice Burger, the Court has achieved some notoriety for its selective non-activism. That is, some of its most notable Burger Court decisions have involved the Court declining to exercise or limiting its exercise of judicial power to establish public policy or to override public policies established by the other branches or divisions of government. But part of the reason that those decisions are notable is because they break with the accepted assumption of judicial activism. Thus, one might distinguish the Warren and Burger Courts on this basis: the Warren Court was particularly concerned with articulating principled justifications for selective judicial activism, while the Burger Court has been particularly concerned with articulating principled justifications for selective judicial self-restraint. Ironically, *Roe v. Wade*, which is probably the most extreme case of judicial usurpation of legislative policy-making power in the modern history of the Court, was decided by the Burger court.
11. G. Gilmore, The Ages of American Law (1977).
12. See supra, note 2, and accompanying text.
13. One of the drafters of the Constitution gave two reasons for granting the judiary the power to review the constitutionality of legislation: (1) the interpretation of law "is the proper and peculiar province" of judges, and the Constitution is fundamental law, and (2) to ensure a separation of powers the federal courts were "designed to be an intermediate body" to keep the legislature within its constitutional limits. Thus, from the beginning it was conceived

that the federal courts would have power and duty "to declare all acts contrary to the manifest tenor of the Constitution void." The Federalist No. 78 (A. Hamilton).

14. Id.
15. "There is no longer room for any remedy where everything which once had been a vice is now a part of the common pattern." Attributed to Seneca in Quay, Justifiable Abortion — Medical and Legal Foundations, 49 Geo. L. J. 395, 421 (1961).
16. Wardle, Restoring the Constitutional Balance: The Need for a Constitutional Amendment to Reverse *Roe v. Wade*. Statement of Professor Lynn Wardle before the Subcommittee on the Constitution Committee on the Judiciary, U.S. Senate, February 28, 1983, at 11.
17. See 15 Fam. Planning & Population Rep. 111 (1983)
18. Wood & Hawkins, State Regulation of Late Abortion and the Physician's Duty of Care to the Viable Fetus, 45 Mo. L. Rev. 394 (1980).
19. Ely, The Wages of Crying Wolf, A Comment on *Roe v. Wade*, 82 Yale L. J. 920, 947 (1973).

"... FROM THE JAWS OF DEFEAT"

Thomas J. Marzen, Esq.*

"There is no simple or perfect legal or political way to protect the unborn. Each possible path has pitfalls that the advocates of abortion might expose either in the courts or the legislatures, and they would no doubt discover and invent many more than the rather obvious few that this essay suggest."

THOMAS J. MARZEN

What legal strategies and tactics would proponents of permissive abortion employ if *Roe v. Wade* ceased to have the force of law? If the pro-life movement should succeed, how would its opponents respond? How would they attempt to use the courts to snatch victory from the jaws of defeat?

In *Roe v. Wade* the United States Supreme Court held

*Thomas J. Marzen is chief staff counsel, Americans United for Life Legal Defense Fund. He received his B.A. from the University of Illinois, and his J.D. from the Illinois Institute of Technology.

that abortion is protected by the U.S. Constitution and that the State has no interest sufficient to warrant any significant prohibition or regulation of the practice. There are two ways to erase the legal effects of *Roe v. Wade*: by Supreme Court reversal or by constitutional amendment. There are, however, an almost infinite number of possible scripts that could be written for either scenario. While only a few are plausible, even within these few the range of possibilities is so great it defies anything more than a general description of the legal terrain over which the enemies and advocates of permissive abortion would maneuver.

Even so, *Roe v. Wade* is based on only two fundamental premises: one is that there exists a constitutionally protected right to abortion; the other is that the human fetus is neither a "person" under the Constitution, nor the proper subject of a state interest weighty enough to justify meaningful restrictions on abortion practices. The former premise posits a constitutionally protected "zone" within which the woman, together with a cooperative physician, may procure abortion without state interference. The latter negates any obligation or power of the State to curtail the woman's freedom to abort based on a contravailing interest in protecting the life of the fetus.

Whether by court reversal or constitutional amendment, repudiation of *Roe v. Wade* logically entails rejection of one or both of these premises. Hence, predicting the consequences of reversal and the nature of ensuing legal strategies must involve speculation that elaborates two themes: the abolition of the "right to abortion" and the recognition of some legally significant status for the human fetus.

This analysis indicates three sets of circumstances — each already suggested by court decision or legislative initiative — in which to answer the questions posed by this essay:

- Suppose, by Supreme Court decision or constitutional amendment, the practice of abortion has ceased to be protected as a "fundamental right" under the Fourteenth Amendment to the U.S. Constitution.
- Suppose, by Supreme Court decision or constitutional amendment, there is said to exist a compelling state interest in the human fetus throughout pregnancy.
- Suppose, by Supreme Court decision or constitutional amendment, the human fetus is declared to be a "person" under the U.S. Constitution.

In each of these three cases, how would the legal advocates of permissive abortion respond?

Abolition of The Right To Abortion

Assume that the practice of abortion has ceased to be protected as a fundamental right under the Fourteenth Amendment to the Constitution.

In the wake of such a court decision or constitutional amendment abortion supporters might take two fallback positions. First, they might argue that the right to abortion is protected, directly or indirectly, by some other provision of the U.S. Constitution. Second, pro-abortion attorneys could contend that at least some abortions remain protected by the Constitution.

Thus, the legal advocates of abortion might argue that the Establishment of Religion and Free Exercise clauses of the First Amendment to the U.S. Constitution continue to protect those abortions motivated or sanctioned by religious conscientious convictions. They might invoke the Ninth Amendment, which reserves to citizens all rights that they were entitled to until the time of its enactment, claiming that a "right to abortion" was recognized in English and early American common law and is, therefore, protected under this Amendment.

If the proposed Equal Rights Amendment (ERA), which purports to abolish all or almost all gender-based discrimination by the State, were to become law, then advocates of abortion might well contend on this basis that abortion may not be proscribed or restricted: Since men do not become pregnant, women may not be compelled by law to remain pregnant. Moreover, because some state constitutions are more expansive than the federal Constitution, abortion proponents might further claim that abortion must remain permissive under state law even if the federal Constitution does not recognize abortion as a fundamental right.

Thus far, federal constitutional amendments proposed with specific intent to abolish the "right to abortion" have anticipated these claims. The "Hatch Amendment" states:

> *"A right to abortion is not secured by this Constitution. The Congress and the several States shall have concurrent power to restrict and prohibit abortion: Provided, That a provision of law of a State which is more restrictive than a conflicting provision of a law of Congress shall govern."*

The "Hatch-Eagleton" Amendment simply states that, *"A right to abortion is not secured by this Constitution."* Each proposed amendment was accompanied by a strong legislative history that clearly stated an intent to foreclose recognition of a "right to abortion" under *any* provision of the federal Constitution, specifically including the First, Ninth, and Fourteenth Amendments. It is, thus, highly improbable that any such claim would be seriously entertained should either amendment become law.

By the same logic, the ERA could not be invoked if it

became law *before* a Hatch-type amendment accompanied by a similar legislative history. However, if the ERA became law *after* such an anti-abortion amendment, the claim that it recognized a new right to abortion might be entertained by the courts, unless clear legislative history or new ERA language foreclosed such a judicial construction. But even in the absence of legislative history or amendment, the ERA should not, by better reasoning, be construed to recognize abortional liberty. Anti-abortion laws would preclude performance of abortion by or on both men and women; they "discriminate" between men and women only insofar as men cannot be aborted because they cannot become pregnant. Yet this circumstance does not arise by virtue of state action. It results from a condition of nature. Hence, it cannot be imputed to the State. Since the ERA represents a constitutional prohibition only on *state* power to discriminate between the sexes, and because the ERA is not intended to correct accidents of nature, it logically should not be construed to affect anti-abortion legislation. Thus, even if ERA should become law after a Hatch-type amendment, it does not necessarily follow that it would be construed to reestablish a right to abortion.

Foreclosing recognition of a right to abortion only under the federal Constitution, a Hatch-type amendment would not preclude recognition of a similar right under state constitutions. (Indeed, the highest courts of New Jersey, California, Massachusetts, and Oregon have already held that a right to abortion exists under their state constitutions.) The language and legislative history of the Hatch Amendment, however, would permit federal anti-abortion laws to apply within state boundaries even if state anti-abortion laws were impermissible under state constitutions. The Hatch-Eagleton Amendment does not explicitly acknowledge such federal authority, although the Interstate

Commerce Clause of the Constitution would seem to provide the Congress with independent authority to prohibit interstate abortion trafficking and to restrict intrastate abortion practices that involve interstate commerce.

Reversal of *Roe* by judicial decision that abolishes a federally recognized right to abortion would probably have an effect similar to the Hatch-Eagleton Amendment. That is, it would no longer be possible to argue that abortion is protected by the U.S. Constitution. Abortion's legal advocates might then press the claim that abortion remains protected by the First or Ninth Amendments, or some other provision of the Constitution, even if it is not under the Fourteenth Amendment.

But success appears unlikely. It is unreasonable to suppose that the Supreme Court would cease to recognize a right to abortion under one part of the Constitution, only to reverse itself almost immediately by invoking another part to recognize such a right anew. At the time it reversed *Roe*, the Court would probably be compelled to reject *all* claims under *all* provisions of the Constitution that a right to abortion exists.

However, reversal of *Roe* by a judicial decision of this nature would not foreclose recognition of a right to abortion under state constitutions or a claim that a constitutional amendment, such as the ERA, enacted after reversal establishes such a right. As under a Hatch-type amendment, abortion advocates would also seek to secure state constitutional decisions recognizing a right to abortion.

Quite apart from any claim that there exists some independent basis in state or federal constitutions for a full-scale right to abortion, it might be argued in the face of *Roe's* reversal that, in some circumstances, abortion remains protected as an aspect of some other recognized constitutional right. Thus, for example, it might be argued that abortion for "health" remains protected and that the use of certain forms of birth control that function as both contraceptives and abortifacients may not be regulated. The recognized right to *prevent* pregnancy is not intended to nor would it be abolished by a Hatch-type amendment or by reversal of *Roe* by court decision. (Nor would it be abolished by declaring the fetus a constitutional "person.") Since use of contraceptives would remain protected by the Constitution, even if a contraceptive method had some incidental abortifacient effect — such as the intra-uterine device (IUD) is alleged to have — regulation of such a method would have to be directed exclusively to elimination of its abortifacient effect. Its contraceptive use would remain protected.

In a similar vein, the State's power to regulate early abortion and menstrual extraction would depend on how "pregnancy" and "abortion" are understood. The legislative history of the Hatch and Hatch-Eagleton Amendments define "abortion" as the destruction of fetal life at any stage of development from the onset of fertilization. Hence, they would permit regulation of menstrual extraction and pre-implantation abortifacients. Should *Roe* be reversed by judicial decision, however, the nature of "abortion" and "pregnancy" might well be the subject of considerable litigation in view of the conceptual complexity of the issues raised by the use of these terms in different contexts.

It should be noted that the issues raised by birth control techniques with abortifacient side-effects are no different than those raised by an almost infinite number of other drugs, devices, and techniques. For example, the currette, drugs customarily used to treat various diseases, prostaglandins, and even certain foods *might* be abortifacients, yet all also obviously have legitimate uses. Thus, a legal doctrine or public policy that singled out birth control drugs or devices as possible abortifacients would seem to be rooted in opposition to contraception rather than in a consistent principle directed at the protection of fetal life. Since contraception would remain constitutionally protected, any attempt to single out contraceptive techniques for regulatory control of their abortifacient side-effects without similar controls on other agents that may have some abortifacient but no contraceptive use would be constitutionally suspect.

There is as yet no generally recognized "right to health." But in the face of rejection of a "right to abortion," advocates of permissive abortion might argue that such a right to health exists. The claim would then be that "health" abortions may not be banned. The legislative histories of both the Hatch and the Hatch-Eagleton Amendments clearly anticipate such a claim, and both state that "health" abortions may be prohibited under both measures. But rejection of the "right to abortion" by judicial decision would, however, leave resolution of the question more in doubt. Logically, the Supreme Court would have to acknowledge a general "right to health" in order to grant that there existed a constitutional right to abortion for "health" reasons. But by the same reasoning entailed in full rejection of a "right of abortion," any claim that there exists a special right to "health" abortions would also appear to fail: If there is no right to abortion at all, there is no right to a "health" abortion.

Moreoever, it is highly improbable that a Supreme Court that would reject the right to abortion, a Court which is likely to be populated by "strict constructionists," would then recognize the existence of a general "right to health." Recognition of such a right would involve the judiciary in unprecedented interference with legislatively developed health-related policies, which violate strict constructionist doctrine. Should *Roe* be reversed by outright rejection of the right to abortion, it seems unlikely that a right to a "health" abortion would survive in its immediate wake. However, should *Roe* be reversed by recognition of a compelling state interest in the unborn, the prospect for recognition of such a right is considerably greater.

A Compelling Interest in the Unborn

Assume that the unborn child, although lacking the status of a constitutional "person," has been recognized as the proper subject of a compelling state interest throughout all of pregnancy.

The existence of such a compelling interest would tend to justify state prohibition of abortion. But because the "right to abortion" remains intact, there may remain important limitations on the power of the State to proscribe abortion. Certainly, the legal advocates of abortion would raise claims similar to those they would advance were the "right to abortion" abolished. Most would be resolved in similar fashion, but one would be far more persuasive: that there continues to exist a constitutionally protected right to a "health" abortion.

In *Roe v. Wade* the Supreme Court held that the State may not ban abortions performed to preserve maternal life or *health* even in the third trimester of pregnancy when there exists a compelling interest in the life of the fetus. Balancing rights and interests, the Court evidently felt that the woman's interest in "health" abortion is always superior to the State's interest in fetal life. Hence, should the Court decide that there exists a compelling interest in the fetus throughout pregnancy, it could nevertheless be convincingly argued that there continues to exist a right to a "health" abortion throughout pregnancy.

This is a major trap laid in the path toward protection of unborn life.

The courts have so far defined "health" to encompass almost every conceivable physical, psychological, familial, and even economic factor. Moreover, if a "health" abortion were recognized as a fundamental right, it would probably be necessary to prove beyond a reasonable doubt that an abortion was *not* performed to preserve maternal health in order to enforce any anti-abortion law. Finally, the experience of states and nations that have permitted "health" abortions demonstrates that there is no significant practical difference between a regime in which "health" abortion is permitted and a regime of abortion-on-demand.

Yet it would be far more difficult psychologically to ban "health" as opposed to "elective" abortion. Ironically, therefore, the cause of significantly limiting legal abortion might be subverted, rather than served, by recognition of a compelling state interest in the life of the unborn at all stages of development.

Unfortunately, however, recognition of a compelling interest in the fetus appears to be a most likely "first step" the Supreme Court might take toward reversal. Such a step would not require the Court to hold plainly that it had erred in finding that there had existed a right to abortion.

The judiciary is naturally loathe to admit error so forthrightly. Moreover, it is more likely that there will be a majority on the Court sufficient to find a compelling state interest in the life of the fetus while still recognizing the legality of "health" abortions before there is a Court majority for reversal based on abolition of the right to abortion. (Even Justice White, a consistent opponent to an expansive right to abortion, stated in his dissent to *Roe* that he might find that there exists a right to abortion for life or health.)

Finally, this form of reversal is encouraged by

advancing medical technology. Such technology will extend fetal viability earlier into pregnancy, thereby also extending the power of the State to regulate abortion practices earlier into the pregnancy. Indeed, Justice O'Connor, joined by Justices White and Rehnquist in her dissenting opinion in *Akron Reproductive Health Services v. City of Akron*, anticipating these medical advances, has already stated that she would even now find a compelling interest in the fetus throughout all of pregnancy. (Justice O'Connor would also find that the State maintains a compelling interest in maternal health throughout all of pregnancy that justifies regulation of abortion at every stage. But this interest would obviously not support a prohibition on "health" abortions: It makes no sense to ban abortions performed to protect maternal health in order to protect maternal health.)

Both theoretical and practical circumstances provide the legal advocates of permissive abortion with a clear opportunity to preserve "health" abortion — another term for elective abortion — should the Supreme Court hold there is a compelling state interest in the fetus. Pro-life political and legal strategy obviously must be calculated to prevent recognition of a full right to "health" abortions by carefully framing legislation and litigation designed first, to limit the present expansive definition of health, and second, to lead the Court to reversal by abolishing the right to abortion rather than by recognizing a compelling interest in the fetus.

The pro-life movement must take care to avoid falling into a trap of its own making by reflexively insisting on the assertion of fetal rights and interests without first carefully considering legal consequences. For example, versions of the federal "Human Life" and "Respect Life" statutes have asserted a compelling interest in the fetus. This invites the Court to affirm the existence of such an interest without also answering whether a right to a "health" abortion would survive should the Court take up the invitation.

Personhood of The Unborn

Assume the unborn child has been declared a "person" under the Constitution and, therefore, possesses all rights that the rest of us have. What might ensue?

Clearly, abortion could and, perhaps, must be proscribed by the State. But there may be limitations on the power or the obligation of the State to make abortion illegal. At the very least, advocates of legal abortion would attempt to reduce the status of any allegedly mandatory "personhood" amendment to a discretionary "state's rights" amendment. They would seek to subtract any obligation to protect the unborn from a decision of the Supreme Court declaring them "persons."

From one perspective, their efforts would seem to be pointless or doomed. If the super-majorities necessary to enact a "personhood" amendment were gathered, then the ordinary majorities needed to enact and enforce strict anti-abortion legislation would seem to be available; any Supreme Court that would actually declare the unborn "persons" would be unlikely to brook any attempt to deprive the unborn of full and adequate legal protection.

Yet majorities in legislatures and in courts may shift. There may be residual pockets or resistance to any anti-abortion amendment, and the courts may remain hostile to recognition of fetal personhood even in the face of a constitutional amendment. For these reasons, and because a "mandatory personhood" constitutional amendment is often claimed to be the final and only proper legal solution to the problem of abortion, it is crucial to examine how abortion advocates might react should the fetus become a constitutional person.

In this regard, the steps abortion advocates would take

cannot be predicted without describing the ground on which they must walk. What happens if the unborn becomes a "person" under the Constitution?

At first, nothing. The Constitution contains no penalties, no prohibition on private conduct (except the ownership of slaves). It would be necessary for advocates for the unborn to initiate legal actions to enjoin government entities from funding or facilitating abortions as violations of the due process and equal protection rights of the unborn. Similarly, suits would have to be initiated to attempt to force recalcitrant states to enact legislation proscribing abortion. The extent to which these latter suits succeed would determine the degree to which fetal personhood imposed some mandatory "obligation" on the government through criminal law to protect the unborn from abortion.

In a suit to enforce the obligation of the State to protect the unborn, pro-life advocates would claim that the state homicide code is unconstitutionally underinclusive because it fails to provide protection to the unborn. (The theory here would be the same as in a suit that involved a challenge to a law that, for example, punished murder of whites, but not blacks.) The court would be requested to strike down the homicide code of the State so that it is no longer a crime to kill another human being, born or unborn. It is assumed that the state legislature, threatened with such a draconian court decision, would enact an anti-abortion law in order to preserve its homicide code.

This, the reader will note, is the *only* way in which the State could be forced to provide legal protection for the unborn by virtue of fetal "personhood". It is the *only* sense in which a constitutional amendment declaring fetal personhood is "mandatory."

The State is not *obliged* by the Constitution to penalize any form of private conduct. If the legislature so desired, it could decriminalize robbery, rape, or murder.

The Constitution imposes restrictions on governmental actions — it restrains the *State*, not private individuals. Whether or not the conduct of the private person — be it rape, murder, or abortion — is to be penalized or otherwise restrained by the State is a matter for the legislature. Hence, the day after the unborn child is declared a constitutional "person," abortion performed by private doctors on women would be as "legal" as it was the day before, although it would no longer be a "right" that could not be punished by the State through criminal legislation.

But suppose a legislature does not act? In our legal system, the only way to force it to do so is to threaten some law that has already been enacted and (in this case, the homicide code) that is now defective because it fails to provide some other class of persons (here, the unborn) with equal protection of law.

Observe that the court is requested to strike down the homicide code in this suit. Courts cannot simply create a penalty on any form of conduct, including abortion, where none existed before — this is the exclusive prerogative of the legislature. Moreover, the language of the homicide codes was never intended by the various legislatures to punish abortion; hence, courts could not "cure" the defective homicide codes by reading the unborn child into them. The only remaining option is to strike down the code.

Observe also that "equal protection" is the concept that underlies any alleged obligation that fetal personhood would impose on the State. The requirement of the Constitution that the unborn must be treated by the State in the same fashion as any other person provides the necessary leverage against the state homicide code to force the legislature to act. (The "Human Life Statute" proposed in Congress stated that the unborn are "persons" only for the purpose of due process, not equal protection. Hence, even if such a statute were upheld, it would impose no obligation on the State to protect the unborn, except to provide the unborn with "due process" — such as notice, a hearing, and an opportunity to be heard through an attorney — before the State assisted anyone to abort them. The legislative history of the Human Life Statute stated that the legal effect of the law would otherwise be similar to a "state's rights" constitutional amendment.)

The legal strategy of the advocates of permissive abortion in the face of such a scenario would depend on the nature of the equal protection requirement imposed on the State by virtue of fetal personhood. Does personhood require that the unborn be treated in precisely the same way as any other person? Does it require "perfect symmetry" in the law? Or does it permit some distinctions be made between the unborn and other persons? If so, what are they?

If perfect symmetry is required, then abortion advocates will have no significant options. The courts would be compelled to find that abortion must be punished in the same way as homicide — that state legislatures either must in effect incorporate the fetus into their homicide codes or the codes will be stricken with the result that all forms of homicide will go unpunished.

But it is probably absurd to imagine that a principle of perfect or even near-perfect symmetry would be accepted by the courts or legislatures. No legislature would pass a constitutional amendment that would jeopardize the entire homicide code unless abortion were punished in precisely the same way as all other forms of homicide. In such a setting, the woman who, for example, intentionally aborts herself might properly be charged with murder; she would be subject to the death penalty if it existed in her state. The woman who miscarried as a result of negligence might be prosecuted for negligent homicide. Certainly, no court would require abortion and other forms of homicide to be treated identically unless absolutely compelled to do so by the plain language and unmistakable legislative history of a constitutional amendment — language and history probably impossible to secure. Even if it were possible to secure an amendment that requires that the legal treatment accorded the unborn must be the mirror-image of that accorded other human beings, very few in the pro-life movement argue such a result is desirable.

Thus, it may be safely assumed that "personhood" would *not* require the State to treat the unborn and other persons in the same fashion. But if perfect symmetry is not required, then what is? Abortion advocates would answer: very little. Since the courts would be compelled to strike down homicide codes if they found that the unborn were not adequately protected by state law, they would clearly be inclined to agree that little protection is required.

As a result, the way would be open for abortion advocates to argue in favor of the constitutionality of statutes that permit abortion for life, health, rape, incest, eugenic purposes, population control, that impose a fine of $1.00 on elective abortion, and that require proof beyond a reasonable doubt that a person caused the death of an individual human fetus known to be in existence at the time before any penalty may be imposed. All of these exceptions and qualifications would or might be justified by legitimate and compelling state interests. If all or even some were deemed acceptable, then "personhood" would have little actual "mandatory" effect.

A "personhood" approach also places the authority to protect the unborn in the hands of the traditionally hostile judiciary rather than in the hands of the usually friendly legislature, as an amendment or decision that merely abolishes the right to abortion would do. The naive, underlying assumption is that the courts, although they have hardly been champions of the unborn in the past, will suddenly and enthusiastically force recalcitrant state legislatures to enact anti-abortion laws.

Moreover, power so placed in the hands of the judiciary is a two-edged sword. Abortion advocates could use the requirement that the unborn be treated equally to strike down constitutionally imperfect anti-abortion legislation. For example, they might attack laws that did not penalize the woman who procured abortion, that had a lesser penalty than homicide, that did not penalize negligent abortion by miscarriage, or that contained any exceptions to their application.

If they succeed in such a suit, there would be no abortion law at all, at least until the legislature acted to strengthen it. This cycle might continue for some time — anti-abortion laws stricken, reenacted to conform to court decisions, then stricken again — much like anti-abortion laws are now struck because they are said to burden the right of abortion. Only this time the cycle would go on under the aegis of the right of the fetus to equal treatment. And all the while there would be no effective anti-abortion law. Even if such suits failed, and laws with such exceptions and qualifications were upheld, then abortion proponents succeed in establishing still further what fetal personhood does *not* require, further diminishing any allegedly mandatory effect that would flow from fetal personhood.

Obviously, the virtual uncertainty over exactly what fetal personhood would finally mean radically jeopardizes any possibility that the Supreme Court would hold that the unborn are persons or that the super-majorities needed to enact a constitutional amendment establishing fetal personhood could be gathered. In this regard, the difficulty is similar to that of the proposed

ERA: The unwillingness or inability of its advocates to state precisely what it is intended to do, preferring instead to stand on abstract principle that the courts could breathe life into, permits its opponents to attribute all manner of extreme mischief to it.

Even if this mischief is not likely to result, the proponent of ERA (or fetal personhood) is placed in the awkward and defensive position of continually explaining away "hard cases," losing the argument by default because, for one thing, the affirmative case is never effectively made. And the proponent of legal personhood is paradoxically confronted with the worst of both worlds in the legislatures and in the courts. He must continually counter the parade of horribles that the opponents of personhood would raise. Yet even if he is successful, the probable outcome of establishment of legal personhood is likely to be little different than if only the "right to abortion" were abolished by court action or through a Hatch-type amendment.

The authors of the "Unity" Human Life Amendment and its precursor, the National Right to Life Committee (NRLC) Amendment, were clearly aware of the legal confusion and uncertainty that adheres to attempting to mandate protection of the unborn merely by establishing fetal personhood. Both proposed amendments added in an explicit recognition of fetal personhood a prohibition on abortion followed by an exception to the prohibition: with the NRLC Amendment, the exception was for the "life of the mother"; in the "Unity Amendment" an exception was included that appears to embody the Roman Catholic distinction that prohibits "direct," but permits "indirect" abortion, *e.g.* removal of an ectopic pregnancy or a cancerous uterus.

The prohibition on abortion in these proposed amendments is intended to create a "private cause of action" in order to provide private individuals with the authority to seek injunctive relief against abortion practices. For whatever reason, states might not enact effective anti-abortion legislation. Even if there were anti-abortion laws in effect, they would have no practical effect unless prosecutors enforced them, and prosecutors have almost absolute discretion to refuse to bring charges. Traditionally, prosecutors have been reluctant to enforce the criminal law of abortion; they would probably be even more reluctant to do so after reversal of *Roe* in view of the extent to which abortion has become a widespread and accepted practice. Moreover, there would probably be massive, brazen civil disobedience in the face of any restrictive anti-abortion legislation that followed *Roe's* reversal.

The private cause of action created by the NRLC and "Unity" Amendments would arguably permit those opposed to abortion to seek an injunction against abortion practices even if the legislature, the police, and prosecutors failed to enforce the law. (However it is unclear who would have the legal right to bring such a suit. As the advocates of abortion could convincingly argue, it might be limited to the father of the unborn child under the "case or controversy" requirements of the Constitution.)

The most important practical effect of the "life of the mother" and "indirect abortion" exceptions in these proposed amendments lies not in their content but in the fact that they exist. They would preclude abortion advocates from arguing that anti-abortion laws with other, additional exceptions were constitutionally permissible. Hence, for example, the courts could not permit states to permit "health" abortions, or abortions for rape or incest, as they could if the unborn were merely recognized as persons. Abortion advocates might still successfully claim that a reduced penalty is permissible and that the unborn need not be provided with full equal protection in a host of other ways, but at least the presence of such an exception would limit the permissible scope of the substantive language of an anti-abortion statute.

The NRLC and "Unity" Amendments, by combining the concept of fetal personhood with an explicit prohibition of abortion and an exception to the prohibition, thus approach a political and legal solution that would accomplish all at once almost everything the pro-life cause wants. By establishing a constitutionally-imposed "floor" on the exceptions that legislatures could enact, they minimize the possibility that the legal advocates of abortion could successfully deprive them of any mandatory effect.

Yet for either proposed amendment to become law, legislative super majorities would have to accept the remaining legal uncertainties that attend unborn personhood, a private action provision that apparently permits individual pro-lifers to bring anyone allegedly involved with abortion before the courts at will, and a requirement that each State must either enact an anti-abortion law with a very limited exception or jeopardize the constitutionality of its homicide code. Thus, although the NRLC and "Unity" Amendments may successfully embody pro-life ideals, they would probably encounter almost insurmountable political opposition in the amendment process.

Conclusion

There is no simple or perfect legal or political way to protect the unborn. Each possible path has pitfalls that the advocates of abortion might expose either in courts or in the legislatures, and no doubt they would discover and invent many more than the rather obvious few this essay suggests. It should be clear, however, the more elegant and ambitious the proposed pro-life solution, the more difficulties are likely to arise in successfully implementing it.

The legal and political realities outlined by this essay dictate a strategy designed to save as many lives as possible with the means at hand. They mock stubborn adherence to the perfectionist delusion that there exists some magic language which, if enshrined in the Constitution, would cause the problem of abortion to vanish and relieve the pro-life cause of its moral imperative.

The Supreme Court is not a sacred institution; the Constitution is not a sacred document. What is or should be sacred are the lives of unborn children. In the present desperate circumstances, to decline to take whatever path that is reasonably available to protect the unborn through law because its form may fall short of some preferred ideal that might be embodied in the Constitution perverts this moral order.

The pro-life cause is rooted in the blood of the unborn, not airy abstractions. Its fundamental purpose is to protect human life — to stop the killing. Use of the power of the State through law is one of the tools that might be used to accomplish this end, but a tool withheld by virtue of *Roe v. Wade*. Therefore, *Roe v. Wade* must be reversed. Since the power of the State is exercised primarily through the legislature, the primary political goal of the pro-life movement must logically be restoration to the legislature of full power to discourage abortion, rather than incorporation into the Constitution of some formula that purports to embody pro-life principle.

The proponents of legal abortion will battle to preserve its widespread practice on any front that is chosen. To refuse to join in that battle unless assured of perfect victory is to walk off the edge of history.

PART III

THE NETWORK OF THE OPPOSITION: HOW THE ENEMIES OF LIFE THINK

A separate volume could easily be devoted just to detailing the pro-abortion mentality. Although we specifically address that question in this section, who we're up against, how they think and why is the subtext that runs through virtually every essay in this collection.

All first-rate debaters understand the enormous advantage that accrues to whichever side "frames the question." That is, whoever is able to establish the framework within which the debate is conducted will be difficult to beat. The question of abortion has long been interpreted as exclusively a woman's issue as if the unborn child has no father, grandparents or siblings, or as a matter of individual decision making, as though society has no interest in the purposeful destruction of its citizens.

In this section John Walker and Robert Morrison dissect the fallacies of this kind of thinking. They show what kind of assumptions contribute to such a truncated view of the value of life and demonstrate that pro-life principles are in harmony with the core values of America. Professor John Dunsford's Swiftian satire deftly illustrates the expansionary potential of the rationale for abortion.

If there is any one factor which was the linchpin of the successful campaign to legitimate abortion in the 1960s — and maintain it ever since — it would unquestionably be the unholy marriage consumated between the media and the women's liberation movement. Although it might seem otherwise to pro-lifers, it was not written in the stars that the women's liberation movement would establish its secular church on the right to "pulverize a 20 gram fetus," as Rosemary Bottcher observes in her essay. Why the media swoons in the presence of the women's liberation movement and holds its collective nose in the presence of the pro-life movement is the subject of the concluding essay in this section by Dave Andrusko.

BENEATH THE PRO-ABORTION LOGIC

John Walker*

"...Use a language to conceive, organize, and justify Belsen; use it to make out specifications for gas ovens; use it to dehumanize man during twelve years of calculated bestiality. Something will happen to it... Something of the lies and sadism will settle in the marrow of the language."

GEORGE STEINER, "The Hollow Moral," from *Language and Silence.*

I started this essay modestly: addressing the rhetoric used by both pro-lifers and pro-abortionists. How do our "languages" differ? How can we oppose or use points in their rhetoric?

Nice. But in going on, I found I wasn't really concerned

*John Walker is Research Director for Libertarians for Life. He maintains a busy debate schedule among libertarians on the issue of abortion. He is currently employed as a technical editor for a computer magazine. He has an extensive background in conservative and libertarian politics, both in Washington and in Rhode Island where he was raised. He served on the staff of Senator James Buckley in 1975-76.

with rhetoric. True, it's important. We should re-check everything we write to see whether (taken strictly literally or taken emotionally) we're conceding points to the enemy.

But I found that I was really concerned with what's going on *underneath* the rhetoric — and *why* the two sides express themselves differently. To look at that, however, we have to ignore the abortion debate itself to some extent. Listening to it, we can sometimes be overwhelmed by the sheer number of questions involved. Besides the philosophical questions of life and rights and the person, there are the scientific ones. There are the medical ones that involve professional judgment suited to particular situations, as well as knowledge of the general facts. It's easy to get snowed under.

But underneath the diversity, there are certain recurrent themes. Time and again, people seem to use similar arguments and show similar perspectives, however different the questions may be.

Two Different Ways of Describing Things

Without oversimplifying too much, the pro-lifer is willing to consider "internal" elements. The pro-abortionist relies on purely "external" data. For instance, when pro-lifers try to say what a person is, or what life is, or what rights are, they tend to try to "get into" life or the person or rights. They try to find out and describe what it is like to be alive or to be a person or to have rights. Pro-abortionists, however, tend to handle such questions in a totally different manner. How do persons *behave*? What do we, outside, *observe* in a creature we call "alive"?

Let's take those two examples: "life" and being a "person." When pro-lifers talk about being alive they talk about feeling pleasure and pain, growing, seeing colors, hearing sound. Think of a picture showing an unborn child in the womb. When she raises her hand to shade her eyes from a bright light outside, that's important to pro-lifers. It shows what's going on in that unborn child's experience, "inside" her.

These things are important because they show that this creature is like *me*, like *us*. We feel pain, heat, and so forth. She does, too. Of course she's alive! The "external" facts are evidence for an "internal" state which is what really counts in being alive. It's what distinguishes us and all living things from mere matter, from rocks and atoms.

For pro-abortionists, a popular test is "viability." Statistically, so many children at so many weeks will live so long outside the womb. Easy. If they can live for some specified period of time, they're "alive." Here, being alive is essentially a relationship of the child to the outside world. If he needs the womb (or some mechanical surrogate) in order to survive, then he's not "alive." And being alive can be absolutely measured from "outside." That's all it *means:* just being able to survive without certain kinds of assistance.(I agree that this idea is self contradictory. The child has to be alive already in order to die. But let's ignore that.)

When we are dealing with "personhood," a similar dichotomy takes place. Both sides generally agree that something like reason and choice is necessary for someone to be a person. (Call it what you will: consciousness, volition, intellect, and so forth. Most of the terms talk about much the same thing.)

But pro-lifers and pro-abortionists approach reason and choice in radically different ways. Pro-abortionists, explicitly or implicitly, demand a manifestation, a display of reason and choice. Or they demand physical development to the point where we have display of things associated with reason (brainwaves or certain brain development, say). Being a person is a matter of what you display to *me.* Your being a person is dependent upon my *recognizing* it.

So, there's a problem for the "pro-choicers" who recoil from things like infanticide or euthanasia. They have problems with infants, the mentally handicapped, the senile, the comatose, and so on. They obviously don't *display* much reason and choice. Yet they know very well that these are persons with the right not to be killed.

Pro-lifers, however, talk of things like "capacity," "potential," "power," and the like. Something the child has, but needs time and growth to display. Being a person is a matter of what you *are*, a matter of *kind*, not just *degree*. Whether I recognize it or not doesn't change that. And it comes to us with our very biological existence; with our genetic makeup, if you will. Moreover, that "capacity," that "power," that "spark" is what distinguishes us from mere animals. Even if it's not yet displayed, as in the young, or if it's actually been impaired, as in the aged or ill, it's still there.

Facts Versus Appearances

This difference between the two views is hardly coincidental. It reflects a debate within philosophy that has been going on for at least the last 500 years or so. One school — loosely called "realism" — holds that we can find out truths about the world around us. The other school — "subjectivism," "relativism," and their variants — holds that all we have are the sensations and images that bounce around inside our heads. Maybe the conventions of society can make do as a substitute for facts.

Some people are only ethical subjectivists. Some will drag it into other fields, poisoning biology perhaps, but leaving physics intact. Still others will have these ideas affecting them in every aspect of reality. How, then, can subjectivists know whether their neighbors are really persons like themselves? Well, they can't. All they can say is that their neighbors *appear* to be like them externally. Words come out of their mouths. (But is there reasoning going on inside?) Their faces form smiles. (But is there joy or humor?) They grimace or scream when jabbed with a knife. (But is there pain?)

Pushed to it, some pro-abortionists would admit that, no they can't *really* be sure that the rest of us are anything more than appearances. We might be some weird robots. Upon being jabbed, their pain may be real enough, but ours is merely a matter of our grimacing or what not. Their reasoning is real enough, but ours may be merely words on the air. Sometimes the effects of this view are gross and instantly observable. Sometimes they are subtle and barely noticeable. They have produced a world in which "I" am not merely the center of my universe. I *am* the universe — there isn't anything else.

A War of World-Views

Now, this may be plowing old ground for many of you. This is the Age of Permissiveness. Ethics was the first field to fall to the subjectivists. The gospels of permissiveness and subjectivism have dominated our colleges and universities for most of this century. They are the faith of our intelligentsia. So what else is new? What is new is that many of us have had to argue against academically trained opponents before audiences whose perspectives and language have been shaped by the same forces that have produced the abortion movement. And many times these ideas masquerade as biology or science.

This situation is frequently described as a conflict between "world-views." To some extent, that is true. We confront something that is a way of looking at the whole world — at all of reality. Yet it is also, in some sense, a conflict of *worlds*. It is almost as if pro-abortionists and pro-lifers lived in different universes. There are whole chunks of our world which seem missing from theirs. We live in a world in which pain and joy take place — not just ours, but other people's too. In their world, there are only grimaces and smiles, only images on a screen.

Now, we all know that this is not the case. Their world has all the same fixtures and features as ours. It's the same world. The problem is that they have an intellectual apparatus that has no way to explain much of reality. Indeed, it explains it away. And we also know that when their intellectual apparatus proves inconvenient, they will ignore it. Do they address war and peace as things the rightness or wrongness of which are forever in doubt? No. In certain cases, words like "just," "unjust," "moral," and "immoral" are as easy for them to use as for us. They certainly *act* as if these words told us something about reality, and not just about their state of mind. They use the traditional language of ethics because it allows them to describe reality.

A similar dynamic goes on in the abortion debate. But with a strange difference. When they discuss the underlying questions, they are still good subjectivists. ("Who can say what 'life' is?") But when they discuss the *conclusion*, they speak with a fervor and certainty that would make any absolutist blush. Abortion is a *right*. It is a matter of *choice*. This response is not accidental. Nor is it merely hypocritical. They *must* do something like this. Subjectivism is a jolly theory. It can't be lived.

I cannot will rocks out of my path. Nor can I will rights and obligations out of existence, either. In order to defend abortion it is convenient to deny that we can find anything out about "life" or about "rights." But in order to give any meaning to that defense, the language of rights and personal choice must be invoked.

Making War on Logic

They have done this by choosing words which carry the power of traditional ethical language. But they have been applied systematically in a sort of "first-person" context. *I* (or you, or he, or she) have this right. There is no reference to how rights arise or what obligations they may entail. I *choose* (or you, or he, or she). There is no reference to what alternatives are chosen among or whether they entail consequences (or which ones).

A notion, then, is "chopped off." It is taken without any reference to its correlative terms and concepts. Unchallenged, that makes for a very powerful rhetorical device.

To retain the full power of words like "rights," I must repeat words that emphasize *me* and confer moral value on my actions. Yet I must also suppress the logical implications of those words (e.g. obligations). Again, nonsensical, but powerful if unchallenged. I have all the benefits of moral reality without the restraints.

The sad thing in some respects is that our opposition is trapped by reality, however popular their views are. Their own behavior bears it out. The more militant pro-abortionists are not characterized by anger or rage or even sorrow at what they pronounce to be threats to their rights. Rather, it is bitterness that marks them. And bitterness is most often the product of betrayal. Bitterness may be produced by betrayal by other people. Or it may be produced by the "betrayal" of events that destroy hopes.

People trapped in the contemporary mindset are set up for bitterness because reality will continually "betray" them. For men and women alike, pregnancy is an ultimate betrayal since it comes without asking whether we want it or not. It is self-betrayal, too, since it occurs because of our own action. And it destroys utterly the myth that we are our own universe — secure, able to decree whatever we will. Even in imposing death as the penalty for such a betrayal, we must approach life on its own terms. Much of the pro-abortionists' intellectual activity goes into speaking and thinking in such a way as to pretend those facts and limits on our actions do not exist. The very existence of rights which we must invade stands as the ultimate rebuke and "betrayal."

So our opposition has an intellectual structure, a world-view, that denies the existence of an enormous chunk of reality. To a large extent, they have crippled the language as a means to describe reality. Yet they, too, are drawn along by the forces of the real world and wish or need to employ traditional ethical language to defend their position. They have done so by taking certain concepts while suppressing those concepts' correlative terms. So what should we do?

How Do We Fight It?

First of all, we can't simply drop language that looks unacceptable to our audiences — mainly, that which looks religious or philosophical. We cannot and should not keep the debate restricted to the nature of fetal brainwaves at "x" weeks versus so many weeks later. The scientific and medical debates may be essential to an informed pro-life position, but, alone, they are not *sufficient*.

Life is sacred. So say it. But we have to realize that our language needs to be *explained*. We cannot escape philosophy. And people are willing to recognize its importance and necessity. Personally, I will use "sacred" along with "special," "having rights," and any other term that comes to mind, in order to describe a central aspect of the person: persons are not to be treated as mere things. Even the nonreligious can recognize the force and descriptiveness of words like "sacred" and "sanctity." They will accept them so long as they do not feel they're getting theology under the guise of a political debate.

(Quite frankly, I don't think that many people object to the presence of religious values in public discussion, so long as "religion" is not a mask for refusing to engage in genuine discussion of issues: "If you don't agree with me, you're damned." This is the way pro-abortionists like to paint pro-lifers. I think most people can recognize that most pro-lifers are innocent of the charge.)

Turning Their Words Against Them

If we wish to go on the offensive, and use language used by the pro-abortionists, then we have to keep our audience uppermost in our minds. At the outset, the main difference is between those committed to the pro-abortion cause, and those relatively uncommitted — even if they call themselves "pro-choice." In this regard, the emotional forces at work in the committed may be too strong to counter by merely rhetorical means.

But for the relatively uncommitted, there is still the possibility of catching hold of the language of the opposition in order to turn it against them. I think that this can be done by emphasizing the correlative concepts of each of the terms they employ. When they employ "choice," we must remind the audience of alternatives and consequences. It is not a private choice when we take another's life. When they talk of "our rights," we must emphasize the equal rights of others. How can we have rights without others having the obligation to respect them? And without having the obligation to respect their rights? When they say that having an abortion is the "responsible" thing to do, we've got to point out that "taking responsibility for our acts" can never imply imposing our will on others. Would killing someone be all right if I were willing to go to jail for it?

Regarding our hearers, we have to find out where we agree with them, and build upon it. Even if only as an abstract principle, many "pro-choicers" are willing to agree that *if* they thought the preborn were persons, then, yes, they'd have to agree that killing them would be the worst form of aggression. Some of those who believe in the "right" to abandon children may concede that abortion as it takes place in the real world is killing and not abandonment.

We are going to have to *listen*. Because many on the other side are not really on the other side — at least not all the way. They are not the ones who will casually endorse infanticide as a convenient method to control population and welfare costs. Yes, they do like the "me-first" aspects of rights and given the opportunity, will ignore the less comfy points of ethics and justice. But given the opportunity, they are also willing to recognize "responsibility," and "obligation," and the need for limiting our choices in the light of these principles.

That doesn't give us very much, you say? True. But in the long run, *we* cannot persuade anyone of anything. We must present the truth effectively and clearly. Our hearers must decide whether *they* will accept it or reject it. That fundamental ability and liberty of persons to choose good or evil is, after all, why we fight abortion. Abortion is what stamps it out.

THE WORD MET THE TIME

Robert Morrison*

"Man is the animal that speaks. Understanding language is then the key to understanding men; and the control of language, to the control of men."

THOMAS SZASZ, *The Second Sin.*

"We knew that abortion wasn't just central to a woman's right of choice. It was central to *everything in life and how we wanted to live it."* (Emphasis added.) Thus did Lawrence Lader, the father of abortion on demand, describe what was at stake for him and his followers in today's irrepressible conflict. Lader aptly subtitled the book wherein that quote appears "Making the Revolution." We in the pro-life movement must give Lawrence Lader his due: he understands the importance of abortion.

Frequently, political scientists discuss issues in terms of High Politics and Low Politics. High Politics involve

*Robert Morrison is executive director of Connecticut Citizens Concerned for Life. He received his B.A. and M.A. degrees in Government and Foreign Affairs from the University of Virginia. He is a frequent contributor to pro-life journals.

fundamental issues like the nature of the constitutional system and the means of providing for the common defense. High Politics inevitably touch on grand questions of who has power, who has sovereignty. Initially, at least, the abortion revolutionaries were skilled in representing this issue as one of High Politics: Can the state exercise sovereignty over the bodies of half its citizens in such an intimate way?

Low Politics, on the other hand, are the stuff of day-to-day public life. Low Politics involve every mundane question from how best to deliver the mail to how to zone for industrial development. Having achieved their constitutional coup in the *Roe* v. *Wade* decision, the abortion revolutionaries became the abortion party. They sought, with great success, to convert the abortion issue to one of Low Politics. Taking abortion-on-demand as a given, they moved to such questions as funding all choices in every imaginable arena: For example, may the state pay for all other Medicaid operations but deny it arbitrarily to one — abortion? Can the state refuse to include all "reproductive options" in its mandatory sex education curriculum?

But, as Lader said, abortion is central. And as it is central to our enemies, so it is central to us. But it is more than that. Because abortion attacks the intrinsic worth of human life at its most vulnerable, it is a prime issue, for human life is the prime value from which we derive all other values. Abortion, therefore, is *metapolitical.* Metapolitical questions are defined as those which provide the context in which politics takes place. It can even be argued that metapolitical questions by their very nature border on the theological. Lawrence Lader and his fellow abortion revolutionaries have done more than achieve a stunning political victory. They have thrown down the most radical challenge to America's political justification since slavery. If the born can sell or slay the unborn at will, then this nation is no longer dedicated to the proposition that all men are created equal.

Instead, we will have a new doctrine as stated by Lader's ally, Balfour Brickner: "We affirm the right to life, *when wanted.*" Clearly, such a conditional, feeble, alienable right is no right at all. When Justice Blackmun wrote his bicentennial opinion denying fathers the right to protect their unborn children *(Planned Parenthood* v. *Danforth)*, he ruled that the state cannot delegate any rights it does not possess. Whether or not fathers ever possessed the right to protect is only *part* of the question. The ominous import of Blackmun's decision is that our rights are said to be granted or denied by the state.

Abraham Lincoln came to political maturity at a time when the truth or the relevance of the Declaration of Independence was being debated. How could we reconcile the phrase "all men are created equal" with slavery? How can we reconcile it today with abortion? Lincoln said that he based his whole political philosophy on the ideas expressed by Jefferson in the Declaration. So, safely, can those who defend unborn life.

In the 1840s, the nation's political life was dominated by men like John C. Calhoun. Like some modern defenders of abortion, Calhoun simply denied the truth of the Declaration. "There is not a word of truth in it," Calhoun stated. The philosopher of slavery went on to attack Jefferson's famous phrase by changing the words: "Men are not born," he said. "Infants are born. They are not born free. While infants, they are incapable of freedom." Calhoun went on to liken blacks to infants and to justify their permanent enslavement by arguing that they were eternally incapable of freedom. In just this way, today's pro-abortionists finesse the question of createdness and stress the limitations of the fetus. What are the concepts "personhood," "viability," and "meaningful life" but cloaks to cover the act of killing?

Ironically, Calhoun is increasingly recognized by political scientists as the father of American Pluralism. It is to just this "pluralism" that the abortion party constantly appeals for justification of its own peculiar institution. The pro-abortionists ask: since we are a nation of many faiths, many beliefs, how can one doctrine ever cover all? In practical terms, what they have done is to destroy the ideological consensus that made this one nation indivisible: no longer can our motto be "E pluribus unum" — from many, one. Rather, we must accept their fractured version, from one, many.

At least Calhoun was willing to take the Declaration head on. Today's most prominent exponents of abortion, like the most successful defenders of slavery, argue seductively that the words of the Declaration do not apply. Jefferson could not have meant the unborn any more than he could have meant blacks. This attack on the Declaration is more dangerous because it is more subtle. Chief Justice Roger B. Taney established the precedent for this line of attack in the *Dred Scott* decision of 1857. There, he pointedly read black men out of the family of man. A century and a quarter later, Justice Harry Blackmun trod the same path in saying, "We need not decide the difficult question of when human life begins."

Historian Carl Becker showed in his classic study of the Declaration of Independence how vigorous was the political and intellectual effort in the 19th century to escape the implications of the phrase "all men are created equal." Those words not only embarassed slavery's American apologists, but they were also a stinging rebuke to Europe's rising imperialists. Failing to rebut the truth or the relevance of the Declaration, opponents of human liberty fell back on the argument that Jefferson's words were only "glittering generalities." The abortion party today is no more inclined to consider the meaning of those words. Yet pro-lifers could readily re-adopt them, for we are a Right to Life Movement because we are a Created Equal Movement.

The pro-abortionists cannot look back. Nor can they look to the future. They live only in the present. They cannot bear even to let justice sleep overnight for fear that too many will choose life in the light of a better morning. Pro-lifers can look at our nation's history. We can examine the ideas of our greatest American thinkers — Jefferson and Lincoln — and we will find support. We must search the past to rescue the future. When we do this, we will see that the cause we defend today is the same cause they defended. It is the cause that has always needed our defense: the cause is mankind.

We should begin our search for meaning with the words of a thirty-three year old Virginian who had been chosen to draft the unanimous declaration of the thirteen colonies. His draft was to be uniquely his own, but the ideas he expressed represented — as he would modestly confess decades later — the common sense of the matter.

Thomas Jefferson, with what John Adams called his "peculiar felicity of expression," gave us a political statement that was also a philosophical one and — dare we say it? — a religious one.

> We hold these truths to be self evident, that all men are created equal, that they are endowed by their Creator with certain inalienable rights, that among these are life, liberty, and the pursuit of happiness....

Perhaps some of us put a different construction on these words today than the one they clearly had when they were written. We can determine what the words meant by referring to Samuel Johnson's famous first dictionary. Let us analyze the text as it was understood in the eighteenth century:

Self evident: We don't have to prove these truths, we take them as axiomatic; they are the foundation of our national faith.

All men: Included is the whole class of human beings, regardless of age, regardless of sex.

Created: The key distinction between the more legalistic Constitution and the philosophic Declaration. We can safely rest our case here, for "created" clearly means conceived, made, brought into being, not merely born. How wildly unscientific would our cerebral Mr. Jefferson find today's pathetic, feigned uncertainty about when men are created men.

Equal: Here we ascend to the moral heights of our national existence. One of the most exciting discoveries imaginable is to learn that Jefferson said equal and meant equal. He did not mean a baser equality of wealth, intellect, lineage, or physical capacity. Rather, he meant moral equality — the capacity to come to know what is good and to do what is good. Some people, he conceded did not trouble themselves to know or to do good. Still, he maintained, that just as some people are blind, sightedness, not blindness, was a characteristic of humans.

Jefferson made his philosophic paper a religious argument when he wrote that we are all endowed with our inalienable rights by our Creator. Here, this most undogmatic of believers, this disestablisher of the state church, unequivocally put our new nation under God. More than that, he regarded all the rights he defended as inalienable *because* they were endowed by God.

Jefferson ordered his enumeration of life, liberty, and the pursuit of happiness in this way for reasons that go beyond euphony. For it is only in the realization of life that we can experience liberty. And only in liberty can we truly pursue happiness. But, as successfully as the Declaration of Independence has been as a literary effort, it would have failed if it did not embody a core of profound political beliefs which the American people accepted as true. We are well-favored as pro-lifers. Can anyone imagine a ringing declaration for "choice, liberty, and the pursuit of happiness"? It would be a literary — as it is already a political — abortion.

With no hope of justification in the text or the spirit of the Declaration, pro-abortionists have attempted to place the Constitution above the Declaration and to suggest that there is some kind of conflict between the two. They are different documents, it is true, intended to serve different purposes. So, while right-to-lifers take their name from the Declaration, abortion advocates strike a pose of defending sacred constitutional rights.

Where are these constitutional rights to abortion? Can the pro-abortionists point to the words? Can they quote the phrase? Of course not. It is enough for the learned Justices of the Supreme Court to say that an unmentioned right to privacy can be found within the "penumbra of the Fourteenth Amendment." And within this shadow, the learned Justices discovered a right to abortion. Who could have anticipated that our venerable old Constitution would suddenly give birth to such an unlikely new right? Few of us even suspected she was pregnant.

In order to serve as midwife to this unexpected arrival, however, the Justices had to hurry past the explicit text of the Preamble to the Constitution. One of the original purposes for which "We the People of the United States" were ordaining and establishing this Constitution was to "secure the blessings of liberty to ourselves *and our posterity.*" [Emphasis added.] Posterity has been getting short shrift lately. Professor Henry Steele Commager, shortly after his strong endorsement of John Anderson for President, lamented the lack of concern for posterity in our present day political rhetoric.

Who is posterity? *Black's Law Dictionary* defines posterity as "all the descendants of a person in a direct line to the remotest generation." The reference to "our posterity" would not have caused mystery at the

Constitutional Convention. It certainly did not refer to Secretary James Madison's posterity or to President George Washington's posterity since both men were childless. "Our posterity" clearly refers to the descendants of the same "We the People." Small wonder, then that politicians like John Anderson, who aggressively promote abortion, have little use for the term.

The Declaration of Independence and the Constitution are not antagonists. They are as compatible and complementary as were Jefferson and Madison. To attack the Constitution, one must first subvert the Declaration. This is what the Supreme Court did in *Roe v. Wade* and its progeny. Neither in the Second Continental Congress nor in the Constitutional Convention do we find even passing reference to abortion, yet our opponents would have us believe that this practice has always been accepted among us. Jefferson, the great stylist, does use the word. In a letter to a friend, he speaks of "...the abortion of all our hopes." And Jefferson wrote of pregnancy, too. In the last letter of his life, he wrote: "The Declaration of Independence is pregnant with our own and the fate of the world."

The relevance of the Declaration of Independence was still at issue in the 1850's. But it was an obscure, one-term ex-Congressman from an untried political party who used the language of Scripture to defend the noblest ideals of the Enlightenment.

When Abraham Lincoln made his most important speech on slavery, he quoted the words of Jesus: "A house divided against itself cannot stand." Lincoln, of course, was speaking to frontier people, who, even if they could not read, had at last heard and understood those words. Lincoln went on to say that he did not expect the house to fall, but he did expect it to cease to be divided: it would become either all slave or all free. The "House Divided" speech is credited with lifting Lincoln out of defeat and obscurity and making him a presidential contender.

Lincoln based his argument not on the Bible, as we might suppose, but on logic. He argued simply that when the Supreme Court decided in the *Dred Scott* case that black people were property, there was no legal or constitutional way to prevent slaveholders from taking their property into any free state and no practical way to prevent them from using or abusing their property as they saw fit. "The black man has no right which the white man is bound to respect," said Chief Justice Roger B. Taney.

Lincoln poked fun at the Supreme Court of his day. "Verily, verily, thus saith the Court," he said, mocking the pretensions of the justices to infallibility. Chief Justice Taney had argued that Jefferson did not mean blacks when he wrote "all men are created equal." Lincoln said Taney's opinion was ridiculous. Certainly, Lincoln said, some people didn't *agree* with what Jefferson wrote in the Declaration of Independence, but nobody had ever before said that Jefferson didn't *mean* what he wrote.

And Lincoln debated Stephen Douglas all over the state of Illinois while a divided nation listened. Douglas, the leading Democrat of his day, was pro-choice on the issue of slavery. He said the people of each state should decide whether or not human beings should be property in that state. Although he might be *personally opposed* to holding slaves — he never really did say — Douglas did not think he should impose his beliefs on those who chose to hold slaves. The important thing, argued Douglas, was freedom of choice. Whichever way the people of a state decided, Douglas would respect that decision. Further, he said, "I don't care" which way they decide. For Douglas, "the People" could never include Blacks. For Lawrence Lader, "a woman's right to choose" could never be shared by her unborn daughter.

Seven debates were held. Seven times Lincoln and Douglas met to discuss slavery. No one then complained about "a single issue campaign." Everyone seemed to recognize that upon the outcome of this vital question rested the very destiny of the United States. Lincoln pressed Douglas hard. What he said, in effect, was: you can only be pro-choice if the thing that is chosen is neither bad nor good, if it is neutral. If it is bad, then you cannot logically say "you don't care" if it is chosen. You must logically wish for good and not bad to be chosen.

Lincoln said it plainly: "If slavery is not wrong, then *nothing* is wrong." He would describe the controversy as "the *eternal*" struggle between right and wrong." In one of the last debates Lincoln said: "...eighty years ago we began by declaring all men equal; but now [as steadily as a man's march to the grave] we have run down to that other declaration, that for some men to enslave others is 'a sacred right of self-government.' These principles cannot stand together. They are as opposite as God and Mammon, and whoever holds to the one must despise the other."

The question of abortion is fundamentally no different than the question of slavery. The Supreme Court of 1973, like the Supreme Court of 1857, said that a whole class of human beings were not "created equal." "Unwantedness," like blackness, was sufficient to deny them any rights at all. The logic of the Supreme Court in both instances is that some human beings can be viewed as property.

Does it surprise anyone, therefore, that the pro-abortionists so often defend "choice" but so rarely defend the thing that is chosen? The slaveholders demanded the right to control their property. The pro-abortionists demand the right to control their bodies. What started out even for slaveholders as a "necessary evil" became less evil as it grew more necessary. Eventually, some slavers argued that their institution was a "positive good," that they were doing the poor blacks a favor by enslaving them. We hear echoes of this argument today. Some ardent pro-abortionists say that every child has the right to be well, the right to be well-off, the right to be wanted, and the right to be killed rather than suffer the deprivation of any of these strange new rights.

Lincoln asked why the slavers were so alarmed by what he was saying. He was a moderate. He did not ask for immediate emancipation of all the slaves. But he answered his own question. The slavers desperately needed the respectability of being *thought* right. Lincoln refused to grant them respectability. And for that refusal they hated him. He said: "Their thinking it right and our thinking it wrong is the precise fact upon which depends the whole controversy. Thinking it right, as they do, they are not to blame for desiring its full recognition as being right; but thinking it wrong, as we do, *can we yield to them?* Can we cast our votes with their view and against our own?"

If abortion is not wrong, then nothing is wrong. It is more than a singular or separate wrong — it is the source of all wrong. To kill the small, the weak, the sick, the dependent, the defenseless violates all that our people's faith and our nation's history tells us is right. If we can choose between one human being's right to life and another human being's life *style* and give death to one and absolute power to the other, then how can we ever again claim to be what Lincoln called us: the last, best hope of earth?

With even a casual reading of the arguments Lincoln confronted, we are struck by their familiar hollow ring. We face so many similar arguments in the abortion conflict today. Time and time again, in lofty phrases, and in homely parables, Lincoln framed the issue of slavery in terms that put the life of the nation first. And he resisted the vigorous efforts of ordinary politicians to divert attention away from the vital issue. In Harford, Connecticut, in 1860, he said:

> I think one great mistake is made by them all. I

> think our wisest men have made this mistake. They underrate its importance, and a settlement can never be effected until its magnitude is properly estimated. Now what is the difficulty? One sixth of the population of the United States is slave. One man of every six, one woman of every six, is a slave Those who own them look upon them as property, and nothing else.

Certainly we can find few wise men or women in government today who can properly estimate the magnitude of the abortion issue. One third of the pregnancies in the United States are aborted. One boy in every three, one girl in every three is killed before birth. One pregnant woman in three consents to the killing.

Lincoln said that looking at the slaves only as property exerted a powerful interest over the minds of those who held them. We see this today as well. Gloria Steinem told the readers of *Ms.* magazine, "we have *become* the men we wanted to marry." This statement is more clearly understood by advertisers in *Ms.* who are encouraged by the fact that the average reader of *Ms.* earns more than $25,000 a year. Abortion is essential to the property interest of some wealthy people. No questions of the "feminization of poverty" or of women's political opinions — the "gender gap" — is addressed in *Ms.* without reference to the preservation and extension of abortion rights. Without malice, Lincoln said that public opinion was always formed relative to a property interest. A similar interest in property would affect our thinking, too.

With Lincoln, as with us, the question of rightness or wrongness could not be examined without reference to religion. But, like Jefferson, Lincoln called for no religious revival. Nor did he seek to impose an orthodoxy of religious belief. He stated it simply:

> I think that if anything can be proved by natural

> theology, it is that slavery is morally wrong. God gave man a mouth to receive bread, hands to feed it, and his hand has a right to carry bread to his mouth without controversy.

There is nothing here to conflict with Jefferson's famous phrase: "The God who gave me life gave me liberty at the same time." Today both these sentiments are unbearably controversial. They can hardly be repeated without inviting a charge of violating the sacred separation of church and state. The established irreligion would have American history taught fairly — minus Jefferson, minus Lincoln. But just as insistently, just as unapologetically, pro-lifers must press the question; Life, liberty, hands, mouths — these were given by God, these are destroyed by abortion.

We must never forget that when we fight for life, the life we defend is not only that of the smallest child, but also that of the greatest republic. Nations, like men, die. This nation has been an especially vital one because it is constantly renewed by new peoples. This was never a community of common blood, like China or France. "You cannot spill a drop of American blood without spilling the blood of the world," wrote Melville of an even younger republic.

To a nation conceived in liberty and dedicated to the proposition that all men are created equal, the *Roe* v. *Wade* ruling is as inimical as the *Dred Scott* v. *Sanford* ruling was. The Supreme Court of our time, like the earlier one, has placed the rattlesnake in the cradle.

Can America die? *Time* magazine, which once asked "Is God Dead?" would find the very idea incomprehensible. But classical political theorists have written that a republic is based on justice. When justice departs, the republic dies. St. Augustine used this pagan argument, rather than Christian doctrine, when he said that Rome was not done in by the attack of the Goths *because she was already dead.*

She died when she became totally unjust.

The advocates of "Choice" only pretend to be neutral. It is feigned indifference. In reality, they have zealously fought to expand the right to abortion. The more they expand the "right," the faster they spread the deadly toxin of injustice. Lincoln described slavery as a wen — a tumor — on the neck of a man who sat in front of him on the New Haven railroad: eventually it would kill him. We can see abortion as a cancer which is now rapidly metastasizing. New growths appear — infanticide, euthanasia — but all stem from the primary source: abortion.

When Edmund Burke, the great English parliamentarian, urged conciliation with the colonies then in revolt, he recognized the danger *to Britain* posed by a policy of narrow, constricted self-interest. "Great empires and little minds go ill together," he said in 1775. Now we have an American jurist, Lewis Powell, who not only regards a policy of narrow, constricting self-interest as appropriate, he terms it fundamental. Our republican system cannot stand without it. Justice Powell writes lyrically of the new means of achieving that policy when he praises the ghastliest abortion method of them all : dilatation and extraction. By this procedure, the head of a struggling unborn child is forcibly crushed and the limbs are hacked away. Such is the decadent use to which intellect and legal scholarship have been put two centuries after Burke: "Great republics and little skulls go ill together," we respond.

One of our best popular historians, Page Smith, has written of Lincoln's time in words quite fitting for our own:

> To be divided against oneself is death; in the language of the psychiatrist it is schizophrenia. The United States was in its deepest being, divided against itself, unto the agony of death, death to its

> ideals and principles, death to the Union, death to its soul. Whatever the costs, it must look into the terror. [In Abraham Lincoln,] The Word met the Time."

What we fight for, therefore, is not only the right of humans to live, but for the concept of humanity to survive. The United States is either the keeper of that light or she dies. And we may permit ourselves to state boldly that we hate Choice; we hate this evil word which comes to us from the lexicon of butchers and not that of philosophers. It is a hateful idea.

Lincoln hated no one, but he hated "choice":

> This declared indifference, but as I must think, covert real zeal for the spread of slavery, *I cannot but hate* [emphasis added]. I hate it because of the monstrous injustice of slavery itself. I hate it because it deprives our republican example of its just influence in the world... and especially because it forces so many good men amongst ourselves into an open war with the very fundamental principles of civil liberty, criticising the Declaration of Independence, and insisting that there is no principle of action but *self-interest.*

As we love and defend life, so we must hate choice. To do less is to join our adversaries as they try "to blow out the moral lights around us."

A YOUNGLING SOLE: A SHORT STORY

John E. Dunsford*

"She explained that a woman must not only have a right to control her body but also the products of her body as well, at least for a period of time sufficient to make an adequate assessment of the impact of parenthood on her lifestyle. Such an awareness sometimes takes eight or nine years to acquire, though she readily conceded there is a general consensus in the community that a period of ten years would be unreasonably long."

From "A Youngling Sole."

On the morning of August 12 six-year-old Scott Morrow Klein did not make his customary raucous appearance at the breakfast table. The housekeeper, Mrs. Rose Sanchez, pretended to take no special

*John E. Dunsford is the McDonnell Professor of Law at St. Louis University. He is a nationally known labor arbitrator. He has taught law since 1956. He is married and the father of five children. "A Youngling Sole" is Professor Dunford's first work of fiction.

notice of his absence, having been forewarned not to expect him or prepare a meal for him. She ate alone in stony silence, Shredded Wheat and Prune Danish. Her face wore a perplexed look and she was slightly annoyed. Why had the family instructed her to stay over and follow the regular routine under the circumstances? It made no sense.

Mr. and Mrs. Klein had scheduled themselves out of town for three days, pending the event. Arrangements had already been consummated with a small local firm specializing in such matters: an expert in the cosmetics of the domestic adjustment. When Mrs. Sanchez packed up and departed on her holiday later in the morning, uniformed representatives of the firm quickly materialized to remove the personal effects and redecorate the room. The Kleins had great plans to turn it into a hobby and entertainment center. A casual visitor would never be conscious of the change.

"The transition period for ex-parents normally lasts about three or four weeks," a spokesperson for the Reproductive Control Association explained. "Obviously this period varies considerably from one couple to another, in dependence on the character of the relationship which existed between the former parents and the youngling or sibling. The important thing to emphasize is that this is an agonizing decision for the parents. Adequate recovery time is essential to relieve any irrational doubts. At all costs their privacy must be respected during the transition."

Approximately 650,000 younglings (or siblings, as the case may be) have had their potential maturity terminated in the two years since the "Quality of Life" program went into effect in this country. A recent study by the Rauschitter Institute of Population Control reveals that 89 percent of the participants in the program expressed "strong satisfaction" with the results of the decision to prune their families. However, a few of the parent respondents did give negative answers, inexplicably reporting hallucinations in which they imagined they saw a child at a distance waving to them, or heard a muffled sob in the night. The reasons most often advanced by respondents for nominating a youngling for the program were "career impediment," "abnormal personal attributes," and "health deficiency." In over two-thirds of the cases covered by the study, the subject of the procedure was a youngling sole.

Despite intense curiosity on the part of the general public, the details of the procedures for terminating the latent maturity of younglings have been a closely guarded secret of the sponsoring organization. (Editors of the *New York Times* took the unusual step of denying they were suppressing a story and spread of pictures which would describe the terminating practices step by step.) A program brochure distributed by the Reproductive Control Association reassures that the apprehension and dispatching techniques followed by its facilitators are in every respect painless for the subject, at least within the known limits of consciousness. For humanitarian reasons, the organization restricts eligiblity for the program to younglings nine years and younger.

There is a speculation that this limitation may also be due to the intractability of subjects who have passed their tenth birthday, rendering the procedures more difficult to administer. Inquiries about the nature of the initial approach to the youngling, and the mechanics of the teminating methods, are politely but firmly rebuffed by the Reproductive Control Association. "All that we will say is that each of the selected younglings was unwanted and otherwise would have been doomed to a life of neglect and disadvantage," a spokesperson volunteered. Interviews with some of the participating ex-parents reveal that, as a matter of policy, they themselves are not informed by the organization of any of the particulars of the implementation of the program. Apparently none of the parents have challenged this policy.

Last week a national committee of pediatricians formed by the Reproductive Control Association called a press conference to issue a formal statement defending the program against mounting public criticism. "These senseless attacks from fundamentalists constitute a blatant attempt to interfere with the professional relationship between a doctor and the parents of his or her patients," the statement said. "What is under assault is a sacred relationship which goes to the financial stability and security of the profession itself. We want to repeat that the 'Quality of Life' program centers on intimate personal decisions which are best left to the parents in consultation with a medical doctor." The statement went on to condemn any attempt by the government to promulgate rigid rules in this area, since "such attempts can only be mischievous, an effort to treat simplistically what is an extremely complex matter."

Political figures have been reluctant to take a public position on the program. This situation may change in the light of a recent comment by an official of the Democratic National Committee. While he is personally opposed to youngling termination, he believes it is a matter for individual choice in a pluralistic society. The official scoffed at suggestions of a contradiction between that position and earlier statements regarding child abuse, quipping to reporters, "The only person who confuses child abuse with youngling termination is Jerry Falwell." State interference with the program would represent a further threat to the integrity of the American family, he said.

A few of the mainline religious groups in the society have expressed reservations about the morality of the program. In a brief homily at a Sunday ecumenical service in the former chapel of an Eastern college during spring break, an Episcopalian priest questioned the consistency of the program with the premises of the Judeo-Christian tradition. "Without wishing to be unduly judgmental on this subject," she preached, "one must state in all candor that a very grave reason indeed is necessary to justify interruption of the latent maturity of a ... er ... youngling. At the same time who cannot empathize with the pain and trauma experienced by the parents who are contemplating such a choice? These are sincere and caring people, seeking only to allocate the burdens of life equitably."

Sharp attacks have been directed against the Roman Catholic Church for its opposition to the program. "No one is forced to terminate the potential maturity of a youngling or sibling if that is against his or her principles," the Reproductive Control Association spokesperson pointed out. "The Catholic Church should live and let live, so to speak."

According to the spokesperson, it is particularly ironic that a celibate clergy would venture an opinion on family matters. "One can hardly think of an issue more appropriate for a final solution in the privacy of the home. Yet once again we find religious zealots endeavoring to impose their morality on others. It is our urgent hope that the American peole will reject any return to the Inquisition and the Middle Ages." A common charge that the executioners of the program are murderers was dismissed as "religious rhetoric." The spokesperson noted that no one truly knows when a youngling becomes a person "in the whole sense." That is a legal problem which even the mind of Justice Harry Blackmun could not resolve because there is such disagreement among those who are learned in theology, philosophy, comparative medicine, and statistics.

A fear that religious groups are determined to strip

away all of the civil liberties of Americans was expressed by a feminist supporter of the "Quality of Life" program. Declining to be identified because of her concern over personal harassment, she appeared masked and robed at a conference in the Crisis Center Building. She explained that a woman must not only have a right to control her body but also the products of her body as well, at least for a period of time sufficient to make an adequate assessment of the impact of parenthood on her lifestyle. If intelligent choices are to be made, she said, they ought to be made in full awareness of their consequences. Such an awareness sometimes takes eight or nine years to acquire, though she readily conceded there is a general consensus in the community that a period of ten years would be unreasonably long.

Pro-choice advocates in Congress have rushed to defend the program by reference to its promise of long-term scientific advancement. They are readying a resolution calling for the creation of a Special Committee to evaluate the types of medical information obtainable through a program of experimentation on younglings whose parents have registered them for the "Quality of Life" program. Guidelines for implementation of such a program have not been worked out, but a Congressional spokesperson said that the research possibilities are virtually limitless.

FEMINISM: BEWITCHED BY ABORTION

Rosemary Bottcher*

"Removing a right from one diminishes the rights of us all."

GLORIA STEINEM

Modern feminism has been bewitched by abortion. Mesmerized by its evil spell, many feminists have been tricked into advocating the Orwellian notion (everyone is equal, but some are more equal than others) that has been the excuse for all discrimination. Their insistence that the lives of unborn children have no significance poisons the roots of feminism by betraying the very essence of the concept of equality.

Pro-abortion feminists open themselves to charges of crass hypocrisy and insincerity by indulging in the very same behavior for which they condemn men: the

*Rosemary Bottcher is an analytical chemist whose major professional interest is protection of the environment. For several years she also wrote a column for the *Tallahassee Democrat*, and her articles on bioethics have been widely reprinted. She lives with her husband, an attorney, and their four children on a farm in north Florida.

unethical use of power to usurp the rights of those less powerful. To disguise the shameless inconsistency, feminists are forced to use the language in an overly creative manner that disintegrates into dishonesty. Not since the time of Humpty Dumpty have words been so emancipated from their definitions, so free to mean anything their utterer fancies them to mean.

Feminists force themselves into the unenviable position of arguing that the behavior they find indefensible in men is perfectly acceptable, even laudable, when practiced by women. This attitude can be interpreted as an admission that feminists do not really believe that women are mature enough to be judged by the same standards as are men. It is a confession that feminists believe that women, like children, are persons of "diminished responsibility" because of their inherent lack of judgment; therefore, they cannot be held strictly accountable for their behavior.

When arguing for their own equality, feminists condemn the unethical use of power by which men have usurped the rights of women. The price of men's privilege, they conclude, has been paid by women, and the price is too high. Feminists believe that rights must be ranked; no one can demand for himself the right to deprive another of a more important right. Decency requires that men make some sacrifices to prevent greater sacrifices being unjustly imposed upon women.

This is a reasonable position, but pro-abortion feminists sabotage their own case by hypocritically refusing to grant the unborn the same rights they demand for themselves. They resent the discrimination practiced against a whole class of humans because they happen to be female, yet they themselves discriminate against a whole class of humans because they happen to be very young. They deplore that the value of a woman has been determined by whether some man wants her, yet insist that the value of an unborn child is determined by whether some woman wants him. They resent that women have been "owned" by their fathers or husbands, yet claim that the unborn are owned by their mothers. They believe that sexual freedom cannot include a man's right to rape women, yet proclaim that it does include a woman's right to kill her unborn children. They lament men's reluctance to recognize the personhood of women, yet steadfastly refuse to acknowledge the personhood of the unborn.

Pro-abortion rhetoric is utterly without respect for facts, language, logic, or women. Abortion apologists disregard the rules of reason and present us with a very unflattering view of women. Faye Wattleton, president of Planned Parenthood, states, "If we don't win [the abortion fight] millions of women will be forced to bear unwanted children, and many of them will be condemned to lives of trauma, abuse, hopelessness and despair." This remark implies that women are incompetent, unresourceful, incapable of handling stress, and cannot be good mothers except under ideal circumstances.

This well worn contention — that women denied legal abortion will produce hoards of unwanted and therefore worthless children — is contradicted by another favorite argument: Restoring abortions to the status of crime will not reduce their numbers; women will have them anyway. The claim is frequently made that prior to 1973, over one million illegal abortions were performed in this country each year, and ten thousand women died as a result. I had always wondered where these figures came from — how can the incidence of an illegal activity that leaves no trace be accurately calculated — until Bernard Nathanson, a cofounder of NARAL, spilled the beans:

"We made it up," he confessed. "We knew those

numbers would impress legislators." The actual number of illegal abortions prior to 1973 is unknown and probably unknowable, but the true figure for deaths due to these abortions is probably fewer than 500 a year, according to Dr. Nathanson. Nevertheless, the argument that it is futile to criminalize abortion tells us that women are irresponsible and undependable. They cannot be trusted to obey the law; they never have and never will. In fact, if abortion should be made illegal again, women will be "forced" to have them at the hands of those awful back alley butchers. Who forces them? Are they dragged to the butchers against their will? Are they so weak and witless that they cannot resist this strange "force"?

The abortion rhetoric presumes that women cannot resist any force; they are forced to have sex in the first place. A Tallahassee feminist wrote, "We can't say 'no' because we will be called prudes, frigid, or cruel, ... or beaten up." One feminist associated with a Tallahassee abortion clinic made this remarkable statement: "All pregnancies are the result of rape — if not physical rape then psychological rape." Here, again, we have a woman who claims to be a feminist making a comment that depicts women as being stupid, gullible, vulnerable, and powerless. Women are so insecure that they will risk unwanted pregnancy to avoid displeasing men.

The suggestion that women surrender their mistimed children for adoption is greeted with indignation by pro-abortion feminists. They believe that women have the right to be frivolous and self-indulgent. They cannot be asked to endure any hardship or even inconvenience for the sake of joy for a childless couple or life for a blameless child. Women cannot be expected to conform to a standard of minimal decency, much less one of selflessness.

Nearly all pro-abortionists are opposed to the concept

of informed consent. Information about the risks of abortion and about prenatal development is a "parade of horribles" which "merely adds to her stress." One reason the D&E is the preferred technique for late abortions is that this method "allows her to continue her pattern of denial." A woman delivering a salt-poisoned baby is "forced to come to terms with the significance of her decision." A woman considering eugenic abortion must not be shown sonographic images of her baby because "this will bias her decision." Fetology is one of the fastest growing medical specialties, and the media frequently report new discoveries about the majesty and complexity of prenatal life; nevertheless, women are so dumb that they will never be able to figure out for themselves the obvious connection between babies and abortion. The less women know about abortion the better off they are; they have a right to their ignorance.

By failing to recognize, much less criticize, the unmitigated misogyny of their own rhetoric, pro-abortion feminists betray their very low opinion of themselves and of all women. They believe that being born a woman is life's cruelest blow, a terrible handicap. Abortion is of crucial importance because it negates the one irrefutable difference between men and women: childbearing. Childbearing is an onerous, crippling burden inflicted upon women by a male-oriented society. Motherhood is ridiculed as a form of enslavement. Tenderness, caring, compassion, and selflessness — these are qualities associated with women and are therefore signs of weakness. Abortion symbolically destroys the perceived essence of womanliness — nurturance — which these feminists despise with venomous vehemence.

The separatist feminists, who are the most avidly pro-abortion, are classic examples of Eric Hoffer's "true believer." Consumed by self-hatred, true believers join a movement which allows them to transfer their unbearable feelings of worthlessness onto some other group, which is blamed for all the true believers' failures — indeed, for all the troubles of the world. Nazis blamed Jews, Klansmen blamed blacks, and radical feminists blame men and children.

These feminists suffer from the "kick the dog" syndrome. They express their frustration and feelings of powerlessness in the adult world by insisting upon their right to pulverize a 20-gram fetus. They *do* have power over somebody, by golly! Like the Hindu goddess of revenge, these feminists revel in their destructive power by making necklaces of the skulls of their children.

Thoughtful feminists are embarassed by the excesses of their more strident sisters. They realize that the abortion brouhaha is threatening women's quest for equality. The same cowardly, hysterical women who will abort themselves, lose their minds, commit suicide, or abuse their children if denied legal abortion can hardly be trusted with adult responsibilities. It is irrational to argue that women are capable of managing corporations, but not contraceptives; that they can handle the stresses of a presidency, but not those of a pregnancy. This vacillation about the competence of women makes it much more difficult to press for genuine equality.

Betty Friedan argues in *The Second Stage* that feminists must now soften their tactics of belligerent confrontation and come to terms with the profound importance of families to the happiness of human beings. She urges feminists to redirect their energy into changing the structure of their everyday lives so that women (and men) can combine career and family. Friedan hopes for more equitable marriages, workplaces that recognize and make concessions to the obligations of parents, and men who are more willing to accept an active role in the rearing of their children.

Legal abortion threatens every one of these goals. Accessible, socially-acceptable abortion gives reluctant employers more leverage to resist demands for a working environment that recognizes the needs of working parents. Abortion is easier and cheaper than accommodation. A society that promotes abortion is not likely to aggressively seek positive solutions to the problems of pregnant women and working parents.

At present, the fathers of unborn children have absolutely no right to participate in the abortion decision. Men whose rights as fathers have been so severely curtailed are not as likely to be enthusiastic about accepting the responsibilities of fatherhood. A marriage that does not recognize a father's right to protect his unborn children is not equitable. Women are free to abandon their unborn children, but if they decide to let their children live, men are given no option but to recognize their obligations to these children. Women who think they can't be equal without their abortions forget that the law expects and requires that a man provide for his children, even though doing so may cause him much inconvenience.

A man cannot demand that he be excused from his duty because his career might suffer. He can't say, "I'm not ready for children," or "I have enough already," or "I don't want that child." He knew what he was doing when he did it and he should expect to be held accountable. Men are expected to be mature, and the mark of maturity is the willingness to accept the consequences of one's actions, even though doing so may cause sacrifice and even hardship. Women who want equality can demand no less of themselves.

Though men have certainly abused their power over women, they have never done so to the extent that women have abused their power over unborn children.

This is the grotesque hypocrisy of the feminist demand for unfettered abortion.

ZEALOTS, ZANIES, AND ASSORTED KOOKS: HOW THE MAJOR MEDIA INTERPRETS THE PRO-LIFE MOVEMENT

Dave Andrusko*

Journalists have always been specialists in immediacy, chroniclers of the day. This, too, is an honorable calling. Out of frustration of trying to deal with complexity and perhaps out of a feeling that what they do is less worthy, good journalists may become bad social scientists. The market in bad social science is already glutted."

STEPHEN HESS, *The Washington Reporters.*

Pro-lifers take their disputes seriously. Because the issue at hand is literally a matter of life and death, they very earnestly study every nuance of proposals, strategies, and ideas. Scratch a pro-lifer and you'll

*Dave Andrusko is editor of the National Right to Life News and editor of this volume. He is married to Lisa Schultz Andrusko. They live in Virginia with their daughter, Emily Susan.

find a man or woman ready to expound on the superior merits of the Human Life Bill or the Hatch-Eagleton Amendment, whether the Garn or the Unity Amendment is the ideal ultimate Human Life Amendment, whether it is wise or foolish to use "the pictures," and whether or not it is a smart use of energy to try to convene a Constitutional Convention.

Whatever the differences over strategy, however contentious the debate over tactics, there is one subject about which there is total uniformity: pro-lifers fear, mistrust, and even despise "the media." It is no exaggeration to say that if you gather two or more pro-lifers together, it is even money that within the hour they will be trading horror stories about the media.

Indeed, so universal is the anger at the media, so uniform is the opinion that the pro-life movement never gets a fair shake that many pro-lifers would rather spend their time lambasting the media than trying to understand why we receive such shoddy press coverage. While understandable, such attitudes are self-defeating. The media, particularly the "Media Elite," are the information gatekeepers in our society; they explain to the general public which ideas, attitudes, and social and political actors are legitimate and which are not. With a few well-chosen verbs and adjectives, the media tells their readers whether the cause is worth taking seriously and whether its proponents are honorable or wont to cut corners ethically.

The likelihood of favorable coverage is in direct proportion to a cause's success in the media's "compassion/adaptability index." One gets points for being spontaneous, liberal, pragmatic and willing to live and let live. One loses points if described as "rigid," "reactionary," "ideological/extremist," or bent on "imposing morality." Needless to say, the pro-life movement fares poorly. Our motives are invariably suspect, our membership stereotyped, our values caricatured, mocked and maligned. The understandable reaction is to lash out at our tormentors. However, aside from temporarily relieving our rage, such blanket indictments accomplish little.

If we are to move beyond anger, we must document the manifestations of conscious and unconscious bias, and — more important — search out their origins. Only if we have some understanding why we are battered from *New York Times* pillar to *Washington Post* will we be able to forge that knowledge into a tool for gaining better, more objective coverage.

Now to be sure, complaints of media bias from cause groups are as old as the hills. Writing in the *Washington Journalism Review, Baltimore Sun* reporter Fred Barnes does an admirable job of documenting the complaints of "ideologues of the Left and Right" about media bias. Interestingly, Barnes argues that both sides of the abortion issue "claim that their clout is badly analyzed by the press." Yet a close reading of each side's critique is most revealing.

Nanette Falkenberg, NARAL's executive director, complained to Barnes that the press was less interested in writing about what NARAL felt was important in the 1982 elections — individual contests for state legislative seats — than it was about which U.S. Senators NARAL had "targeted" for defeat. But Falkenberg's lament lacks both persuasiveness and weight. Is it unfair that given the enormous change in the complexion of the Senate in 1980, due in no small part to the abortion issue, the media would focus on the 1982 senatorial elections when interviewing partisans of both sides. Notice, too, her complaint is not really about fairness; it is a mild grousing over the fact that the media did not choose to concentrate on that part of the 1982 electoral process which NARAL felt made it look best.

How does such a quibble stack up against the ongoing media campaign to delegitimize the pro-life movement, the endlessly repeated assertions that it is comprised almost exclusively of kooks, religious fanatics and assorted zanies? It is one thing to have abundant attention given to developments one would rather see ignored. It is quite another thing not to be accepted as a legitimate player in the political arena.

Barnes, no doubt unknowingly, was pandering to reporters' worst self-congratulatory instincts. He was telling his colleagues what reporters love to hear: both sides are unhappy. Such comments are prima facie evidence that the reporter is doing a good job. Why? "Because both sides hate me." However, as the previous example illustrates, the facts give us a very different picture than the one painted by Barnes. If the media were any more flagrantly pro-abortion, they would be on Planned Parenthood's payroll. (Several of the media's most influential members already are not shy about accepting speaking engagements at various pro-abortion gatherings, presumably for pay.) Although we will take a moment to talk about the evidence of media bias, in fact the only debatable question is not *whether* bias is evidenced but *why* there is bias, and *how much* of it is conscious, and how much unintended.

An immediate distinction must be drawn between the so-called "media elite" and virtually everybody else, particularly the smaller dailies and the weeklies. While the latter are hardly bosom buddies of the pro-life movement, ordinarily they do at least go through the motions of playing fair. With the media elite ... well, all is fair in love, war, and abortion politics. With the elite — the *New York Times*, the *Washington Post*, the *Wall Street Journal*, the three television networks and *PBS*, and the three weekly newsmagazines, *Time, Newsweek*, and *U.S. News and World Report* — the gloves come off.

Even the most cursory research makes it obvious that we have no cultural authority with the elite reporters, anchormen, commentators, producers, and so forth. In a word, they have not taken and do not now take pro-lifers seriously, except as menaces to the political process. Our most eloquent pleas, our most soaring rhetoric in defense of liberty and justice fall on deaf ears. Most of the media elite clearly do not believe we have anything worth listening to. We have been tuned out. Why? For one thing, because we have been tarred with the "anti-pluralist" brush; we are said to violate the cultural compact to live and let live(!) The media elite see in wellsprings of our concern not an unyielding belief in the dignity of human life and a desire to help women facing problem pregnancies, but a wish to turn the continental United States into one giant Puritan Commonwealth.

To jump ahead briefly, the explanation why the media elite comes down so hard on the pro-life movement is a complex mixture of conscious bias, shared values (among themselves and with the pro-abortion leadership), familiarity — or lack thereof — with the principal parties to the abortion battle, the legends of the journalist's trade, and the genuinely superior ability of the pro-abortion establishment to use language in a highly effective, if dishonest and misleading, way.

The importance of this last point can scarcely be overstated. Abortion proponents shrewdly take advantage of the fact that most reporters have a very limited stock of categories into which to locate ideas, people, and movements. Abortion proponents assiduously cultivate the press and never forget that most reporters are generalists, not specialists, much less moral philosophers.

Conscious Bias

Since we can not very well get inside a reporter's

brain, there is no way to document conscious bias except in those rare cases where they come right out and tell you. There are indirect measurements, however. One example of this would be the continued use of patently incorrect evidence after that error has been repeatedly brought to the attention of those making the error.

On this score, we have nearly ten years of press accounts that reflexively observe that the Supreme Court decision legalized abortions in the first three months of pregnancy only. No amount of letters to the editor, phone calls, or personal visits seems able to make a dent in this stereotype, although it will probably begin to break down somewhat now that the Supreme Court has explicitly ruled that states cannot require second-trimester abortions be performed in hospitals. (This illustrates an iron rule of thumb with the media. Cliches and mistakes, like bad news, travel fast. Not only that, once a mistake enters the public domain, often it is virtually impossible to get the matter straightened out.)

But there are many reporters whose personal agenda is so clearly the promotion of abortion that we need not resort to indirect evidence to prove bias. Take the chief congressional correspondent for the *New York Times*, Steven V. Roberts. So widespread is the pro-abortion poison in the editorial veins of the *Times* that Roberts does not even bother to feign objectivity.

One classic example is Roberts' new analysis following the battle over Sen. Jesse Helms' Human Life Bill. Roberts' thesis was that because the HLB had failed to overcome a pro-abortion filibuster, the pro-life movement probably crested politically. "Pro-choice" forces had ridden out the storm engendered by the 1980 elections and were now no longer on the defensive. His sources for this important analysis? Planned Parenthood, a pro-abortion senator's aide, the American Civil Liberties Union, the National Abortion

Rights Action League, the Religious Coalition for Abortion Rights, and pro-abortion knight in shining armor, Sen. Robert Packwood. Although Senator Helms secured 50 votes in his effort to override the filibuster, Roberts' story contained not a single pro-life voice.

Roberts' hype job had barely cooled before its author was off to address the annual convention of Planned Parenthood. Playing to an adoring audience, Roberts praised the "courage" of Packwood and Senator Lowell Weicker who were willing, he said, to "really throw their bodies across the train (tracks) two years ago when the New Right was riding high." Not content to cite the contributions of others, Roberts made a startling admission. He confided to his compatriots that he was partially responsible for convincing the *Times'* editorial page editors to support the Senate's number two pro-abortionist, Weicker, over Toby Moffit in the closely contested 1982 Connecticut senatorial race. Sad to say, Roberts is only the most egregious example of an all too pervasive pattern.

Yet the question remains, does the presence of repeated factual errors for as long as a decade and the partisan reporting of journalists such as Roberts conclusively demonstrate that the primary reason for most media bias is deliberate attempts to slant the news? Surprisingly, in conversations with pro-life journalists, many say no! A great many believe their colleagues are innocent of bias on the abortion issue. The immediate response by those who take a dimmer view of the media's objectivity might be that such a belief flies in the face of the results of Stanley Rothman and Robert Lichter's survey of the media elite.

But does it? Do their findings buttress the case for conscious bias? Let us see. Rothman and Lichter conducted a now-famous survey of 240 members of what they described as the aforementioned media elite. The responses were fascinating. An overwhelming ninety percent of the media elite agreed that a woman ought to be able to decide for herself whether to have an abortion. Seventy nine percent felt so strongly. Their answers to the abortion question were consonant with their responses to kindred questions about sexual ethics. For example, fifty-four percent did not regard adultery as wrong.

Rothman and Lichter concluded, "Thus, members of the media elite emerge as strong supporters of sexual freedom or permissiveness, and as natural opponents of groups like the Moral Majority, who seek to enlist the state in restricting sexual freedom." (Any suspicions Rothman and Lichter were closet pro-lifers ready to cook the figures can be dispelled by the end of that remark.)

But do these results prove the presence of widespread conscious bias? Not really. They do demonstrate that the media elite is "liberal," even ultra-liberal on a wide range of public policy questions, including questions of sexual ethics. The results also show that most of the media elite share a common set of cultural values and assumptions; because they do look at the world through very liberal eyes, it may color the way they interpret people whose values are so completely different. What can be argued fairly is that, like the rest of humanity, they are going to be easier on those who think as they do and harsher on those who don't.

How Reporters See Themselves

Reporters are notorious for a reluctance to examine their own motives. If forced to answer pro-life allegations, most reporters would strongly deny they are biased. Most would say they are merely trying to do a job. In a sense, most would be giving sincere responses. But as you talk with reporters about the issue, it is clear that most have a way of seeing the question that virtually precludes a balanced presentation.

The best example of this is when pro-lifers try to point out that the results of a survey which frames the abortion liberty as extending only through the first trimester is grossly misleading. Newspaper ombudsmen will look at you like you have a screw loose. They'll say, "But we're not saying that abortion isn't legal after three months; abortion is legal the first three months of pregnancy, isn't it? Therefore, what we choose to ask them *is* accurate and you're too close to the issue to see the distinction." You try again. Support falls off dramatically for abortions performed after the first trimester. If you report support for first trimester abortions as indicative of support for the Supreme Court decision which legalized abortion throughout the entire pregnancy, you distort the real position of the American people on abortion. The response to this line of argument is usually indifference or hostility. You have been dismissed as a fanatic who is unable to understand a simple declarative sentence.

The most plausible conclusion is that serious distortion comes less in the form of conscious, deliberate, agenda-furthering bias than it does in an unacknowledged willingness to cast in the best possible light what pro-abortionists say or do and to subject to the most withering criticism the activities — and especially the motives — of pro-lifers. It seems that no matter how patently absurd or self-serving the pro-abortionists' description of themselves and their activities, all too many media outlets will report it uncritically. How many stories have we endured about the courageous efforts of abortionists to bring abortion facilities to the hinterland? (In their secular proselytizing fervor, Planned Parenthood's minions are not unlike traditional missionaries; each is bringing "the fruits of civilization" to the natives.) By contrast, how many times has the *New York Times* played taps for the pro-life movement?

A closer look reveals that the media elite's receptivity to the siren call of the pro-abortionists goes far deeper than conscious bias and a commonality of values. Judging from their stories, the elite shares with pro-abortionists an extremely distorted and warped view of who makes up the pro-life movement.

One needn't read extensively or watch many 7:00 p.m. newscasts to understand that the media elite has a very definite composite picture of who the opponents of abortion are. Pro-lifers (and even more so, pro-family people) are synonymous with repression, political and sexual. The buzz words practically leap off their typewriters: puritan, prudish, Victorian, rigid, repressed, hysterical, etc.

Thus, it is no surprise that the pro-life movement is most often compared not to the abolition or to the civil rights movement but to Prohibition. To the media elite, we are self-evidently a band of latter-day Comstockians, ill-at-ease with the twentieth century and, therefore, irrelevant.

But why? Why are we pegged as prigs and not as civil rights crusaders? One possible explanation for this is suggested by Rothman and Lichter in their book, *The Roots of Radicalism*, in which they offer convincing evidence for the enduring importance of the early 1950's study by Max Horkheimer and T.W. Adorno, *The Authoritarian Personality.*

Essentially an explanatory tool to analyze the rise of European totalitarian regimes, the idea of an authoritarian personality made a successful migration to the United States where, in a slightly different form, it was applied to a vastly different context. Although the subject of ferocious dispute virtually from the day it was first espoused, the notion of an authoritarian personality structure had, as Rothman and Lichter pointed out, "a major impact on American social science by identifying some traditional American social values with an authoritarian personality structure."

This traditionalist-as-closet-fascist idea persists today and makes its appearance in an attenuated form whenever liberals are "explaining" what motivates those who are traditional, especially with regard to matters of sexual ethics. Tucked away in the sarcasm and cheap-shots, is the media elite's quite correct assumption that most pro-lifers do not share the elite's libertine sexual ethics. The penalty for this disagreement is to be identified, often explicitly, with the stunted psycho-social personalities Horkheimer and Adorno attribute to those who adhere to traditional values.

Moreover, as indicated earlier, the values and positions of the typical member of the media elite and members of the Abortion Establishment are similar. This is made clear by comparing Rothman and Lichter's results with those of sociologist Donald Granberg. Granberg surveyed the leadership of both the National Abortion Rights Action League and the National Right to Life Committee. Without attributing conscious motivation, the results of this similarity between the values of the media elite and the Abortion Establishment have been a media elite willing to wipe away all the unsightly blemishes of abortion proponents and, when that has not proven feasible, to ignore them altogether. Thus, when perfervid abortionists routinely utter the most outrageous racist remarks; or when abortion supporters testify that aborting women have the "right" to a dead fetus; or when a professor like Peter Singer unfavorably compares the capacities of a severely handicapped newborn with a pig or a dog, nary a word shows up in the *Washington Post*, or on *CBS*, or in *Newsweek*.

As eagerly as the media elite pats the pro-abortion movement on the back, it goes for the pro-life movement's throat. We can do nothing right. We are forever imposing morality, manhandling and bullying women, forcing compulsory pregnancy on unwilling women, etc., etc. Every once in awhile a bone of sorts will be thrown: we are sincere if deluded fanatics. On the whole, the message is unambiguous: pro-lifers are exceedingly dangerous, particularly to the political system.

What little chance pro-lifers do have rests on the slender reed of journalistic "objectivity." Unfortunately, this formerly sacrosanct rule of journalistic ethics has been eroded beyond recognition. A detailed explanation of this most regrettable turn of events is beyond the scope of this essay, but it begins with the fact that many reporters have convinced themselves that too often the rule of objectivity has turned them into unwilling dupes of right-wing politicians.

All this changed with Vietnam and Watergate. One of the many aftershocks of these traumatic experiences was enhanced reportorial freedom. Under the guise of "giving context," reporters now had the right to interject an interpretation of what the speaker's "real" motivation was rather than merely rehashing what he had said. The possibilities for abuse are as prevalent as they are obvious.

Equally important when trying to comprehend our problems with the media elite is that when we talk about the right to life of unborn children, about the responsibilities that accompany rights, about justice for a tiny unseen victim, we offer life in all its complexity. It is not conducive to the simple black and white, good guy, bad guy categories so favored by the media.

Yet are we not told (interminably) how well-educated the new breed of reporters are? No more shady, besotten characters out of *The Front Page*. What is there, then, about Washington reporters and/or the media elite that make them so ill-at-ease with complexity and imperfect solutions? It is, I would suggest, the media personality type.

According to Stephen Hess in his book, *The Washington Reporters*, the typical reporter lusts after "instant gratification," understandable in a profession that is expected to produce wisdom on a daily basis in forty column inches or less. Uncomfortable with abstractions, these reporters (some of whom would fall into Rothman and Lichter's media elite) are action-oriented, ever on the prowl for variety and excitement in their work. What Hess has to say about the exceptional self-absorption of Washington reporters is worth repeating. There is, Hess writes, "a solipsistic quality about reporters and politicians, their sense that nothing can exist if it is not part of their own experiences." What ought to be obvious by now is that we are decidedly *not* part of the elite journalist's experience.

Compounding the difficulty for us is what Hess accurately describes as the Washington reporter's comically-inept journey into "social science" journalism. By the very nature of the daily journalistic grind, even the elite reporters vastly simplify reality in their accounts. The real rub comes when they try to get the "story behind the story": that is, to explain what forces "cause" the events they report. Not trained in the techniques of original research, temperamentally unsuited for a time-consuming search after evidence, what all too often happens is that "good journalists may become bad social scientists," as Hess observes. Essentially storytellers, "specialists in immediacy, chroniclers of the day," the media elite is like a fish out of water when attempting to deal with multifaceted, complex phenomena like abortion and infanticide.

The beauty of the pro-abortion position vis-a-vis reporters is its claim to simplistic, twenty minute solutions. Come in over lunch, they tell young women, and we'll remove that troublesome growth; it's of no more significance than having an unsightly mole removed. Pro-lifers never pretend there are easy answers; their solutions are always less than perfect because people — and life itself — are not simple. Pro-lifers would never kid themselves or women by denying there are problem pregnancies. Many times, making the right decision requires great courage and character. What individual pro-lifers do promise is to do whatever they can to help women in their time of need to make life-affirming decisions. [See the final section of this book.]

Although dismissed as a routine medical "procedure," abortion not only has short and long-term dangers to the mother, it entails and reveals more about basic human needs and emotions than any other single social act. Abortion, in short, is profoundly complex. To ask reporters to understand that the woman is victimized not when she is *prevented* from abortion but when she *does* abort is asking a lot. But it is nigh on impossible to expect generalists to comprehend the pain of an unseen victim.

Abortion proponents save reporters the trouble of delving deeply. It is no accident that the level of pro-abortion argument has not advanced in twenty years past the coathanger and the picture of a politician elbowing his way into your bed. Such propaganda is intellectually indefensible, but we must remember that the mind is not the pro-abortionist's target. What they desire are images that preclude reason, that are so emotionally charged that the mind quickly accedes and moves on to other issues.

One final point is worth mentioning. Whether one is

talking about the 1960's NARAL demagoguery about 1,000,000 illegal abortions per year and the deaths of 10,000 women or the current nonsense about imprisoning women who have miscarriages, the pro-abortion movement has never felt constrained by such niceties as truth. For them, language is a tool to be used in whatever way furthers their objectives. This brings to mind George Orwell's great essay, *Politics and the English Language*. Orwell warned that "the great enemy of clear language is insincerity." Replete with meaningless words, euphemisms, and hackneyed phrases, such language, Orwell wrote, is employed by those determined to hide the gap between their real aims and their declared aims.

Orwell's remarks shed a great deal of light on the remarkable successes of the modern pro-abortion movement. What is most astonishing about the enemies of the unborn (and increasingly the handicapped newborn) is the extent to which they successfully alternate between examples of what Orwell would instantly recognize as outrageous duplicity and an almost barbaric candor.

In the first instance, the listener is disarmed by the reassuring sound of words like "privacy," "freedom," and "choice." A recent example is the extension of the "right" of privacy to justify infanticide. Even the handicapped newborn, it is alleged, has these privacy rights. Unable to exercise them, the child needs his parents to make his privacy rights operational. Only in this instance, the right under discussion is the right to die chosen *for* the baby *by* his parents.

On the other hand, when the anti-life types go too far, the message tends to be so revolting to most people's sensibilities that they are apt to dismiss the comments as the babblings of a slightly deranged mind. An example of this is the aforementioned Singer commentary. But in either case, the damage is done. We begin to think about the unthinkable either because of the loving way it is packaged or because we feel the need to denounce the idea. In the "liberated" media elite, pro-abortionists find an enthusiastic ally. Daily journalism, by definition, is the chronicler of the new, the different, and the immediate. This is even more true with the media elite, which is ready at the drop of a hat to exlore new ideas, the more provocative and the more outrageous the better.

What is Ahead

After outlining the media's chronic weaknesses, bias, and tunnel vision, it may seem strange to conclude on a hopeful note. But a close reading of media coverage of our issue of late suggests our press clippings will improve. This is for reasons that have little to do with a new found appreciation for pro-lifers but with the nature of the information coming to light.

For example, there is the revolution in medical technology, reports of which are virtually saturating the popular and scholarly press. Notice that no matter what a reporter's position or intent, when he or she, obviously amazed, writes of the reality of unborn babies learning while in the womb, or when they detail the miracle of *in utero* surgery, the reader is propelled to consider the common humanity shared by himself and the tiny passenger in the womb. (One can also hope some of the life-affirming message of this incredible research will rub off on reporters.)

In addition there are a myriad of little signs suggesting the picture is getting brighter. Reporters needn't like pro-lifers to have a grudging admiration for our refusal to fade away. That theme shone through unmistakably in many stories detailing the tenth anniversary of *Roe v. Wade*. Just by stubbornly holding on, the movement forced the media to deal with the question, "What about abortion after ten years and 15 million "procedures?" Just by keeping the case for the unborn alive, the pro-life movement forces reporters to talk about both sides of the controversy.

Another example of more balanced coverage were the stories written about the 1983 National Right to Life Committee convention. All in all, the stories were quite positive. The story in — of all places — the *New York Times* was not only accurate but, in some ways, highly complimentary. Part of the reason this gradual transformation is occuring is that pro-lifers have taken a leaf out of the pro-abortion book: they, too, are cultivating the media. Since it is impossible to be as bad as they believe we are, contacts with the press will inevitably break down media stereotypes.

Moreover, the language of civil rights is creeping into coverage of the pro-life movement. This breakthrough is of towering importance, for not only are most representatives of the press corp favorably disposed towards civil rights groups, it is the truth. The pro-life movement is *the* civil rights movement of the 1980s; the more this is known the better are the babies' chances.

This is not to say everything is coming up roses. By and large, the political press will never have any use for us. The substance of what we are fighting for — the lives of unborn children — is almost a nuisance to them. They are locked into what I have called anti-anti-abortionism, and the prospects for change are not bright.

Yet even the political press is not immune to the stories about fetal therapy and the efforts of pro-life groups to aid women in need. Whether they ever moderate their vituperation is problematic, but it is becoming increasingly difficult for political reporters to maintain the fiction that the abortion issue is little more than an irritant, an obstacle to the consideration of more important items.

Unlike our opposition, we will never enjoy a boisterous, vocal media cheering section. But we will settle for a media that reports the abortion issue factually and truthfully. The media need not like the pro-life movement. That is their right, provided they print the untainted truth. When they do, when the blinders come off and the unborn are recognized as fellow human beings, then the "long night of discrimination, injustice, and oppression" will at last come to an end.

PART IV

TECHNOLOGY: THE DOUBLE-EDGED SWORD

Medical technology, progressing at breakneck speed, is "rehumanizing" the unborn child. Replete with space-age-sounding names such as sonography, fetoscopy, hysteroscopy, amniography, amniocentesis, and ultra-sound B-scanners, these breakthroughs are proving beyond cavil that the unborn child is alive, human, an individual entity separate from his or her mother, and the tiniest member of the human family. So self-evident is the unborn's status that some doctors now speak of the need to recognize a new stage in human development — "prenatality."

In this section, Professor William Brennan and Dr. Bernard Nathanson explore the life-affirming and life-denying potential of the new technology. Both warn that technological data and scientific perceptions do not exist in a moral vacuum. In the wrong hands, these techniques can be used to further exploit and ravage the smallest humans. Nancy Koster worries about the consequences for humanity of the quest for perfection, the blurring of what it means to be human, which is at the heart of genetic engineering.

BIOTECHNOLOGY AND THE SANCTITY OF HUMAN LIFE

Nancy Koster*

"We have paid some high prices for the technological conquest of nature, but none so high as the intellectual and spiritual costs of seeing nature as mere material for our manipulation, exploitation and transformation. With the power for biological engineering now gathering, there will be splendid new opportunities for a similar degradation of our view of man."

DR. LEON KASS

Suppose you are trying to describe for someone the beauty of the Mona Lisa. Suppose also that when your listener looks at the painting, he doesn't see the lady with the mystic smile, but only a collection of brush strokes and random splotches of color. How can you convince him that daVinci's masterpiece, rather than a page from the Sunday comics, deserves a place on

*Nancy Koster has a degree in journalism and for ten years has been editor of Minnesota Citizens Concerned for Life's monthly newsletter. She also serves as a vice-president of MCCL. She and her husband, an attorney, live in Minneapolis with their five children.

the wall of the Louvre?

Those who have engaged in debate with an advocate of abortion undoubtedly feel they have faced almost as arduous a task. Where the sanctity of life proponent sees in the unborn child a beautiful, complex, well-ordered marvel truly to be wondered at and protected, the pro-abortionist sees a piece of protoplasm, a clump of cells, or, in one Minnesota woman's words, a "black cancer."

This myopia clouds not only the vision some people have of the unborn but also many of their other views: fertility and pregnancy are not seen as normal, essential human processes, but rather as diseases to be controlled, prevented, or thwarted by almost any means. A handicapped newborn is not regarded as someone with problems to be overcome; instead, the baby *is* the problem, to be hidden away or perhaps destroyed. And an old person is viewed not as venerable and valuable because he remains a human being, but as an intolerable drain on emotional and financial resources because he is senile and sickly. Yes, it has been difficult to defend life when some do not see its beauty. And yet, forces at work in our post-*Roe v. Wade* society threaten to scramble perceptions even further and to make the task of the pro-lifer, already difficult, even more formidable.

Early arguments defended abortion as more or less a necessary evil; the child's death was decided supposedly "in necessity and sorrow." More sophisticated apologias are emerging today aimed at enthroning it as a positive good, a course of action as defensible as giving birth, if not more so. It's not the first time advocates of an untenable moral position have sought justification by encouraging others not only to tolerate such views but eventually to affirm their moral rightness.

As Professor John Noonan has pointed out, pro-slavery forces could have been content to confine the practice to the South where it generally was accepted.

Instead they were compelled to insist on its spread westward and northward, not so much to create new markets for the slave trade as to secure approbation for their challenged morality.

Nevertheless, one senses that something deeper is precipitating the metamorphosis from abortion as a tragic necessity to abortion (and kindred evils) as a beneficence. It may well have something to do with the explosion in biotechnology that is attacking the very foundations of traditional regard for human life.

In his book *Algeny,* Jeremy Rifkin propounds a theory that may shed some light on the path we are traveling so rapidly. Its relevance to the abortion question may not be immediately clear, but it positively jumps out when considered thoughtfully and carefully. Rifkin argues that throughout history, societies have developed cosmologies to describe the operation of nature and to define man's place in it. Although it is never recognized at the time, each of these world views has been a deception — not an objective description of nature's laws at all, but rather a means to justify the way society happened to be operating at that point in history.

Thus Darwin's theory, for example, with its emphasis on "survival of the fittest" and "natural selection," reflected the British industrial society of his day, in which those who worked hard got along and passed the fruits of their labor on to their children, while those who didn't work or somehow were unable to function in the new age of the machine fell by the wayside, thus freeing the social body of their "undesirable influence."

Darwin saw nature as moving with glacial slowness, each evolutionary change depending on the happy chance that a deviant characteristic might prove beneficial to an organism, allowing it to survive longer and leave more progeny to perpetuate the useful trait. Although in this scheme unfit individual organisms were doomed, the process in the long run was seen always to promote the common good. To attempt radical change in nature or in the social fabric, especially with the aim of benefiting the "unproductive," then became an "unnatural" and futile exercise.

Questions of scientific validity aside, Darwin's theory, like other cosmologies, was a way for man to convince himself that how he was behaving was the way nature intended — and because it was "natural," it was unarguably right. Rifkin argues that gradually the Darwinian world view is being replaced by a new and equally deceptive cosmology. The concept of evolution, remains the core to be sure, but grafted on are elements of the new and rapidly developing fields of genetics and cybernetics. Its metaphor is no longer the machine but — what else? — the computer.

No parent, surely, can doubt the pervasive influence of the computer on daily life. Kids, some not much more than toddlers, can be found in rec rooms and arcades across the nation in mesmerized oneness with beeping, flashing, and buzzing devices of all description, the function and operation of which many of those raised pre-Atari can only surmise.

Besides helping the child recreate, computers are a fixture of his learning environment (is there a school that doesn't use them to teach math and reading skills?), and "computer literacy" is an established goal of secondary and even primary education.

Rifkin argues that children (like many of their elders) are coming to see the world as a computable domain. Their world becomes less a place to be born into than something to program. The advent of the computer parallels in importance the invention of writing as an influence on how man will conceptualize and communicate with his world. In the machine model of the industrial age, nature was the sum total of individual, distinct organisms doing specifically what their heredity had equipped them for. In the computer model, organisms instead are temporal systems containing millions of bits of information capable of being rearranged in an almost infinite number of ways. Because he is fast acquiring the power to do so, man feels entitled to assume the role of programmer.

Just as the alchemists of an earlier age thought their tinkering could create gold, the "perfect metal" (a goal they believed every other metal was striving for in its own, less efficient way), the "algenists" of the age of biotechnology believe that through genetic tinkering they can help give rise to a perfect human being. The implications of this perception are as ominous as they are obvious. For the algenist, no living creature is a finished product. Everything is a temporality, and each organism is merely on its way to becoming something else, struggling toward perfection or, in this world view, optimum efficiency. The new cosmology eschews Darwin's natural selection, a ponderously slow business, for a theory of "punctuated equilibrium," which holds that the evolutionary process remains relatively static for long periods, occasionally undergoing rapid periods of speciation.

Scientists' developing control over human heredity and reproduction, in addition to their new-found power to cross species boundaries by combining genetic material from one organism with that of a totally different one, are projected onto nature; if man can redesign living creatures and the way they procreate without taking millions of years, nature must be able to do likewise. Further, since survival of the "best informed" is the watchword of the new cosmology, bioengineering merely speeds up nature's processes by putting more and better information into an organism quicker. It's a logical extension of, rather than a radical departure from, the way nature works ... or so the theory goes.

So it is, Rifkin says, that the algenists err as the Darwinists did. They take a small piece of reality and enshrine it as a universal truth. Then they justify what they are doing and want to do by demonstrating its "naturalness." They silence critics by pointing out that it's futile to stand in the path of Mother Nature and the inevitable.

Every daring new venture — from cloning lower animals, fashioning genes from laboratory chemicals, synthesizing cells, fusing cells from different species, and changing the original instructions of a cell by introducing extraneous material (which is being done), to curing disease by repairing or replacing defective genes, building "better" human beings by changing their genetic make-up, and altering human germ cells to improve the heredity of offspring (which are envisioned) — all of this and more becomes not "playing God" but merely enhancing natural processes.

If Rifkin's theory has validity, and I believe it does, there are profound implications for the issues which traditionally have concerned the pro-life movement.

The quest for perfection, the notion that man is the architect of his own heredity and the blurring of what it means to be human are mainstays of the new world view. They also underlie many of the justifications for abortion, infanticide, and euthanasia and the increasing attempts to make objections to them obsolete if not reprehensible.

After all, if every living thing is merely "in potentia," it can't matter much if you end its existence. (Abortion advocates claim that like the egg and sperm, the fetus is only "potential life" and therefore expendable.) If it's nature's way to move ever closer to optimum efficiency, it cannot be wrong to facilitate the process. (They argue that defective fetuses routinely are eliminated through spontaneous miscarriage, so eugenic abortion precipitated purposely is also natural.) And if being human requires the possession of an ability to use sufficient information to carry on a meaningful relationship with one's environment, those who have never developed or have lost such ability do not qualify. (It is suggested that those lacking cortical function be classified among the "brain dead.")

Hence, to abort a "defective" child (especially one with mental handicaps), to fail to feed an injured newborn, or to withdraw treatment from a dysfunctional old person (and eventually to require others to do these things) all are merely giving nature a helping hand. Further, those who may still feel a bit squeamish about the methods by which nature is to be assisted are accused of irresponsibility. If there were a concept of sin in the new cosmology, the most mortal sin would have to be allowing a defective being to exist (and possibly to procreate) if you could do something about it. "Not to control when we can is immoral," as bioethicist Joseph Fletcher asserts.

Cecil B. Jacobson, a George Washington University geneticist, has said he "can't imagine any reasonably responsible person arguing against the abortion of mongols (sic)." Even if the unborn child is not afflicted with but is only a carrier of a genetic anomaly, Jacobson sees an obligation to deny survival. He suggests that daughters in a family of hemophiliacs, who don't exhibit the disease but can pass it on to sons, should be eliminated. "Unfortunately, only by aborting normal people in this generation can we spare the next generation from the burden of some forms of genetic disease," he contends.

As if this were not enough, he asks what parents would want to bear a child who will die of cancer at age 40 if the tendency to develop the disease could be detected before birth (a possibility well within the grasp of scientists working today). If potential cancer victims could be identified, Jacobson says, "I would favor aborting them now. That would eliminate some types of cancer forever."

The inherent fallacy in all of this is pointed out by Mayo Clinic geneticist Dr. Hymie Gordon, who says that because every person is the carrier of a number of "bad" genes, the only way to eliminate genetic diseases is to abort or sterilize everyone.

But what's important is not whether we actually can "cleanse" the gene pool or significantly alter the human genome, but rather the idea that it's "natural" to try. If we accept this notion, we change basic, concepts of what it means to be human, and in the process we cannot help but seriously devalue our offspring and ourselves. For example, one "human" characteristic we traditionally have prided ourselves on is our concern for the weak and the young. Elephants may abandon an injured herd member and gerbils may eat their babies, but we humans (theoretically, at least) take care of our own, especially our "flesh and blood."

However, when our children may be conceived in the laboratory from genetic material donated by others; when they probably soon will be transferred into and out of our wombs almost at will, our physical connection to them becomes less and less. Furthermore, when we can eliminate them pre- or even post-natally when they don't meet specifications, our emotional identification is diminished as well. Home, once described as the place where, when you went there they had to take you in, now bolts its doors against you if you lack the qualifications for family membership and then draws its drapes so those within will be spared the sight of you succumbing to your imperfections. The implications for the nuclear family, already beset from all sides, and for the obligations owed by parents to their children (and vice versa) are staggering.

Not the least of them is the burden placed on siblings of babies aborted or denied care and feeding after birth for eugenic reasons. How is a child to bear the knowledge (which may come to him in a number of overt and subtle ways) that his parents deliberately rejected a sick brother or sister (or, likewise, an ailing grandparent)? For as the late renowned fetologist Sir. A. W. Liley has pointed out, there is nothing a baby is born with that others can't develop through disease or accident.

For that matter, how do parents themselves bear these decisions, even if freely made? Some research, notably that by geneticist John Fletcher of the Hastings Center, suggests that trust relationships are indeed damaged in many families when amniocentesis is used to detect genetic abnormalities. "Even if the diagnosis ... were negative, you have nonetheless entertained the idea of the death of your baby," he says.

When you do eliminate a genetically damaged offspring, you kill, literally, a part of yourself. And afterward the defect still lurks deep within you, capable of manifesting itself again for as long as you are alive. Also, traditionally, we have valued our human imperfections and peculiarities, commending ourselves for our toleration of those who are "different." Just as we recognize that diversity is necessary for a species to adapt to changing physical environments, we have looked upon it as necessary to the success of our social organizations as well. (Despite our pride in the great American melting pot, we decline to throw into it many of our cherished ethnic and cultural treasures.)

We have also recognized that many of the things we value — from a Toulouse-Lautrec painting to the inspiration of a Helen Keller to the unconditional love received from a child with Down's syndrome — all this and so much more have come from "imperfect" people. When someone pleads, "I'm only human," he's not just excusing a mistake or lapse in conduct; he's saying something profound about our very essence that, until now at least, we have not been eager to give up.

What does the algenist's promise of a perfect human, achievable or not, do to this self-concept? The whole brouhaha over who qualifies as a "person," and thus is deserving of legal protection, gets a lot stickier when the definition of "humanness," whether applied to the unborn or the born, may depend on what characteristics the biotechnologists are seeking to engineer in and out at a particular time.

Also devastating to traditional conceptions of humanity is the growing notion that most behavior is genetically determined ("There can be no twisted thought without a twisted molecule," says a prominent neurophysiologist) and that we literally *are* our genes. It even has been argued that the body is but a vessel to contain the genes until they are passed on to progeny (a chicken is merely an egg's way of making another egg, it is said).

Things become even more problematical when we add in the ability to combine genetic material between species. The worry is not that scientists will produce a monkey-man or a human cabbage, but rather that we are fostering a mind-set that sees life, human or otherwise, merely as a collection of chemicals and that anything one might wish to do with them is not only acceptable but another step up the evolutionary ladder.

Thus the pro-life advocate in the age of biotechnology faces a double challenge. His adversaries will continue to oppose legal protection for the lives of all human beings, but they will also dispute the very fact that many of those lives can be classified as human in the first place, and they will fight for abortion, infanticide, and euthanasia as practices in perfect accord with the laws of nature.

So, back at the museum, what *are* we going to say to the fellow bent on using the Mona Lisa as a dart board? Although the communication gap is widening to a chasm, we must attempt to bridge it, bolstered by the conviction that unlike Leonardo daVinci, who is no longer able to defend his work, the Artist who fashioned man and nature still has a hand in His creation.

I think I might start by assuring the brave new biotechnologist that there are many of us left who, although we may not be able to define precisely what a masterpiece is, know one when we see one. And I would tell him that we will not go gentle into a world that refuses to give such a masterpiece the respect it deserves.

ABORTION TECHNOLOGY AND FETAL THERAPY: ON A COLLISION COURSE

William Brennan, Ph.D.*

"The killing center is the reductio ad absurdum of all health planning."

LEO ALEXANDER, *Medical Science Under Dictatorship.*

Contrary to pro-abortion mythology, the greatest threat to today's abortion-industrial complex does not come from heavy-handed tactics of the so-called radical right or the imposition of sectarian morality by alleged religious zealots, but from fetologists and surgeons pioneering radical new methods of treating unborn children.

The life-enhancing thrust of fetal surgery stands in stark opposition to the life-denying emphasis of

*William Brennan is a professor of social services at St. Louis University. His first book, *Medical Holocausts* (1980), is a thorough analysis of medical involvement in the destruction of unwanted human life in Nazi Germany and contemporary America. His most recent book is *The Abortion Holocaust: Today's Final Solution.* He has written numerous articles for both professional and popular journals.

abortion technology. Each advance in fetal therapy will crystallize the inherent contradiction between the therapeutic medicine of fetologists and the exterminative medicine of the abortionists. To understand why fetology is threatening the very foundation of abortion, it is important to understand the "genius" of mass destruction.

To be able to kill human beings on a massive scale requires many things, but most of all the ability to dehumanize the victims and to kill them in secrecy. In the Third Reich, Jews were described as "useless eaters," "trash," and "subhuman." Most Jews were asphyxiated inside gas chamber walls where their death agonies could not be seen or heard. Similarly, in the past twenty years, the healthy, vibrant unborn child has been transformed linguistically into a "parasite," "a black cancer," and "fetal tissue." Most abortion victims are also killed quietly, in this case, inside the walls of the uterus where the process of dismemberment and salt poisoning goes on out of sight both of the mother and of society at large.

This awesome ability of modern destructive technology to keep the victims' plight concealed goes a long way toward explaining and reinforcing the myth that there is no victim. The Nazis took then-current technology such as gas ovens and expanded their size and "efficiency" enabling them to kill on an unbelievable scale. Similarly, today's abortionists were unable to kill on a massive scale until the importation of the suction curettage machine, a "gift," ironically, from the Communist Chinese.

Modern Medicine Against Itself

The womb as a surgical theater for the unborn is the perfect paradigm for the schizophrenic world of contemporary medicine where killing and curing share a perverse state of professional compatibility. Developments in fetal therapy will, however, make it increasingly difficult to ignore, let alone tolerate, the deplorable condition of modern medical ethics in which too many physicians have regressed back to the dark age of pre-Hippocratic medicine where they once again function in the schizophrenic role of killer-healer.

The miracle technologies of ultrasound, fetoscopy, and hysteroscopy have opened up unprecedented windows on the womb. They reveal compellingly that the tiny passenger within is nothing less than a bona fide human being from the very onset of pregnancy, and they make the surgical treatment of that unborn human being increasingly routine. Planned Parenthood executive Alfred Moran warned his cohorts at a National Abortion Federation meeting in 1982 that "we are going to find ourselves isolated" unless "we are prepared to begin to recognize that technology and medical sciences and perceptions of fetal viability are radically changing in our society." He was particularly horrified by the potential that the new life-promoting fetal therapy has for jeopardizing the right to abortion: "We begin to see the fetus as a patient; which tends to personalize it," he observed.

Every time the unborn child becomes the beneficiary of treatment formerly reserved for those after birth, a spotlight of increasing intensity is focused on the inherent humanity of life in the womb. The implementation of abortion technology — built on a depersonalized, anachronistic perception of unwanted unborn children as pregnancy tissue or subhuman entities — is running on a direct collision course with the science of fetology, which is forging powerful, personalized images of the fetus as a legitimate patient deserving the best care and treatment possible. The consequences of this strongly emerging perception are far-reaching. It is but a short step from the image of the fetus as a legitimate patient to a view of the fetus as a legal person with constitutional rights.

A New Phase of the Human Life Cycle

Progress in fetal surgery contains the seeds of even more profound revolutionary and long-term outcomes than saving human lives in the womb and personalizing the unborn. In the *New England Journal of Medicine* (February 17, 1983) Drs. Mark I. Evans and John C. Fletcher report on the cases of two pregnant women (one in the late first trimester and the other in the early second trimester) who decided against abortion after seeing ultrasonic pictures of their unborn children. The authors indicate that such an experience precipitated the onset of maternal bonding — the propensity of the mother to form a close emotional attachment with her baby.

Such evidence of intrauterine bonding during the early stages of pregnancy may well represent, according to Evans and Fletcher, part of a vast evolutionary process which will result in the establishment of a new stage of human existence — "prenatality" — a phenomenon as momentous as the many centuries of cultural and biological evolution leading to the recognition of childhood as a differentiated stage of the human life cycle. Dr. A. W. Liley's brilliant portrayal of the fetus as a personality in *Australia and New Zealand Journal of Psychiatry* in 1972 was a major forerunner of this development. His characterization of the unborn as a splendidly functioning baby rather than a poorly functioning adult provided much of the attitudinal and empirical legacy responsible for the dramatic increase in today's therapeutic efforts on behalf of the unborn now viewed as a human being existing at a legitimate phase of the human life continuum.

Through the creation of such semantic distortions as "products of conception" and "only the potentiality of life," pro-abortionists have been alarmingly effective in blocking recognition of intrauterine life as a legitimate stage in the human life cycle. To confer a status on prenatal development comparable to childhood, adolescence, and adulthood strikes at the very foundation of pro-abortion rhetoric. Such recognition would deal the anti-life forces a devastating blow.

Anti-Life Responses and Pro-Life Counter-responses

Pro-abortionists are building a set of powerful justifications for the continuation and expansion of abortion technology even in an era when the saving of unborn children will become a dominant activity of many doctors. It behooves members of the pro-life movement to get a handle on these rationalizations for killing the unborn and learn how best to counteract them. Reading the annals of Nazi medicine offers a promising approach for challenging the pro-abortion arguments, which are strikingly similar.

Although the spectacular advances in fetal therapy may force more of those in the pro-abortion camp to acknowledge the destructive nature of abortion technology, it is unlikely that they will relinquish their commitment to destroying the unwanted unborn in the most efficient manner possible. All indicators point to the increased promotion of abortion as a noble endeavor containing many indispensable benefits. This strategy will be particularly intensified in two areas: prenatal diagnosis for the detection of defects, and fetal experimentation.

Amniocentesis in conjunction with ultrasound expand the capacity to identify a growing number of abnormalities and handicaps before birth. These techniques of identification are being hailed as making significant contributions to the prevention of birth defects because those identified as defective in the womb can then be aborted. This has the effect of elevating destruction of the "unfit" to the highest level of altruism.

A blatant instance of sophisticated technology in the service of killing-redefined-as-benevolence was reported on at a press conference in June 1981. Drs. Thomas Kerenyi and Usha Chitkara of Mount Sinai Medical School in New York City announced they had killed an unwanted unborn twin with Down's syndrome by piercing his heart with a needle and extracting half his blood. Amniocentesis diagnosed Down's syndrome in one of the twins, and ultrasound enabled these medical executioners to "hit a moving target [the afflicted twin's heart] less than an inch across." This phrase surely smacks of a precision-type military operation directed against an enemy! This act of scientific barbarism was characterized by those who perpetrated it as "a very gratifying experience" on two counts: the elimination of an unwanted unfit twin and the saving of a wanted normal twin.

At this point it needs to be emphasized that eugenics as a justification for destroying the afflicted before birth did not originate with the doctors of Mount Sinai. Eugenic abortion was pioneered by the physicians of the Third Reich as one of the beginning steps toward purging Germany of its unfit elements. The echoes of Nazi-style medicine are unmistakably clear today: the "curing" of afflictions by eradicating the afflicted.

Another tactic can be seen in the attitude of a growing number of doctors and abortion proponents who concede that abortion is unpleasant and even destructive, but nonetheless maintain that the list of benefits to be derived from experimentation on unborn babies slated for death transforms abortion into a worthwhile endeavor after all. Dr. Lawrence Lawn of Cambridge University explained it this way: "We are simply using something which is destined for the incinerator to benefit mankind." Fetal research advocates Drs. Willard Gaylin and Mare Lappe declared that the death of the "doomed fetus" chosen for abortion "can be ennobled" through experimentation because the information produced can be utilized for "the saving of the lives (or the reduction of defects) of other, wanted fetuses."

It should be pointed out that the Nazi doctors, although expressing some regrets, invoked a similar justification for experiments conducted on concentration camp inmates destined for the gas chambers: they held great potential for making significant contributions to humanity. "These condemned men will at least make themselves useful," stated Nazi researcher Dr. August Hirt. "Wouldn't it be ridiculous to execute them and send their bodies to the crematory oven without giving them an opportunity to contribute to the progress of society?" At the Nuremberg Doctors' Trial, Dr. Gerhard Rose asserted that "the victims of this Buchenwald typhus test did not suffer in vain and did not die in vain." Countless numbers of people, he assured the court, "were saved by these experiments."

There seems to be no end to the "altruistic" reasons put forth for exploiting the bodies and organs of aborted babies. Medical researchers at the University of California at Los Angeles are working on a technique involving transplanting the pancreas from aborted children for the purpose of curing diabetes. Scientists at Clark University in Worcester, Massachusetts reported that they have dramatically improved the learning ability of rats with severely damaged brains by implanting fresh brain tissue from rat fetuses. The next step in this therapeutic-sounding "Brave New World" of unlimited experimental exploitation is the extraction of brain tissue from aborted human beings for treatment of people with brain damage.

This is not the first time, however, that the bodies of the unwanted slated for obliteration have been utilized as spare parts for the wanted segments of society. It was the Nazi medics who trail-blazed the removal of body parts from unwanted, doomed human beings. Their professed motivation for doing so was just as beneficent as that of today's researchers. In what became known as the "Bone, Muscle and Nerve Regeneration, and Bone Transplantation Experiments" conducted at the Ravensbrueck concentration camp, the arms, shoulder blades, or legs of female inmates were amputated and transported to a nearby hospital where they were used "in the attempt to heal the injured limbs of wounded German soldiers."

A tragic irony intrinsic to concentration camp and fetal research is that, in both cases, the victims have not been considered important enough to merit the right to life, but their value jumps dramatically when it comes to draining out of them every possible ounce of information, blood, and tissue for the benefit of science and humanity. Auschwitz survivor Dr. Gisella Pearl put it aptly when she related how the fear of contamination with "inferior Jewish blood" was forgotten in the process of extracting blood from Jewish inmates to aid German soldiers: "We were too 'inferior' to live, but not too inferior to keep the German army alive with our blood."

It cannot be reiterated enough that many in the pro-abortion movement are hard core fanatics totally dedicated to the right to choose to kill the being in the womb. Abortion proponents are not about to give up their commitment even in the face of revolutionary advances in prenatal surgery. Abortion will be increasingly promoted as a humanitarian method of preventing many social and other problems associated with *unwanted* individuals, while intrauterine therapy will be welcomed because it helps children *wanted* before birth to survive. In arguing that fetal surgery has moral considerations only for "wanted" babies, staunch abortion supporter Judith Pasternak of the American Civil Liberties Union's Reproductive Freedom Project, put it this way: "For thousands of years, healers have been trying to preserve the lives and health of fetuses whose mothers wanted them; only the sophisticated techniques and the rate of success are new."

The employment of physicians and medical procedures for both killing and healing, based on the criterion of wantedness, reflects a blatant form of doublethink straight out of George Orwell's *1984*. It is also this same kind of perverse compatibility between killing and healing which made the Third Reich possible. Many of the German doctors responsible for crimes against humanity in euthanasia hospitals and concentration camps had also made outstanding contributions to combating diseases.

In the latter part of 1939, for example, four mentally ill patients were gassed to death. This was the first successful gas chamber experiment. It was not conducted, however, by Nazi sadists, but by distinguished psychiatrists from the leading medical schools in Germany. It took place at Sonnenstein, a psychiatric institution with a long tradition of humane treatment of mental patients.

Killing and healing are running on a technological collision course. They must not be allowed to co-exist; one is the very antithesis of the other. The survival of a truly civilized society where all human beings are respected and protected by law demands that abortion technology be thoroughly repudiated and recognized for what it truly is: an atavistic barbarity comparable to the worst excesses of Nazi medicine.

The sole role of technology, especially medical technology, should be to cure, care for, and heal human lives whatever their status, condition, or stage of development. Unless this sanctity-of-life ethic is established as the prevailing norm, destructive technology run amuk will continue to engulf in its wake an ever-expanding universe of unwanted expendables before and after birth.

TAMING THE RESTLESS BEAST

Bernard Nathanson, M.D.*

"Things fall apart; the center cannot hold.
Mere anarchy is loosed upon the world ..."

The Second Coming: W.B. YEATS

On November 24, 1859 Charles Darwin published his monumental masterwork: "On the Origin of the Species by Means of Natural Selection." The book had germinated in Darwin's mind for a period of twenty-three years, and the published work was a closely reasoned compelling exposition of how the varieties of life on our planet seek out the environment most suitable to their biology, how they struggle for reproductive success, and how minute biological changes brought about through mutations will allow certain varieties to adapt more readily to the environment. The book relied for its authority on the massive collection of

*Dr. Nathanson is a New York Obstetrician-gynecologist. He was co-founder in 1969 of the National Association for the Repeal of Abortion Laws, later renamed the National Abortion Rights Action League. He has since reversed his views on abortion and is one of the best-known and most articulate pro-life advocates in the United States. He is the author (with Richard Ostling) of "Aborting America," and has authored a new book titled "The Abortion Papers."

scientific observations and data which Darwin had accumulated during his five-year voyage of biological exploration between the years 1831 and 1836, on H.M.S. Beagle.

Despite the impeccable scientific reasoning which informed his presentation of the revolutionary theory of natural selection as the dominant force in organic evolution, Darwin was attacked and derided by many of the intellectual lights of the era. Notoriously quick to identify heterodoxy and threatened by what appeared to be an audacious refutation of the teachings of Genesis, clerics in particular assailed him personally and denigrated his theory. The respected natural scientist Samuel Wilberforce, Bishop of Oxford, publically debated the merits of the book at the University Museum of Oxford barely six months after it had appeared, and in the course of the debate the Bishop sarcastically queried of his opponent: "I should like to ask you if you really believe your ancestor was an ape. If so, I should be interested to know something: did that ape come into the family on your grandfather's or grandmother's side?"

The sheer malice of the question, the unbridled vitriol of the debate and the cavalier display of ignorance of the unshakable scientific framework of the Darwinian thesis are strongly reminiscent of the color and tone of the national abortion argument today. With the advent of fetology as a full-fledged medical specialty in 1973 — the year in which ultra-sound technology and electronic fetal heart monitoring emerged from the laboratory and became the everyday clinical tools of modern obstetricians — an immense store of scientific data regarding the human unborn has been compiled.

As an example, Dr. Lyndon Hill at the Mayo Clinic has published a comprehensive review of all the new data we have accumulated regarding the developing organ systems of the unborn by means of ultra-sound technology. His review appears in the July 1983 issue of the journal *Obstetrical and Gynecological Survey*, and his bibliography lists one hundred and sixty-three different sources of information for this one article alone. Hill reviews for us the now-familiar facts: cardiac activity begins in the fourth week of life, muscular movements begin at five weeks of life, and taste buds appear on the tongue at that stage; at five weeks one can stroke the region around the mouth and the unborn will reflexly pull away its head and neck. Electrical activity in the brain begins at six weeks. At ten weeks the ear is fully formed and the palms of the hand are sensitive to light touch. Swallowing commences at ten weeks. He concludes his article thus:

> The fetus can no longer be considered ... as a relatively non-functioning organism until delivery. From an early gestational age the fetus is capable of reacting to and within its environment.

First generation fetologists such as Hill have charted for us the anatomical and functional qualities of the smallest human unborn. Second generation fetologists — fetal physicians and surgeons — have utilized these data to diagnose intra-uterine illness, to medicate the unborn, transfuse it, even perform surgery upon it. Brain surgery on the unborn is no longer a media event, and the administration of drugs and medications to the unborn is rapidly becoming everyday practice in modern fetology and obstetrics.

But technological data and scientific perceptions do not exist in a moral vacuum. It is for humans to draw the morally correct conclusions from these discoveries and to apply them in an ethically acceptable manner. Second generation fetologists have compelled us to regard the human unborn as simply another patient, a person in his/her own right. Now ethicists have emphasized for us the various complex bonding mechanisms which mark the emergence of the unborn as patient. The celebrated editorial piece of Fletcher and Evans in the February 17, 1983 issue of the *New England Journal of Medicine* was the first to call attention to maternal-fetal bonding which establishes itself during ultra-sound examinations in early pregnancy.

Regrettably, the authors were a bit timid in applying these apercus to the larger question of the ethical acceptability of permissive abortion (can a human being to whom another human being becomes bonded fail to be a person?) and left these extra-ordinarily persuasive scientific observations bumping lightly around in the moral vacuum. Other observers have not been quite as reluctant to draw the necessary conclusion and act conscientiously upon them: I, myself, had noted some years ago that a curious bonding occurs during ultra-sound examination in early pregnancy between the unborn and the physician who watches the screen with the mother. It became impossible for me thereafter to regard the unborn — at any stage in the pregnancy, from conception on — as nothing more than meat.

Still other observers have chronicled bonding between fathers and the unborn during ultra-sound viewing, and more recently Dr. Wulf Utian working in an *in-vitro* fertilization program at the Mount Sinai Medical Center in Cleveland has documented bonding between the prospective mother and the dividing fertilized egg. When informed that the division of the egg had ceased, that the egg was no longer viable and therefore unsuitable for implantation into her uterus, one mother stated that she felt as if she had, "... just suffered a stillbirth." Even more astonishing is Utian's entirely unsolicited observation that the medical team conducting the *in-vitro* fertilization program — the physicians, nurses, laboratory technicians and sonographers — became caught up emotionally in the work to the extent that they experienced a bonding to the developing unborn themselves. He states it thus:

> As eggs are collected and fertilization is attempted in the laboratory, there are strong feelings by the team toward the early cleaving embryo ... My experience with an *in-vitro* fertilization program, although also anecdotal, would confirm that "bonding" may occur even before the embryo is placed in the mother's uterus.

Could anyone now deny that the human unborn — even at the earliest stage of its existence — is infinitely more than a mere collection of cells? Defined by the narrow chilly criteria of the Abortion People, "persons" are, after all, nothing more than collections of cells with the capability of establishing social and psychological relationships with other human beings. Now the human unborn has met even that cruel test. What further credentials can the Abortion People demand before the unborn is welcomed into the human community?

Several years ago, in the epilogue of "Aborting America," I concluded that fetology had established beyond cavil that the human unborn was a person inviolable within the moral and legal perimeters of Western civilization, and predicted that technology would lead us out of the abortion dilemma: that the abortion of the future would involve the non-injurious atraumatic removal of the unborn at its earliest stage from the uterus of the unwilling mother for transfer to the uterus of a woman desirous of a child — or to an unimaginably complex life-support system where the child would remain until all organ systems were fully mature. With the perfection and general application of this technology the rights of both parties — mother and unborn — would be respected. The mother would not be required to bear a child against her will and the right to life of the unborn would be fully preserved.

But I cautioned that although a technological breakthrough of this magnitude would defuse the bitter abortion conflict of the past ten years, it would raise a host of difficult and perhaps equally divisive questions: what if the pregnant woman refused this type of abortion and insisted upon the "old type" of suction procedure in which the unborn is churned through the Berkely apparatus and sent to the pathologist as a bag full of scraps? Should a pregnant woman have the power to make the decision regarding the type of abortion to have? If she opted for an "ovum transfer" type of abortion, to whom would the child eventually belong? Who would bear the cost of maintaining tens, perhaps hundreds of thousands of unborn on these enormously expensive machines?

These questions — provocative but yielding finally to conventional ethical analysis — now seem almost endearingly simple, the relics of a more innocent time. A third generation of fetologists has appeared with its baggage of technological tricks so stunning as to alter irretrievably the terms of the abortion conflict, to wit:

Experimenters in Australia have succeeded in freezing human embryos, for later implantation into an appropriate human uterus. Genetic engineers are racing ahead with techniques for switching off defective genes and substituting healthy or more desirable ones. A group of investigators at Johns Hopkins University is working on methods to obtain tissue samples (biopsies) from the placentas of early unborns and analyzing the tissue for genetic defects — a simpler and more universally applicable version of amniocentesis.

The abortion of the future now promises no defusion or resolution of the abortion conflict; it looms instead as a procedure so revolutionary, so macabre that the human mind literally balks at examining it within a traditional ethical framework. In that surrealistic landscape the woman who applies for "abortion" (the word itself may be an anachronism) will first have a placental biopsy made to determine the genetic quality of the unborn. If unsatisfactory, ovum transfer will allow the unborn to be removed, quick-frozen and then either genetically remodeled for future implantation into a recipient uterus, or else cannibalized for component parts at some time in the future: in this post-Huxleyan nightmarish society organ transplant will be big business. If, on the other hand, the biopsy proved satisfactory then the unborn would be transferred to another uterus, or to the life-support system, the "fetal farm."

The questions raised by such technological thaumaturgy will not be the pellucidly clear, uncomplicated ones of life and death, the rights of the unborn versus the rights of the woman, the legal wrangling over persons and non-persons. In this Orwellian world we will be forced to grapple with such Gordian tangles as: who will set the standards for "satisfactory genetic quality"? To whom does the frozen unborn — existing in a cryogenic limbo — belong? How much and what kind of genetic remodeling must a person undergo before he or she is another, different person? Should the desideratum of the technocratic society be a physical and intellectual super-race? If healthy animal genes are substituted for defective human ones what is the nature of that composite individual, that chimera?

I have no ready answers for these and the myriad other issues that such futuristic alchemy will raise. But I find it a bitter irony that that same science which so aided us in proving the humanity of the unborn — in ushering the unborn into the community of mankind — now threatens to dehumanize all of us, born and unborn.

The ethical questions must be answered *before* science is unleashed. Only then can science serve humanity, and not enslave it.

I know a riding instructor, an unusual woman so in tune with her animals that sometimes I believe she reads their minds. She keeps reminding me that the horse may not make the decisions: only the rider may. If science is the beast then we must ride it firmly and wisely. Never should we allow the beast to fling the saddle across the back of humanity.

PART V

ABORTION'S DISRUPTIVE INFLUENCE ON THE FAMILY

It is hardly a secret that the beleaguered American family is under siege and has been for nearly twenty years. What may not be as fully recognized is the crucial role abortion plays in destabilizing family life. After all, what could possibly put a greater strain on normal family bonds than the decision to destroy the life of a new member? The tension between parents, especially when the decision to abort is made unilaterally and/or in secrecy, can be fatal to a relationship based on mutual responsibility and concern for the future. The deception and lies that are associated with a teenager's decision to abort without her parents' knowledge or consent can permanently disrupt their relationship, as both Gordon Jones and Professor Rue observe.

ABORTION'S MUDDY FEET

Gordon S. Jones*

"Death, once invited in, leaves his muddy bootprints everywhere."

JOHN UPDIKE

Since the Supreme Court's historic 1973 *Roe v. Wade* decision, the abortion liberty has been used to (1) deny any substantive interest the father of an unborn child might have in the birth of his child; (2) deny any substantive interest the parents might have in protecting the life and health of their daughter; (3) deny parents any procedural interest — even knowledge — of their daughter's pregnancy and abortion. In these cases, the Court has refused to acknowledge the unity of the family, but has instead subordinated that unity to the individual rights of family members. These abortion-related cases are part of, perhaps a culmination of, a clearly discernible trend in recent case law in the United

*Gordon Jones is Executive Director of United Families of America. He has degrees from Columbia, Stanford, and George Washington Universities. He has been a legislative assistant to a number of congressmen and senators.

States, an ominous trend in which the family as an institution is denigrated and the individual family member is exalted.

Some have suggested that Justice Blackmun's decision in *Roe* was made in ignorance, that its implications for the family were not thought through. That is, of course, possible. It may only have been Blackmun's intent to exalt the role of the medicine men, not to attack the family. Whatever the truth may be, it seems indisputable that abortion has been used as a potent weapon to destroy the notion of the family as it has traditionally been understood.

Until fairly recently, the idea of the indivdual as the basic unit of society was unheard of. Families were the constituent elements of society, at once the bulwark against the power of the state and the object of its ministrations. The intervention of the state into this basic unit to "protect" an individual member of the family against the family unit is a revolutionary development, one about which not enough has been remarked. As we will see below, the results are a weakened marriage bond, a lessened commitment to the family as an economic unit, and a profound uncertainty among children.

The family has always had its attackers, of course. Plato was not too fond of it. Nor was Rousseau. In fact, most of the great thinkers who concerned themselves with the question of equality (Marx springs immediately to mind) have criticized the family, seeing it as the engine for perpetuating social inequalities. Those interested in a radical restructuring of society have (correctly) mistrusted the family, recognized it as a conservative institution, preserving and transmitting values, opinions, ethics, attitudes, and of course wealth.

This equalitarian attack, which includes an attack on marriage as well as on the raising of children within the family, spread through the intelligentsia throughout the 19th Century. In the 20th Century, however, the intellectual distaste for traditional families found a channel to the common man through the mass media. The televised anti-family propaganda of soap operas and sit-coms coincided with the development of radical feminist ideology, a development which reached its peak at about the same time as the 1973 Abortion Decisions. Just the titles of some of the most influential feminist books of the 1960s and 1970s (*Marriage is Hell, The Baby Trap,* etc.) are illuminating, as are the names of such political organizations as the Society for Cutting Up Men (SCUM).

But the attack was not limited to men and children. One feminist author described mothers as tending to "small-mindedness, petty jealousy, irrational emotionality and random violence, dependency, competitive selfishness and possessiveness, passivity [never mind the contradictions], a lack of vision and conservatism." In these writings, the family is the principal instrument by which "society" (or at least half of it) oppresses women, and imprints that pattern of oppression on children. To these radicals, the only way out of this horrible, oppressive cultural condition is through the destruction of its chief institution, the family. Thus the campaign for liberalized divorce laws is part of a campaign for individual rights against the family unit. So the increasingly popular "marriage contracts," under which the marriage partnership is reduced to an economic arrangement in which obligations, responsibilities, and benefits must be carefully balanced and which can be abrogated by either party if the arrangements are perceived to be inequitable.

Unfortunately, as the experience of the last twenty years clearly proves, when the destruction of the marriage bond is complete, women are far from being "liberated." They find themselves more alone and exposed than ever before. That reality may explain the shift, one might almost say reversal, in radical feminist sensibilities we see going on right now. With the weakening of the marriage bond, women are finding themselves alone and isolated, without the economic protection the family has always provided to the individual. They are finding emotional isolation as well, and many appear to be trying to find some accommodation with traditional family arrangements. For the moment, at least the overt denigration of the family by feminists is receding.

Radical feminists were not alone in trashing the family. They were not alone in seeing the family as confining and oppressive. The "marriage trap" has long been a staple of country club/bar room talk among men. Men have felt trapped by their responsibilities, chafing under the obligations of steady work and the security required by a wife and children. Beginning in the 1950s, pornographer Hugh Hefner (to strip him of his pretentions) began to popularize a liberationist philosophy of his own. The Playboy Philosophy was, and remains, rank hedonism and escapism. It turned women into objects who exist for the sexual pleasure of men, or as a passive audience for male accomplishments in the world of sports or business. This "philosophy" systematically avoided any suggestion that men might derive comfort or strength from a permanent commitment to one woman, or that the joint enterprise of conceiving and raising children might provide satisfaction and comfort. The word "child" seems not to appear in Hefner's dictionary.

Hefner's considerable success in making this kind of narcissism respectable is truly remarkable. Millions of men were exposed to his destructive childishness and took comfort in the knowledge that the urge to escape responsibility was well-nigh universal. Hefner was able to persuade political thinkers (William F. Buckley), politicians (Jimmy Carter), churchmen (Martin Luther King), and philosophers (Buckminster Fuller) to contribute to his magazine, thus further expanding his aura of respectability. More and more men were encouraged in their fantasies of liberation from their legal and moral relationships with women.

The results of this "liberation" go far beyond their effects on specific couples. In fact, they have implications for the stability of society as a whole. George Gilder argues that the function of marriage, as far as the man is concerned, is to civilize him. His sexual horizon is short-term. He lives for the moment, so to speak, taking his pleasure where he may, and sowing wild oats. Marriage, by imposing upon him long-term responsibilities, forces him to adjust his view to a much longer timespan, in light of which he will subordinate his short-term drives to the longer-term needs of his sexual partner and offspring. (Such honesty may grate on the feminist ear, but it is a fact we ignore at our peril.)

Taking Gilder's analysis another step, if the male has no offspring, or if his offspring is aborted, his view remains perpetually short-term. He continues to take his pleasure where he can find it and refuses to make the long-term commitment required by marriage and by the demands of civilization. In addition, the economic pressures which once encouraged men and women to stay together have been eroded by welfare and by the fact that well over half of the mothers work. The expendability of children dissolves more of the glue keeping families intact. Finally, the familial rearing of children, made less necessary by the expansion of education and child-care services, and eliminated by the mundane acceptability of abortion, can no longer serve as the unifying joint enterprise of man and woman. Thus abortion unravels the single strongest strand in the ties that bind the male into the family unit.

We have recently seen the formation of such groups as Women Exploited by Abortion (WEBA), as women who have undergone abortion have come to recognize (belatedly) what they have done to themselves and to their children. Part of the reason women feel exploited by abortion is precisely because they are! Men are using abortion as a way out of their problems. It is increasingly a way for the male sexual partner to avoid responsibility for his actions. That is particularly true before marriage, but may well be a factor during marriage as well. The recognition by women of their exploitation may also explain the fact that opinion polls consistently show support for abortion on demand to be stronger among men than among women.

Abortion also permits the woman to adopt the same sexual pattern as the male, although it is a pattern alien to her nature. Blessed by God with a much longer view of society and the world, the woman is normally the stabilizing force in a male-female relationship, insisting that the man subordinate his sexual passions to the need to provide for the family over the long run. When the children are removed, or limited, through abortion, his need to make provision is reduced. Her need to provide for herself is increased, further reducing the need for his presence in the home.

One result is the inevitable weakening of the male commitment to the marriage relationship. Another is the weakening of the collective male psyche. The economic independence of women from the marriage relationship undermines the feelings of self-worth of all men, thus further reducing the pool of acceptable partners for serious women. This is not an argument for the economic enslavement of women, but a recognition of the superior economic harmony that comes with the traditional family relationship, especially when that relationship includes dependent children. Once again, the male needs to know that others depend on his willingness to overcome his short-term perspective. In other words, ready access to abortion has gone a long way towards transforming marriage into its caricature, the Marriage Trap. With children gone and the economic independence of the childless woman, there is very little reason to resist the variety that is the spice of life.

Once marriage was identified as a "trap" for the parents, it was inevitable that its alleged confining effects would be found for children as well. The push to permit easier escape from the Marriage Trap has been expanded to permit children to escape more easily from the Family Trap. In recent years, the state has become much more willing than it used to be to interfere in family relationships. Part of that willingness comes from a genuine concern over the well-being of children and a greater willingness to recognize child abuse, both physical (including sexual) and psychological, as an actual fact. But part of it derives from the philosophical argument that family life should be a "chosen" arrangement like any other, out of which not only either parent, but also the children, may opt. Thus Dr. Adele Hoffman, representing the American Association of Pediatricians, testified before a Senate subcommittee that children should be able to assign parental rights to "another adult of the minor's choice."

Even the thrust for early childhood education and universal day care has to be seen as part of this philosophical argument over the family. Some of the proponents of Head Start programs are truly concerned about the lack of stimulative environment in the families of poor people and are motivated by a desire that every child get at least one hot meal a day. But some of them are quite plainly opposed to the kind of socialization children receive in any family and would rather that that early socialization be carried on by social workers and properly "sensitive" educators.

Children are, of course, seriously affected by the loosening of the familial bond, to which abortion contributes. But abortion has other implications for children. There are at least three serious and direct consequences of abortion on the other children of the family. The immediate, physical effect of abortion is to reduce the possibility that there will be future children. Despite the claims of the "pro-choice" lobby, abortion is by no means safe for women. A woman who has an abortion incurs a substantial risk of sterility or complications in future pregnancies. The risk has been understated largely because those who should follow the future problems of women undergoing abortions have a direct interest in understating it. A clinic making hundreds of thousands of dollars a year performing abortions has little incentive to closely monitor the future health of its "patients." Finding problems would have the effect of making the case against abortion, their bread and butter.

Secondly, when there are children already in the home and a couple has an abortion for socio-economic reasons, those children quickly recognize that their presence can and is used as the excuse for the abortion. They may easily develop serious guilt feelings about it. Children may say to themselves that they were the "cause" of the abortion. If they were not already there, they may reason, their parents would have been able to afford the new baby, which is virtually always desired by the existing siblings, particularly the younger ones. Thirdly, later children may well develop serious feelings of insecurity, knowing that their parents have already destroyed a sibling. This insecurity can infect existing siblings as well. After all, if parents could destroy an unborn child, why not a four-year-old?

Abortion is often promoted as an alternative to child abuse. However, there is a growing body of evidence that, far from reducing child abuse, abortion in fact encourages it. Abortion is widely regarded as the ultimate form of child abuse, of course, but beyond that feeling, there is some evidence that abortion, by lowering the value of life in general, makes it easier for parents to abuse their children, either those already born or those subsequently born. The sequence is perfectly understandable; the decision to destroy the life of an unborn child is a decision that the parents may hurt, even kill, children when their presence is an inconvenience. Child abuse is psychologically much easier after the ultimate step has been taken.

The growing liberty of abortion has to be seen in this context. It is part of a radical attack on the family as an institution. It is also a physical and spiritual attack on specific children. Combined with the cultural attack on marriage (easily perceived in an evening's television watching), it has so weakened our societal commitment to marriage that a substantial and growing minority of our rising generation intend (at this point, at least) to do without the great unifier and socializer: the family.

In this respect some comfort can be taken from the newest shift in the thinking of radical feminists. It is not too much to say that the tide may have turned. Many recent writings reflect a certain dissatisfaction with the antagonisms created by the kind of society prefigured in the earlier feminist writings. Some of the most outspoken and influential of the feminists (Betty Friedan, for example) do not seem to like what they see, as the weakened commitment to marriage and family leaves women alone, disadvantaged and, increasingly, poor. Women are striking back against pornography and its intellectual exponents (although to far too great an extent they appear willing to accept Hugh Hefner's money and to hold up his daughter, now publisher of *Playboy,* as an exemplar). If they have so far refused to make common cause with political conservatives (and pro-lifers) against pornography, at least they have recognized the destructiveness of pornography on some human values. If feminists are willing to be this honest with themselves, perhaps middle class men, Playboy's target audience, can find it in themselves to overcome their biological urges, for the benefit of families and civilization.

If they do so, there may be hope for the family. Many women are once again talking about marriage as a partnership and appear willing to recognize its virtues and strengths as well as its weaknesses. If men will rejoin them, perhaps in time we may all come to accept the family as Churchill described democracy: the worst possible system, except for all the others.

What remains to be seen is the effect this recent shift in thinking will have on the abortion liberty. The scientific picture is now clearer than it was in 1973: the child is present from conception; it is a human being. If a renewed acceptance of children, of child-bearing, and child-raising accompanies the resurgence of sympathy for the family, the unborn child can only be the beneficiary. Is it too late? Have too many women (and men) already bloodied their hands with abortion to be able to admit the reality?

I am, myself, hopeful, even in the face of the most recent disappointment by the Supreme Court and the

Senate vote on the Hatch-Eagleton Amendment. There are a few encouraging signs in the way the Court decided, and the debate on the floor of the Senate exposed the issues in the debate in a way they have not been exposed before.

Most encouraging of all is the continual stream of local ordinances and state laws restricting the liberty of abortion, indicating the breadth of discontent with abortion on demand. I see no reason to think that that tide will abate. The Reagan Administration continues to search for ways to limit abortion directly and to curtail the institutional support for pro-abortion organizations which have for so long been funded by tax payers.

Finally, I retain my faith in individual men and women, and their ability to admit mistakes and repent, to cast the issue in theological terms. As a nation we have done it over the slavery issue, and we can do it over abortion. It is my belief that men and women will not forever deny reality and their own nature. If they do, the punishment will be terrible, and not long in coming.

THE ABORTION DECISION: A CRISIS TO BE SHARED

Vincent M. Rue, Ph.D.*

"Unlike any other dimension of human consideration, abortion has within a decade, become nothing less than a national fissure."

VINCENT M. RUE in testimony before the U.S. Senate Subcommittee on the Constitution

Shocked by the news of an unplanned pregnancy, many women react with intense anxiety. Time to make a careful and deliberate decision seems all too short. Often impulsively, they make an individual choice that will permanently affect many other lives as well as their own.

Although unspoken, a woman with a problem

*Dr. Rue is a practicing family psychotherapist and Executive Director of Sir Thomas More Clinics of Southern California. He has been an Associate Professor of Family Relations at California State University at Los Angeles and has testified before the U.S. Senate Subcommittee on the Constitution on the abortion issue. In his practice and his research, Dr. Rue has interviewed hundreds of women with problem pregnancies and has lectured widely on the subject.

pregnancy often has a wish to face her parents or her mate with her ambivalence and to draw on their support. Even when such exchanges result in conflict or disagreement, the sharing will in most instances be beneficial. A secret abortion, on the other hand, creates a psychological burden for the pregnant woman and a barrier to her future relationships with those people in her life who are most important to her. As researchers M. Cotroneo and B. Krasner noted in their study of abortion and problems in decision-making in *The Journal of Marriage and Family Counseling*, a pregnant woman cannot be lifted out of her present and future family network for the purpose of decision making. To do so would be to ignore the relationship fallout of her decision on her mate, parents, children (born and unborn), siblings, grandparents and other significant relationships.

To an adolescent,a problem pregnancy is all the more isolating. Feeling ashamed, frightened and alone, these adolescents are unable to communicate their problem to others, largely because of their own fears and self-disapproval. The loss of self-esteem can be devastating, demanding much attention and empathy. Yet, how many teenagers involve their parents in their decision-making on abortion? Estimates vary from one out of five to maybe half. Crisis decision making that takes place in a vacuum is bound to fail. Abortion as a crisis should be added to the list of other crises family members encounter and which need family help in resolving.

Marriage and family life have long been the primary support systems for just such problems. Over the centuries, families have changed form, structure, membership, even functions, and yet have survived better than any nation or institution. Sociologist Reuben Hill writes in *Families Under Stress:*

> In a society of rapid social change, problems outnumber solutions, and the resulting uncertainties

> are absorbed by the members of society, who for the most part are also members of families. Because the family is the bottleneck through which all troubles pass, no other association so reflects the strains and stresses of life. The family today is not only the focal point of frustration and tensions, but also the source of resolving frustrations and tensions... through its capacity for sympathy, understanding and unlimited support, the family habilitates personalities bruised in the course of daily living.

Beyond a doubt, then, both the woman with an unplanned pregnancy and the pregnant minor benefit from developing a realistic plan which takes into account their relationships with their families and their current living situations. To deprive herself of such communication is to deprive herself unnecesarily of the resources of the family bond. While abortion has been heralded as a remedy for problems or unwanted pregnancies, it may well bring about more problems than it solves. Researchers have found that the occurrence of a pregnancy in an adolescent often indicates a psychological need to become pregnant. Abortion does little to help an adolescent work out such a basic conflict and may add to feelings of guilt and depression. Unless the adolescent can find help in addressing that psychological need, the need will persist. Hence, it is not unusual to see teenagers who have had an abortion without counseling return a year later with another unwanted pregnancy.

To a pregnant minor, lack of parental involvement in the decision-making process can promote a false sense of independence and a misguided notion of personal freedom. The pregnant minor is ill-equipped socially, psychologically and educationally to meet the demands of adult responsibility, especially those of marriage and parenthood. Adolescents are insecure about their identities as men and woman and are only at the beginning of heterosexual interaction.

Clearly, abortion does have a profound impact on families. For example, it prevents increases in family size; it prevents or delays family formation by those who might otherwise choose marriage or start a single parent family. Abortion also affects family communication, parental roles, spousal roles, individual and family problem-solving abilities, self-perceptions and future family relations.

Although largely unresearched, the abortion decision also has profound effects on the father/husband. Extensive research has focused on women and abortion, while men have been legally, psychologically, and medically ignored. This is understandable because the Supreme Court has held that a father has limited rights and that a husband has no rights in the abortion area other than those the state might have and which the state deigns to delegate. Those decisions clearly limit the roles of fathers and parents and eliminate the role of husbands in such decisions. As female autonomy is upheld, the structure and function of the family is undermined. This is clearly in violation of an abundant body of research and clinical knowledge that affirms the family as a powerful and effective problem-solving unit.

Sociologist Arthur Shostak observed in an article for *The Family Coordinator* that a sizable minority of males find their abortion experience more frustrating and emotionally costly than public and academic neglect of this subject would suggest. He also noted that three out of four male partner respondents stated that they had a difficult time with the abortion experience and that a sizable minority reported persistent day and night dreams about the child-that-never-was, and considerable guilt, remorse, and sadness. In addition, researcher Emily Milling found that of more than 400 couples who went through the abortion experience, most of the relationships (70%) had failed one month after the abortion.

Male role conflict can be especially painful during the abortion experience. Men generally believe they must be independent, strong and brave; they must not be weak or dependent. Results of a national poll indicate that three out of four respondents still believe that the ideal man is one who will fight to protect his family. This notion of protectiveness is well ingrained in the American tradition of masculinity. Yet how can one protect, when one is not allowed by law to be involved in a life-or-death decision?

The strong, silent "Marlboro Man" does not fare well at the abortion clinic. One young man's experience was recounted in Arden Rothstein's *Men's Reactions to Their Partner's Elective Abortion:* "I thought I was a much more liberated man. I'd be able to walk in here and sit down and say, 'Here's an abortion' and that would be it. But now that I'm here, I'm a wreck... I don't think anyone could depend on me in this situation... I'm shaken... I really want to know what they will do for her... How about me? Do they have something for me to lay on while I die?" For the male involved in the abortion decision, the role strain is great. His natural strivings to be responsible and to protect fall victims to expedience and accession to his partner's insistence. Males become so eager to protect the female's well-being that they tend to discount or suppress their own needs, which, added to the man's unexpressed guilt or anger, can fester for some time afterwards.

In a very real sense, the double standard has been revisited and revised with abortion. While the right to abdicate future motherhood is legally guaranteed, the right to insist on future fatherhood is not. For a number of men, this societal impotency has produced sexual impotency, typified by a feeling of helplessness and hostility. The double standard extends to other areas as well. If women choose motherhood, men are obligated in paternity action. While women may choose an abortion over the male's objection, men typically shoulder the bulk of the financial costs. When men promote abortion for their partners it is typified as coercion, lack of caring, insensitivity and selfishness. Whereas when women choose abortion it is the exclamation of women's rights, an affirmation of the right to health and freedom from male oppression, and a confirmation of sovereign territoriality over the female body and reproductive functions.

Further, in the resolution of a problem pregnancy, both male and female have equal rights in adoption proceedings, but not in abortion. In both adoption and abortion, at least one parent wishes to give up parental rights and responsibilities. When the parents' interests in the child clash, the determination of rights in one conflict should be applicable to the other. On the other hand, the abdication of responsibility fits nicely into the mainstream of abortion thinking. For men who don't care about the women they impregnate, abortion is a neat disposal system for the evidence of their sexuality and a conclusive abdication of any caretaking responsibilities.

Abortion also serves well the erotically compulsive male who strives to maintain his self-esteem and to gratify his ego needs through sexual achievement. This Don Juan male is typically minimally involved in the personality of his partner since his ability to love is sharply limited. After making a conquest, he loses interest in the chosen woman and reacts with hostility toward her, since he devalues her after the successful seduction. Abortion is also functional for another type of person: the uncommitted male and his female counterpart. Strong ambivalence and excessive narcissism are characteristic of the uncommitted individual. Our era of sexual freedom without marriage has helped disguise this uncommitted type to some extent. He no longer needs to marry the woman with whom he starts a relationship or a family. He no longer feels discredited by disengaging from her: he simply goes on to his next affair. Eventually, however, this leaves him depleted of self-esteem and depressed. To the man and woman who have committed themselves to each other, an abortion may well impair their relationship. Because of the basic inequality between the partners in the abortion decision, the capacity to develop trust, enhance communication and problem-solving skills, intimacy, honesty, and companionship is severely handicapped. This same inequality has the potential to breed displaced male aggression via child abuse, spousal abuse, or self-abuse.

In the case of interfaith marriage, or one in which the spouses have differing degrees of religious faith, the decision to abort by the spouse with the less conservative belief system collides with that of the other partner. In a sense, abortion may represent the direct opposite of marriage in that it eliminates procreative responsibility and occurs most frequently among those who merely live together. L. Shusterman, in *Predicting the Psychological Consequences of Abortion* found that 75 percent of the aborting respondents asserted that "a child at this time would interfere with my career, education, or personal freedom." Abortion also disguises and increases marital dysfunction in another way: a problem pregnancy from an extramarital affair can be secretly disposed of, with little else remaining than a large burden of guilt.

Beyond abortion's effect on marriage and families, there are the risks to the individual woman who chooses it. Countless authors have proclaimed the merits of this medical procedure and asserted only temporary, nonpathological, and limited adverse emotional effects. And yet, the only consistent positive reaction reported in an exhaustive literature review is that of *relief*. Virtually no study reported additional positive feelings. However, negative feelings may include: guilt, anxiety, depression, a sense of loss, anger, relational changes with partner, crying, a feeling of being misled by misinformation or lack of information, deterioration of self-image, regret or remorse, nightmares, anxiety about possible infertility, loneliness/alienation, marital disruption, physical concerns, disturbance in sleep patterns, imagining the aborted child, flashbacks, psychotic reactions, hopelessness, helplessness, powerlessness, and changes in significant relationships. According to researchers R. Illsely and M. Hall, abortion and guilt have become virtually synonymous.

From my own clinical experience, many women who have undergone abortion suffer from what is called post-traumatic stress disorder, which can be acute, chronic, or delayed. This disorder was first diagnosed in some Vietnam veterans several years ago and it is only recently that we have come to see this in women traumatized by elective abortion. Characteristic systems develop following a psychologically traumatic event that is generally outside the norm of human experience. These symptoms include: reexperiencing the traumatic event, numbing of responsiveness to the external world leading to reduced involvement, sleep disturbance, impaired memory or difficulty in concentrating, and guilt feelings about surviving when others did not.

This disorder is apparently more severe and longer lasting when the stressful situation is man-made, as with abortion. The symptoms of the disorder often intensify when the individual is exposed to situations that resemble or symbolize the original trauma (for example, cold, snowy weather or uniformed guards for death camp survivors; hospitals, clinics and especially nurseries for women who have undergone abortions). Impairment from the disorder may be either mild or affect nearly every aspect of life. "Psychic numbing" may interfere with interpersonal relationships, such as marriage or family life. Depression and guilt may result in self-defeating behavior or suicidal actions. Drug and alcohol abuse may develop, and "anniversary reactions" are common.

The effects of abortion on society as a whole are difficult to pinpoint because abortion is, in fact, an undesirable symptom of a far greater problem. Society is displaying a tendency to seek the easy way out and avoid the difficult, to pursue pleasure and abhor pain, to make wants synonymous with needs, to allow desires to replace and become beliefs, and to place individual needs over that of the responsibility to others.

Equally disturbing are the parallels between child abuse and abortion. If violence begets violence, and abortion is the violent end to a life, then to what does abortion lead? Should anyone be surprised that abortion and child abuse are increasing at the same pace? Unrestricted abortion diminishes restraint against rage, weakens the taboo against aggressing against defenseless young, and lessens the value of children. It may also increase hostility between generations and break down the pair-bonding ability of mothers with their infants and, hence, promote child abuse. With the recent cultural obsession with self, faulty thinking has led to faulty social rules. Abortion is one of the more painful social lessons to learn. The pied piper of "meism" has nearly led us to our demise, for nothing subverts self-fulfillment more thoroughly than self-indulgence.

Abortion exists for women, yet is against women, men, and children. Like an anesthesia, abortion comfortably numbs all from experiencing the burden of pregnancy. Abortion has become a social eraser, individually, quickly, and secretly eliminating all traces of the problem that is pregnancy. And yet, within the depths of humankind, the indelible scars remain.

PART VI

THE PRO-LIFE ALTERNATIVE: HELPING *BOTH* MOTHER *AND* CHILD

Since so many pro-lifers do double-duty as both pro-life activists and Emergency Pregnancy Service (Birthright, etc.) counselors, it is only natural that they reject the "either-or" mentality of the pro-abortionists. What is so poorly understood by the public at large is that the pro-life movement is dedicated to **both** *the mother* **and** *her unborn child. The media are of little help: they focus almost exclusively on our legislative and political efforts (usually unfavorably).*

But in the years to come, we can expect literally hundreds of thousands of women to reach out for help to deal with soul-wrenching grief over their abortions. It is understandable that those who profit on the blood of the unborn children would not advertise the fact that study after study is demonstrating the adverse long-term consequences for women who abort. But as more and more photos of unborn children grace the cover of magazines such as Newsweek, the enormity of what millions of women have done to both their children and themselves will come home to roost. Only the pro-life movement, rooted in love and forgiveness, will be able to help them work through their remorse.

CHOOSING LIFE

Sr. Paula Vandegaer, S.S.S.*

"To promote and raise the status of family, motherhood, children, marriage, and the intrinsic value of all human life is AAI's major and enduring objective."

DR. JOHN F. HILLABRAND, Co-founder,
Alternatives to Abortion International

"If you pro-life people are against abortion, what are you doing to help the many women who are distressed with a problem pregnancy?" This question has been posed many times and is a very valid one. It points out how important the pro-life service movement is and how essential it is to a pro-life stance. When abortion was legalized in the United States in the latter part of the '60s, many people knew that something had to be done to counteract this negative force in our society. Some of these people started political action work, some began to work in the legal field, some did educational work about abortion, while others began to form centers

*Sister Vandegaer has her master's degree in social work from Catholic University in Washington, D.C. She has counseled young people and pregnant girls for many years. She is currently editor of *Heartbeat* magazine, a periodical for pro-life counselors published by Alternatives to Abortion International. She has written and lectured extensively on pregnancy counseling.

and set up hot lines to counsel pregnant women.

In 1971 there were barely 60 groups in the United States formed to help pregnant women. Trying to help a woman facing a decision whether or not to have an abortion was such a new form of counseling that everyone was trying to figure out how to do it. It was in this context that the organization that I represent, Alternatives to Abortion International, was formed. We are an international organization seeking to promote and assist in the establishment of a sufficient number of emergency pregnancy service centers, so that no woman in distress with a problem pregnancy will ever be without pro-life counselling help.

From a small beginning of 60 groups in the United States, the service movement has grown to 1,400 groups in the United States and over 2,600 worldwide. These groups vary in methodology — some are hot lines, some do short-term crisis intervention counseling and some provide long-term assistance to the woman. All of them, however, have been formed since approximately 1968 and are grassroots volunteer organizations reaching out to protect women. Today almost two new groups a week are starting in the United States. The U.S. centers receive almost 1.5 million calls a year.

Many of these callers come into the centers for pregnancy tests. Of the women who come in for these tests, only a little over one-half of the results are positive. Estimates are that approximately two-thirds of the women with positive pregnancy tests request an abortion. (These are rough estimates based on an analysis of pro-life service center statistics. It is difficult to get precise national statistics because, as yet, statistical procedures have not been standardized from one center to another.) It appears that approximately one-half of the young women requesting abortion have been advised by someone else to have the abortion. Their boyfriend, girlfriends or parents tell them it is the best solution for them. Although they've come requesting an abortion, when we talk to them, we find they are not at all satisfied with this "solution." They are happy to discuss alternatives and very relieved that they do not have to choose this "solution."

The rest of the women requesting an abortion are women who are very serious about abortion as a personal solution to their problem. In this group we begin to see many women having repeat abortions. Repeat abortions are growing and becoming a serious problem. According to the Alan Guttmacher Institute, in 1980, 33% of all women having an abortion in the United States had had at least one prior abortion. We also see women in this group who have adopted sexual activity and abortion as a lifestyle; they need very significant and dedicated care to aid them to choose another style of life. These are difficult cases; however, from time to time in God's readiness and plan, there is the possibility of a significant breakthrough in such a young woman's life. These difficult breakthroughs are some of the most heartening of the cases we work with.

When a woman does decide to have an abortion, we do not refer her or help her with that decision. Instead, we leave her with the understanding that we care about her and are concerned for her. We cannot refer her, not only because we cannot assist in the taking of the life of the child, but also because our concern for her would not allow us to do anything hurtful to her. We tell her she can come back to us after the abortion or if she becomes pregnant again. Many women have returned to us for post-abortion counseling or in a second pregnancy. Women who have had abortions very frequently become pregnant again within one year after their abortion. Sometimes, the second time around they are more willing to face the responsibility, alter their lifestyle, and assume a commitment to another person.

What are the alternatives that are offered to the young

woman who decides to have her baby? There are really two alternatives available to her. After she has her baby, she can keep her baby or she can place her child for adoption.

If she decides to keep her baby, she can be helped with financial aid, medical aid, a place to live, and maternity and baby clothes. Many groups now are starting homes for pregnant women, in an effort to fulfill an unmet need. Right now, housing and finances are probably the most pervasive unmet needs for pregnant women. All over the country, new groups are starting to answer these concerns.

Other women choose to place their child for adoption. In recent years fewer women are choosing this than in the past, resulting in a great shortage of babies available to couples who wish to adopt. All adoption agencies report long waiting lists of couples who desire a child. There are really no "unwanted" babies. However, agencies still struggle to find homes for hard-to-place children such as racially mixed and handicapped children. As a society we still need the generosity and compassion to help "special needs" children.

A woman who places her baby for adoption needs to receive good counseling from a licensed adoption agency in order to make this decision and feel comfortable with it. She must feel she is being a loving person and doing a loving thing for her baby. Through adoption she must feel that she is being a mother to her baby. If she knows and feels this, the adoption decision will be a peaceful and growing process for her, and she will feel good about herself and her baby. Some women believe if they are going to place their baby for adoption they might as well abort the baby. This thinking, of course, does not take into consideration the very different feelings that arise in the woman following the choice of either adoption or abortion. It is very necessary for a mother to feel herself to be a loving mother to her child. The long-range effects of adoption are very different for women than the long-range effects of abortion.

What about the nearly 50 percent of the young women who come in but who are not yet pregnant? Pro-abortion advocates say that since these women are sexually active, you must get them on contraceptives to avoid having a baby. This advice does not work and shows absolutely no understanding of the psychology of teenagers and young adults. What pro-life counselors do with a young woman who has a negative pregnancy test is help her to say "No" and examine her relationships.

There are three distinct stages of sexual activity for young people. I term them (1) the experimental stage, (2) the identity stage, and (3) the lifestyle stage.

(1) *The Experimental Stage* — Most young people experiment with sexual activity for a year before they ever decide to use contraceptives. For most young people this sexual experimentation is spontaneous; it's "no big deal."

"I really love Joe and we are just experimenting," they say. "I am a good girl and this is not a big problem."

If a young woman decides to use contraceptives, her actions are saying,

"I am no longer a good girl just experimenting. I am a *planfully sexually active woman.*" Most young people do not make this commitment to sexual activity or to this identity change, nor do we, as counselors, want them to make that identity change.

Most young people in the experimental stage feel very uncomfortable with what they are doing. It is also a spiritual problem as God does not allow us to feel comfortable with activity that is not good for us. He agitates and disturbs us. Often when talking with a young woman, a counselor is able to find many places where a woman is not comfortable and disturbed about what is going on in her life. It is at this place that we can help her.

There is a common fallacy today that once a young woman starts sexual activity she can never stop. This is not our experience and we have many case examples to illustrate this. Young people today get talked into, rushed into, and peer-pressured into activity that they know is not good for them. They need strength and courage and back-up to say, "No." We find other young women involved in experimenting who come from disturbed family situations or who have psychological problems. For them sexual activity is a symptom of something else. These youngsters need long-term counselling and often their families do too. A pill or an abortion does nothing for them other than confuse and aggravate the problem.

(2) *Sexual Experimentation as an Identity* — Some women that we see have decided on sexual activity as an identity. Usually these women go in for the pill and plan for their sexual experimentation. It is precisely this group who are highly likely to become pregnant. Although pro-life service centers do not have a standard form for statistics, in reviewing many statistical forms coming in from centers, I do find one consistent statistic. One-third to one-half of the total caseload of pregnant women are women who have become pregnant after someone has put them on a contraceptive.

This is not at all surprising. What consistently happens is that a young woman becomes involved in a relationship with a young man without benefit of marriage. As the relationship continues, she becomes more and more insecure and eventually, consciously or unconsciously, she becomes pregnant. This forces the issue and the young man has to make a significant decision as to what his relationship is with her.

Many times we see that this results in an abortion, with subsequent anger at the boy and the baby, or it may result in a strong desire to keep the baby in order to have someone to love. I have had much experience with post-delivery counseling and, believe me, one of the most important concerns of the young woman is the subsequent relationship with men and her unresolved anger, hurt, and betrayal.

(3) *Sexual Experimentation as a Lifestyle* — Some women that we see have adopted sexual experimentation as a lifestyle. These girls may be living with someone or have had different partners. They say they are modern women with total reproductive freedom. Frequently, however, these women have serious character disorder problems and find it difficult to form a permanent, committed relationship. Unless aided, they will probably have a number of marriages and divorces. They will pursue a personal lifestyle whose primary goal is great concern for themselves alone and their personal self-fulfillment.

The pro-life service movement with its emphasis on caring concern, loving both the young woman and her unborn child, is fulfilling a profound need in our society. The type of counseling we are giving, that emphasizes commitment, accepting responsibility and giving support where support is needed, is slowly, but surely, having an effect on our next generation of young women and young families.

Our counseling is much more significant and personal than that of our opposition. Our opposition seeks a mechanical solution to personal problems. But there is no mechanical solution for troubled young teenagers, only a personal solution of giving one's self to this youngster. It is much more demanding to give oneself than to give a pill or an abortion, and it is more effective.

Surely this is the message that Jesus gave us and surely this is what we are dedicated to doing.

CARING FOR ABORTION'S TWO VICTIMS

J.C. Willke, M.D.*

"Because the pro-life movement has long understood that there are two victims in every abortion, it is only natural that it should be composed of two major complementary components. One focuses on education and political action; the other directly saves babies' lives right now by assisting their mothers to choose positive solutions in times of crisis."

J.C. WILLKE, M.D.

Induced abortion represents a murderous assault on the member of the human family least able to defend him or herself. That the best we can offer a woman confronting a problem pregnancy is the death of her child is unworthy of a society that even today is seen as the last

*Dr. Willke is an internationally known author, lecturer, and expert in family life and sex education. He and his wife, Barbara, are co-authors of *Handbook on Abortion* and other widely used pro-life materials, He has just stepped down after serving three years as President of the National Right to Life Committee.

best hope for mankind. It is ironic that while the pro-life movement gets most of its (negative) press attention for its legislative and political efforts to save the babies from destruction, we never hear a peep about that side of the movement which has offered practically the only sustained program of assistance to pregnant women facing life and death decisions.

This work is less well known because it is less flashy and because it is intensely personal. It is the kind of one-to-one counselling that attracts few headlines but does save babies by sustaining and assisting their mothers who may well have no place else to turn. Because the pro-life movement has long understood there are two victims in every abortion, it is only natural that it should be composed of two major complementary components. One concentrates on education and political action: Its ultimate goal is a human life amendment. The other directly saves babies' lives right now by assisting their mothers to choose positive solutions in times of crisis.

So it is that one wing is made up of the pro-life activists best known to the public. Their primary job is to educate. They lecture, teach, picket, lobby, pray — everything necessary to pass the truth along. Everyone in this half of the movement understands that abortion is a classic example of judicial lawmaking. But the legislative branch still has the ultimate power to override such an outrageous example of improper judicial intervention via a constitutional amendment. Thus, the pro-life activists' job is to convince elected officials that the unborn must be protected. This often necessitates replacing pro-abortion lawmakers with pro-life lawmakers.

But every bit as important, and more so in the short-term, are the efforts of the other half of the movement which devotes its time, energies, and sympathies to caring for and counselling women with unplanned pregnancies. The original group, Birthright, has been replicated, copied, revised and adjusted so that there are now over 1400 groups in the United States alone. Its umbrella group, Alternatives to Abortion International, continues to hold annual conventions and attempts to bring a measure of uniformity to their thankfully ever-increasing numbers. AAI also publishes a quarterly journal which helps them to share ideas, experiences, and counselling techniques.

These helping groups are staffed almost entirely by volunteers; most of whom are women. These are compassionate, concerned people deeply distressed by society's callousness toward the pregnant woman and the intense pressure it can exert on her to choose abortion's "quick-fix" solution. These volunteers typically come from caring, loving homes and become involved quite simply to share some of that love with others.

To make help for these mothers as easily available as possible, these groups ask only the woman's first name, charge her nothing, and help her with what she needs most. They'll find her a home, a job, medical or legal help, and maternity clothes. Later, these same people will help her find a loving home for her child if she decides to place the baby for adoption or give her baby clothes and a crib if she decides to keep her baby. These groups advertise modestly, trying to make their presence known. As a result of their involvement, thousands of distressed women contact them daily. Also, because they do offer genuine alternatives to abortion, the assembly-line abortion profiteers and those who staff the Planned Parenthood abortion chambers hate them.

A new and dynamic concept has recently been added to the family of alternative organizations: the Problem Pregnancy center, pioneered by Robert Pierson. These centers really upset the pro-abortionists for they give accurate information about the baby's development and about abortion to women who may have already decided to get an abortion. These storefront-type operations offer free pregnancy tests. When the woman comes in, she is offered the opportunity to view an educational audio visual while waiting for her test results. Within 30 minutes, having been given the facts, a gratifying 60-80 percent change their minds, accept help, and decide to carry their baby to term. Needless to say, those who so loudly claim to be "pro-choice" bitterly denounce these new centers which provide the other side of the argument, enabling a woman to make a genuinely free choice.

If you believe our largely pro-abortion press, the volunteers who make up the tens of thousands of pro-life and "alternatives" cadre are mostly men, religious zealots, red necks and far-right extremists who hate sex and want to punish women for their sins. As is so common with media stereotypes, the truth is exactly the opposite. Most of our pro-life activists are women, Democrats, Protestant, and happily married with children of their own (Mrs. Willke and I are in our late 50s. At times we've been listed among the "parents" of the movement. We're not sure that's because we've been around from the beginning or just because of our age.)

Again, contrary to media stereotypes, while we do concentrate on the issues of abortion, infanticide, and euthanasia, when we take off our right to life hats we are busy in many other caring community activities. In this sense, we are anything but "single issue." Far beyond the average, pro-life people actively help others in our society. Our people frequently take pregnant girls into their homes, care for foster children, adopt, volunteer in nursing homes and hospitals, and work with special children. Indeed, such volunteer work is almost the norm with pro-life activists.

If there is one common characteristic shared by most pro-life activists, it is a deep love for children. This shows up best in the very high percentage who adopt. Our own experience is completely typical. Barbara and I have a great marriage and from the beginning were very much in love. God blessed us in the early years of our marriage with two little girls. We then tried unsuccessfully for seven years to give them another sister or brother. We felt we could easily care for more and wanted to share our love and blessings.

Finally, after two years of effort and a trip to Quebec, Canada, we were notified that a generous young lady, having decided that she could not offer her new son the life, home and family she wanted for him, had given him to us to love and cherish. It was one of the most joyful days of our lives. As it happened, to our equal delight, Barbara had become pregnant again. The agency lady said, "Oh well, if you are pregnant, we'll cancel the adoption."

"No way!" we said. Since our son-to-be is from outside the United States, we will not be depriving any local couple. We have room in our hearts for both."

And so we did. Our natural son, Joe, joined us in the "airworld" just four months after we brought Chuck home from Canada. In the years since, we've always thought of them as equally our natural sons. And just as with our other four (we were later blessed with another daughter and son), Joe and Chuck is each his own, unique person. Perhaps the unforgetable words of a notice in a college newspaper from many years ago will explain how Barbara and I feel: "Our child was given the gift of life by a man and a woman other than ourselves. Our son lives now because this man and woman chose life instead of death. We can never comprehend the suffering they endured. But we shall always be thankful for their courage and generosity. Their gift of life shall flourish."

As we look to the future, we see ever more need for both halves of the pro-life movement. During my three terms as president of the National Right to Life Committee, the largest and most representative grassroots right to life organization in America. I was privileged to set up and help nurture the growth of a nationwide Adoption Committee. Chaired by Mr. David Moynihan (an adoptive father, of course), and with the close cooperation of the National Committee on Adoption, a major effort is underway to prepare for a time when the killing will cease. Such a time *will* come, and when it does, millions of babies will again be allowed to be born and to live. There will then be a great need to place these little children in the outstetched arms of waiting couples.

There is, at present, a monstrously evil attitude being fostered that somehow it is more "merciful" to kill a baby rather than place him or her in an adoptive home. This attitude is part and parcel of the baby-as-property mentality that underlies abortion. We must work until that kind of thinking is changed. We owe the babies no less.

Whenever the death peddlers are backed into a corner, they lash out, "But pro-lifers are not truly pro-life. They worry about only unborn babies." Yes, we do worry — day and night — about unborn babies, and we will persevere until the womb is once again a safe place to reside. But until that time — and afterwards — we will also be just as concerned about handicapped newborns, about the aged, and about desperate pregnant women (and their men) who might be tempted to "solve" a problem pregnancy with an abortion. Because we are thoroughly, completely pro-life we will never rest. We will continue to put our time, our money, and our personal concern on the line to help those whose lives are in danger from a callous and indifferent society.

Can anyone imagine the officials of NOW, of NARAL, of the Woman's Political Caucus, of Planned Parenthood saying and doing as much? Of course not. They are the great simplifiers. They have one answer: the violence of killing.

Our way is better.

POST-ABORTION COUNSELING: A PRO-LIFE TASK

Marshall Fightlin*

"Because of the psychological inseparability of mother and child, there is no opposition between our concern for unborn children and our concern for mothers who have had abortions.

MARSHALL FIGHTLIN

To its everlasting credit, the pro-life movement has always recognized that in a real sense every abortion has two victims — the unborn child and his or her mother. How could it be otherwise when abortion represents the unjustifiable slaying of an unborn child by the person most closely bound up with the baby: his or her mother. While the legal battle must be waged based on the principle of the sanctity of unborn life, a secondary social and psychological battle must be waged based on a humanitarian concern for the devastating effect

*Marshall Fightlin is a marriage and family therapist. He is associate director of Catholic Family Services in Norwich, Connecticut and president of Humana Vita Renewal. Author and lecture-, Mr Fightlin has made numerous public appearances. He is married with two children.

that the abortion may have on the mother. As a movement, pro-lifers from the beginning have involved themselves heavily in pregnancy counseling, where the aim is to prevent the death of the baby and the ensuing psychological and physical damage to the mother. Where the movement has not devoted as much attention is to counseling those women who have *already had* abortions and who are suffering sometimes as long as decades after the abortion.

Why Abortions Deeply Affect Women

Why do abortions produce psychological traumas in women? In many respects, women are the more "together" sex. Mind, emotions and body are more integrated in women than they are in men. Hence, the somatic configuration of the woman has a profound effect on her feeling and thinking. Because she cannot forget that she is a given and sustainer of life, her maternal capacity is an integral element of her self-image. Abortion, as a solution to a problem pregnancy, is a typically "masculine" solution. It is a solution that can be decided on only by a mind that is capable of distancing itself from feeling and from the procreative truth of the body.

When a woman submits to an abortion, she is doing violence not only to her body, but to her innermost feelings. Even if she does not fully understand that she is taking the life of her child, she feels the abortion as a negation of the truth of her body as a lifegiver and nurturer. It is not at all surprising that intense feelings of anxiety, guilt, and shame arise from such a profound experience.

Although the unborn child is the victim in an abortion and the abortionist is the aggressor, the mother's role carries elements of both. That is, she is both victim and aggressor. She is an aggressor because she facilitates and consents to the abortionist's aggression taken out on the unborn child. However, in a less obvious sense, she is also a victim. By destroying the life of her child, she is insulting the meaning of her own body. Since "our bodies, our selves" is especially true for women, when her body is insulted, when its meaning is denied, the woman herself is insulted and her own meaning is denied. Every woman is insulted and devalued by abortion. In this sense the mother is not only a co-aggressor with the abortionist against her child, she is, along with her child, a co-victim of the abortionist.

Because of the psychological inseparability of mother and child, there is no opposition between our concern for unborn children and our concern for mothers who have had abortions. In fact, the one calls for the other. This course of action becomes clearer when we realize that we must distinguish the motivations of the mother from those of the abortionist. Generally, she feels ambivalence about submitting to an abortion, whereas the abortionist feels none. Pro-life people must recognize women who have had abortions as truly victims. This is all the more warranted since pro-life people have rightly accepted former abortionists who have repudiated their pasts and joined the pro-life ranks.

Post-abortion counseling is an important way pro-life people can help women who have had abortions. When this service is provided in compassion and in truth, far from making a future abortion more acceptable to the woman, it helps heal the deep hurt the woman feels over her past abortions and makes future abortions less likely.

The pro-life movement must take up this task because it is based on the truth of the dignity of each and every human person, from conception to natural death. This means that the pro-life person recognizes the dignity of the unborn child, of the aborting mother, even of the abortionist. One can act against one's dignity, but one cannot destroy one's dignity. Submitting to an abortion, however profoundly mistaken and terrible that decision, does not destroy the human dignity of the mother. Pro-life people must help these suffering women precisely because they affirm the dignity of every human being and understand the difference between condemning the act and forsaking the actor.

The pro-life movement has its roots and impulse in the Judeo-Christian concept of love. One characteristic of this love is that it is forgiving. Human beings, unlike animals, have freedom. Human beings are also weak, hence often abuse that freedom. But we are capable of acknowledging our wrong-doing, repudiating it, and making a "new beginning." This is what is meant by repentance. For repentance to have a social impact, there must also be a corollary — forgiveness. Forgiveness is one's recognition of another's repentance. No one has the right to forgiveness, but everyone has a duty to forgive. To refuse to forgive a repentant person is to be blind to one's own need for forgiveness and is totally contrary to the roots of the pro-life attitude.

What is this second victim like? Often she suffers from low self-esteem. She is unaffirmed. She did not receive affirming love from her parents as she was growing up. This is frequently associated with a tendency to be very dependent on others. In many cases this passive dependency can lead to passive aggression; securing one's own wishes by unconsciously chosen "devious" means. One means of securing a shaky relationship with a boy is to be become pregnant.

Sometimes the woman agrees to an abortion as a result of pressure applied by boyfriend, parents, or social workers. At other times the "pressure" stems from the fact that the pregnancy is seen as pointless because it failed to cement the shaky relationship with the boy. The coerced client may be feeling guilty, not only about procuring the abortion, but also about allowing herself to be coerced: "Why wasn't I strong enough to withstand the pressure?" she asks herself.

The post-abortion client may respond to guilt feelings in two ways. She can face these feelings squarely, admit their cause, repent, and forgive herself. Or she can shield herself from these guilt feelings by means of psychological "defense mechanisms." For example, she can deny the reality of abortion in general or of her abortion in particular by refusing to discuss the issue. She may rationalize her action through excuses which are unconvincing. She may also project blame for her abortion onto others, perhaps onto pro-life people (Here, pro-lifers are seen as being responsible for her guilt feelings because they tell the truth about abortion.) She may have a proselytizing reaction and become an ardent advocate of abortion, the very instrument of her wound. Or she may displace her anger at the men who performed or pressured her into the abortion onto safer objects: pro-life workers, religious hierarchies, etc. Finally, she may try to "undo" the abortion by becoming pregnant again.

In every case, the use of defense mechanisms to shield the woman from her guilt feelings involves the distortion of reality and self-deceptions. Underneath the defenses, the guilt feelings clamor for recognition. The psychic energy that is required to defend against these feelings is enormous. Often there is little left over for the joys and challenges of life. In post-abortion counseling, the therapist views abortion as something that threatens the woman. The main work of the counselor is to listen sympathetically. Sympathy and concern for the client are conveyed by the manner in which he or she listens. The fact that the client can tell the counselor about her abortion without the counselor rejecting her is very helpful for the client and is a major ingredient in her being able to accept herself again.

The basic plan of therapy is that guilt be accepted, worked through, and resolved. With clients who freely admit their guilty feelings either from the beginning of the therapy or after some resistance, the therapist must cling to two basic principles. First, he must never deny the reality of an abortion. Second, he must insist that the woman who has had an abortion is entitled to regain her self-esteem and the esteem of others. In the case of the client who defends against her guilt feelings, it is appropriate to probe, but to do so without pushing: "You mentioned that you had an abortion," you may ask. "Was that an upsetting experience?" The whole tone of the counselor's questioning should suggest that abortion is often psychologically very hurtful to the woman who undergoes it, and that she may be in need of sympathy.

The counselor must strike a very delicate balance. He needs to help the woman confront her guilty feelings insofar as she will allow. This will be a very painful process, and it must be gentle and unforced. On the one hand, the counselor should be doing this in order to heal, not in order to punish. On the other hand, he must not avoid leading the client to this painful confrontation out of a mistaken sense of "compassion." For the counselor to reinforce the defenses that the client is using to refuse to acknowledge her guilt out of a misguided sense of compassion is to leave the client unhealed, with the guilt left untouched to fester beneath the defenses.

This country has had more than ten years of legalized abortion. Psychological sequelae often do not surface until years after an abortion. The typical feeling immediately after an abortion is one of relief. However, this is frequently followed by feelings of anxiety, depression, and guilt. These feelings may be triggered by the arrival of the baby's due date, by the anniversary of the abortion, by the celebration of Christmas with its focus on the Divine Infant. Often seeing a pregnant woman, a little child, especially if it is the same age as her child would have been, will trigger a reaction. Becoming pregnant again, especially when the pregnancy reaches the state at which the prior pregnancy was aborted, can also have this result. Discussing prenatal care or the question of legal abortion can often have the same effect.

I have seen women in my office crying five and ten years after an abortion. And we are familiar with the late actress, Gloria Swanson, who, in her 80s, was still grieving over an abortion she had had fifty years earlier. With technological breakthroughs in fetal medicine, the so-called "rehumanization" of the unborn, the media will be forced to present a more honest picture of abortion. It is reasonable to expect an increase of women who have had abortions developing or becoming aware of psychological problems associated with abortions they have had. It is critical for their psychological health that they be helped both to face what they have done and to forgive themselves. This is more likely to occur in a pro-life setting than in one in which the counselor's own unresolved feelings about abortion and, perhaps, also his own complicity in abortion referral, interfere with an honest and truthful resolution of the therapeutic process.

As long as abortion remains legal, we can expect to see an increase of psychological suffering. In compassion and love, pro-life people must reach out to help the many mothers who are now weeping for their lost children. In doing so, we will not only be honoring a sacred duty to them. It may very well be that their insistent voice, like that of the troublesome widow of the Gospel story, will finally obtain justice for the future unborn in this land.

TO BE PRO-LIFE IS TO MAKE OUR LOVE UNCONDITIONAL

John Powell, S.J.*

"You and I are doing what we know to be the right thing. We must now leave the timetables and all the results in God's hands."

JOHN POWELL, S.J.

I remember once a young woman came to see me. She said something that truly astonished me. I know that this may sound contrived to you, but it really is true. She said "I'm pregnant. Since it has been confirmed that I am pregnant, I have not smoked because, you know, nicotine can harm a developing baby. I have not drunk alcohol because of the fetal alcohol syndrome that we hear so much about."

Then she looked down, almost as though she could not

*Father Powell is a well-known author, lecturer, and scholar. He is currently a professor of theology at Loyola University in Chicago. He is the author of twelve books, including *Abortion: the Silent Holocaust*. He is the second best selling Christian author in the history of the United States, just behind C.S. Lewis. This essay is adopted from a speech given at the annual convention of Minnesota Citizens Concerned for Life in November 1982.

believe her own words. She said softly, "But I have an appointment to kill this baby next Thursday morning."

I could hardly believe that the same mind and mouth were thinking and saying those three statements! I felt I somehow had to plead for the baby's life. So I kept stressing that "this baby, this baby you are carrying inside you, is an innocent, living human being." I kept talking about the baby, the baby. "Please give your baby a chance at life," I pleaded.

After a short while, she looked up at me pleadingly, "I know you love my baby. *Do you also love me?"*

Then I realized that I had been debating, pleading a case. I was debating for the life of the baby against all the forces that had led her to the abortion decision. I had really, in fact, not been thinking about or loving her. I did not think about who she was, what she was feeling, or why she was driven to the edge of the decision to destroy the life inside her.

Where did she get those three messages? Who told her about nicotine, alcohol, and abortion? "I haven't smoked. I haven't drunk alcohol. But I have an appointment to kill this baby." Later, it all came clear to me. She got this from the media. That's what we hear so frequently on television, on the radio. We are warned about nicotine and its effect on the fetus. We are warned about fetal alcohol syndrome.

But we are also reassured that it is all right to terminate a pregnancy, to take the life of an unborn child. Those great men in the august Supreme Court, in their long black robes and solemn decision, have proclaimed the legality of such killing. In fact, very recently, in hearings preparatory to forthcoming decisions on abortion Justice Blackmun compared the surgical procedure of abortion to the lancing of a boil. This comparison was carried on the evening news, in the media report on those hearings.

The media deluge the minds of the young with these

three messages. Many young people simply parrot what they have been told, acting out the media morality. What they are really looking for, I think, is not someone to debate them, or to inform them, "You are carrying inside you an innocent, living, human being."

Somehow I think they know that. I don't think that the coverup of the Supreme Court and the media can ever successfully and completely obscure that fact. No matter how the media tries to launder its language or twist the truth, I think that the young know the facts of life and the fact of new innocent, human life. Beneath all the rationalizations is the painful, persistent question: "Do you love me?"

I think that the truly effective pro-life person has to reflect profoundly on and pray about the meaning of this question: "Do you love me, too?" Is love really my motive? Is my love universal and unconditional?

I had to confront this question of love after a recent telephone conversation. As you know, it is suspected that some pharmaceutical houses are taking collagen from the corpses of aborted fetuses. Perhaps this is one reason why those 17,000 infant corpses were found recently, stored in formaldehyde in plastic containers in a California warehouse. As you also know, this collagen is used in beauty creams. This is done in France unashamedly. Collagen was the subject of the telephone conversation.

The lady to whom I was talking said simply that she was ordered frozen collagen from a pharamceutical house in France. The French representative said it could only be sent if refrigerated. So be it. The lady said, "I want to have hard evidence of this horror, and that is why I placed this order. They openly admit that their collagen is taken from aborted fetuses."

Then she added. "You know, I have not joined a pro-life group simply for one reason. My motives are anger and hatred. I know that there is strength in unity, but I don't want to represent a loving group because I feel filled with anger and hatred. I hate the people who would kill innocent babies and make beauty creams from their corpses. So I operate as an individual. If I am criticized, I and not the group will take the criticism."

After our telephone conversation, I thought for a long time about what she had said. She is a good woman, I thought, but she will short-circuit herself with her anger and hatred. Anger and hatred are consuming: they destroy those who harbor them. I think that we have to make love our universal and unconditional motive, as Jesus did. We have to love the very people that do seemingly heartless and subhuman things. The Gospel leaves us no alternative. "Love your friends?" Jesus asked. "The Heathens do this." Love is the only motive recognized, the only force approved by Jesus.

We all remember poor Peter, the Rock, who was actually a disguised sandpile. At the Last Supper he assures Jesus that he would never betray him. He is arrogant and proud in his protestations. But hours later, he raises his voice and hand in an oath before all the people in the courtyard of the High Priest: "I do not even know who he is!" He did in fact deny Jesus.

It was this Peter, who said to Jesus: "Depart from me. I am a sinful man." The only reply of the Lord was, in effect, "I don't care what you have done or where you have been. The only thing that really matters is: Do you love me?"

It was the same question the young woman asked me: "I know you love my baby. Do you love me, too?" We have to love. Jesus loved people when they were at their worst because he knew that it is love that leads people to their best. He knew that the only transforming force in this world is love. Love is always the pro-life motive. It has to be a love that listens: Who are you? What are your feelings? How did you get to where you are? It has also to be a love that shares. Whatever I am or have that is good I want to share with you.

It has to be a careful love, that does not fall into the snares of anger and hatred. When we develop a siege mentality, a win-lose mentality, love always suffers. We really have to be more careful about love than anything else. The woman who said, "I have an appointment to kill my baby next Thursday morning," was hurting, hurting badly. She was pleading: "Will you also love me, please? I need someone to care about me so I can care about my baby."

If the pro-life effort doesn't have the sound of love, of true caring for all concerned, it will only create a polarization. It will make it easy for others to write us off as fanatics. To review and even to question our motives is tremendously important. Is it me against you or am I trying to share anything good that I am or have? If it is an adversary relationship, a debate, a win-lose contest, marred by the sounds of anger and hatred, we will all be destroyed in the tides of death.

I think that, if I were the devil, I would dangle two temptations in the pro-life line of vision. The first temptation would be *discouragement*. I would remind pro-life people that they are a small minority, a lonely voice crying in the wilderness. "You are just a handful of people. What can you accomplish?" Malcolm Muggeridge once said about this: "We must remember that Christianity is an antistatistical religion." A lonely Jew picked out twelve awkward men and started the whole thing. Two-thirds of the world lived in slavery at that time. The most popular spectator sport was watching two gladiators fight until one killed the other. It was a cruel, ugly, inhumane world.

But the idea of *love* was incarnated in Bethlehem. One man and twelve fragile, we-could-go-either-way apostles. (I think, by the way, that if I had been Jesus, halfway through the public life, I would have said:

"Fellas, it's just not working out. I think that maybe you should be doing something with your hands. What about fishing?")

In the Gospel of Mark, Jesus asks the apostles 17 times — I counted them — "Are you yet without understanding?" We would translate: "You don't get it yet, do you?"

But he loved them into greatness. Love became incarnate in this one man and it transformed the whole world. Of course, when we think about our numbers, and we think about the well-funded and celebrity-supported organizations that promote the killing of the unborn, that want a world free of all human burdens, we can feel a bit discouraged. We can feel like the solitary voice crying in the wilderness.

But remember, our faith is antistatistical. That's why Jesus could leave the ninety-nine sheep and go looking for the stray. It's antistatistical. We cannot play or think in terms of the numbers game.

The second temptation I would propose to the beautiful pro-life persons would be *overresponsibility*. In psychology, an overresponsible person is one who takes on all the problems of the world. (By the way, you are listening to the voice of experience. I have suffered for years from a Messiah complex. I thought Jesus needed a rest so I took over. It was a great relief to resign.)

We can't play Lord of human lives and human history. We have to sell the house on Mt. Olympus (where the gods live) and come back down, take on a pilgrim status, work a little corner of the vineyard, light a small candle instead of cursing the surrounding darkness, speak out in a calm voice in the cause of life... and leave all the results in the hands of God.

As the old Zen proverb has it: "We do not do the right thing because of the calculated effects it will have, but only because it is the right thing to do." You and I are doing what we know to be the right thing. We must now leave the timetables and all the results in God's hands. And when the final history of humanity is written, and it is asked: Who spoke up for life, for the unborn, for the special people, for the sick, for the aged?, I want my name emblazoned on that scroll next to yours. I am sure that the Lord smiles upon us and that he will bless our efforts with eventual success.

Meanwhile, I ask: Please remember me as loving you.